ReFocus: The Films of Zoya Akhtar

ReFocus: The International Directors Series

Series Editors: Robert Singer, Stefanie Van de Peer and Gary D. Rhodes

Board of Advisors:
Lizelle Bisschoff (Glasgow University)
Stephanie Hemelryck Donald (University of Lincoln)
Anna Misiak (Falmouth University)
Des O'Rawe (Queen's University Belfast)

ReFocus is a series of contemporary methodological and theoretical approaches to the interdisciplinary analyses and interpretations of international film directors, from the celebrated to the ignored, in direct relationship to their respective culture – its myths, values and historical precepts – and the broader parameters of international film history and theory.

Titles in the series include:

ReFocus: The Films of Susanne Bier
Edited by Missy Molloy, Mimi Nielsen and Meryl Shriver-Rice

ReFocus: The Films of Francis Veber
Keith Corson

ReFocus: The Films of Jia Zhangke
Maureen Turim and Ying Xiao

ReFocus: The Films of Xavier Dolan
Edited by Andrée Lafontaine

ReFocus: The Films of Pedro Costa: Producing and Consuming Contemporary Art Cinema
Nuno Barradas Jorge

ReFocus: The Films of Sohrab Shahid Saless: Exile, Displacement and the Stateless Moving Image
Edited by Azadeh Fatehrad

ReFocus: The Films of Pablo Larraín
Edited by Laura Hatry

ReFocus: The Films of Michel Gondry
Edited by Marcelline Block and Jennifer Kirby

ReFocus: The Films of Rachid Bouchareb
Edited by Michael Gott and Leslie Kealhofer-Kemp

ReFocus: The Films of Andrei Tarkovsky
Edited by Sergey Toymentsev

ReFocus: The Films of Paul Leni
Edited by Erica Tortolani and Martin F. Norden

ReFocus: The Films of Rakhshan Banietemad
Edited by Maryam Ghorbankarimi

ReFocus: The Films of Jocelyn Saab: Films, Artworks and Cultural Events for the Arab World
Edited by Mathilde Rouxel and Stefanie Van de Peer

ReFocus: The Films of François Ozon
Edited by Loïc Bourdeau

ReFocus: The Films of Lucrecia Martel
Edited by Natalia Christofoletti Barrenha, Julia Kratje and Paul R. Merchant

ReFocus: The Films of Zoya Akhtar
Edited by Aakshi Magazine and Amber Shields

edinburghuniversitypress.com/series/refocint

ReFocus:
The Films of Zoya Akhtar

Edited by Aakshi Magazine and Amber Shields

EDINBURGH
University Press

Edinburgh University Press is one of the leading university presses in the UK. We publish academic books and journals in our selected subject areas across the humanities and social sciences, combining cutting-edge scholarship with high editorial and production values to produce academic works of lasting importance. For more information visit our website: edinburghuniversitypress.com

© editorial matter and organisation Aakshi Magazine and Amber Shields, 2022
© the chapters their several authors, 2022

Edinburgh University Press Ltd
The Tun – Holyrood Road
12 (2f) Jackson's Entry
Edinburgh EH8 8PJ

First published in hardback by Edinburgh University Press, 2022

Typeset in 11/13 Ehrhardt MT by
IDSUK (DataConnection) Ltd, and
printed and bound by CPI Group (UK) Ltd,
Croydon, CR0 4YY

A CIP record for this book is available from the British Library

ISBN 978 1 4744 7641 6 (hardback)
ISBN 978 1 4744 7642 3 (paperback)
ISBN 978 1 4744 7643 0 (webready PDF)
ISBN 978 1 4744 7644 7 (epub)

The right of Aakshi Magazine and Amber Shields to be identified as editors of this work has been asserted in accordance with the Copyright, Designs and Patents Act 1988 and the Copyright and Related Rights Regulations 2003 (SI No. 2498).

Contents

List of Figures	vii
Notes on Contributors	viii
Introduction: Intersecting Industries *Aakshi Magazine and Amber Shields*	1

Part I Growing up Industry

1 Loving but Critical: The Empathetic Gaze of *Luck by Chance* *Aakshi Magazine*	21
2 Relocating Bollywood: *Gully Boy* and the Worlds of Hip-hop *Sangita Gopal*	38
3 New Forms, New Stories: Zoya Akhtar's Short Films *Amber Shields*	59
4 Zoya Akhtar as a Screenwriter: Making Niche the New Mainstream *Vyoma Jha*	75

Part II Reworking Bollywood Themes

5 The Heterotopia of Family Relation-Ship in *Dil Dhadakne Do* *Debnita Chakravarti*	93
6 *Sabka Time Aayega*: Language and the City in *Gully Boy* *Kamayani Sharma*	108
7 Queer Love: He is Also *Made in Heaven* *Iqra Shagufta Cheema*	126

Part III A New Era of Gendered Politics

8 Conflicted and Confused: The Changing Complexity of Masculinity in Zoya Akhtar's Films *Amber Shields*	147

9 *Señoritas* at Work: Gendered Work, Aspiration and Leisure in the Films of Zoya Akhtar   164
Sharanya

10 Self-made vs Self-respect: The Politics of Belonging in Zoya Akhtar's Films   180
Vijeta Kumar

Part IV The Word and the Screen

11 Deconstructing the Perception of 'The Elite Class Filmmaker': A Critical Analysis of Mainstream Film Reviews of Zoya Akhtar's Cinema   199
Ruchi Kher Jaggi and Mudita Mishra

12 The Final Word: An Interview with Zoya Akhtar   217
Aakshi Magazine and Amber Shields

General Index   232
Index of Films   238

Figures

1.1	The final conversation: Sona and Vikram	33
2.1	One of the worlds that *Gully Boy* depicts is the space where *gully* rap happens	53
3.1	Sudha hears the whispers invading her confined space	70
4.1	The Mehras board the ship in this tale of the modern Indian family	85
5.1	The Mehras find a space of regeneration on the lifeboat	105
6.1	Murad is shown toiling over his writing, dispelling its mystery	118
7.1	Karan and his lover in the light	139
8.1	Each of the protagonists in *ZNMD* runs towards his own fate	153
9.1	Sona stares at the domestic apparatus Vikram won	175
10.1	Aftab's demonstrations of patriarchal violence are present throughout *Gully Boy*	183

Notes on Contributors

Debnita Chakravarti is Associate Professor (English literature) with a doctoral degree from the University of Reading, UK. She was awarded a postdoctoral Charles Wallace fellowship to the University of Southampton and Chawton House in Alton. She has been published by Pearson, Peter Lang, Ashgate and Routledge (chapters in books) and in several peer-reviewed academic journals. She has reviewed films and books as a freelancer for Indian magazines and dailies and is a regular literary conversationalist at the annual *Kolkata Literary Meet* and in the series *An Author's Afternoon*.

Iqra Shagufta Cheema recently earned her doctorate in postmodernist comparative literature from the University of North Texas. Currently she is working on a book manuscript, *The Films of Annemarie Jacir*, and editing an anthology, *The Other #MeToos*.

Sangita Gopal is Associate Professor of English at the University of Oregon. She is author of *Conjugations: Marriage and Form in New Bollywood Cinema* (2011) and co editor of *Global Bollywood: Transnational Travels of Hindi Film Music* (2008).

Ruchi Kher Jaggi is Professor and Director of Symbiosis Institute of Media and Communication, and Dean of the Faculty of Media and Communication, Symbiosis International (Deemed University), Pune, India, with an experience of two decades in higher education. Her research interests include media representations, popular culture analysis, media and children, television studies, journalism studies, media literacy, streaming platforms and emerging discourses of identity on the new media.

NOTES ON CONTRIBUTORS   ix

Vyoma Jha is a socio-legal scholar who recently graduated from the doctoral program at Stanford Law School. She holds law degrees from Stanford Law School, New York University School of Law, and National Law University, Jodhpur. Vyoma focuses her research on climate change law and policy, international economic law, and India's foreign policy. Her writing has appeared in journals such as *Economic and Political Weekly*, *Journal of World Investment and Trade*, and *Trade, Law and Development*.

Vijeta Kumar teaches English and Journalism in St Joseph's College, Bangalore. Her research interests include Dalit Literature, Auto ethnography, and Narrative Journalism. She is currently working on a book of essays on caste and the city. Her work has appeared in *Huffpost*, *First Post*, and *India Today*. In 2018, she was shortlisted for the Toto award in creative writing, and as of 2017, she has been conducting writing workshops exclusively for Dalit women.

Aakshi Magazine is a writer and academic based in India. She received her PhD in Film Studies from the University of St Andrews in 2020. Her doctoral thesis, *The 1950s Hindi Film Song: Between Transgression and Memory*, is on the relationship of the film song to the contradictions of the Indian nationalist discourse. She has published several journal articles, a book chapter and film criticism in popular publications.

Mudita Mishra is an Assistant Professor and a doctoral candidate at Symbiosis Institute of Media and Communication, Symbiosis International (Deemed University), Pune, India. Her research interests and areas of work include consumer culture and audience studies for video streaming platforms.

Sharanya is Lecturer in Theatre at Brunel University London. Her work has previously appeared in *Theatre Research International*, *Performance Research* and elsewhere. She is part of the editorial team of *Contemporary Theatre Review*'s online platform Interventions. In 2021, she was a Fellow at the Mellon School of Theater and Performance Research at Harvard University.

Kamayani Sharma studied philosophy and gender studies at Fergusson College, Pune and has a Master's from the School of Arts and Aesthetics, JNU. A former text editor with *ART India*, Sharma has written for *Artforum*, *The White Review*, *Momus*, *The Caravan*, *Open* and *Firstpost*. Her academic articles have appeared in or are forthcoming in *Studies in South Asian Film and Media* and in an edited volume on the South Asian Gothic being published by the University of Wales Press. She has been a research associate to a Brown University anthropologist, taught philosophy at Ashoka University, and been a researcher with the media studies organisation, Sarai (CSDS).

Amber Shields received her PhD in Film Studies from the University of St Andrews where she focused on how fantasy is used to tell stories of individual and collective trauma in films from around the world. She has taught Film and English courses at Mount Tamalpais College and currently works with nonprofits reimagining education and supporting the development of young leaders. She has published several journal articles and book chapters.

Introduction: Intersecting Industries

Aakshi Magazine and Amber Shields

Zoya Akhtar's directorial debut *Luck by Chance* (*LBC*)[1] (2009) is not a glamorised view of the Hindi film industry. It is not the rose-tinted world of *Om Shanti Om* (Farah Khan 2007), in which love of the stars and the industry triumphs over all. Nor is it a world that openly welcomes and preserves bright-eyed innocence and 'true love' as in *Rangeela* (Ram Gopal Varma 1995). Instead, the film is a critical love letter to an industry that only one who knows it intimately can write, at once capturing the appeal of this enticing lover yet also the high price that this all-consuming relationship can cost.

A film about newcomers trying to make their way in an industry that is like (and in many cases, literally is) a family, *LBC* is an intimate portrayal by somebody who, having grown up in the industry, knows the good, the bad and all the nuances in between. The film opens with the complexities of loving an industry that is at once an intangible dream to millions across the world and yet is at the same time a daily reality that operates just as much in the mundane as the magical. While the opening shot shows the newcomer actor Sona (Konkona Sen Sharma) being seduced in more ways than one, as she is told by producer Satish (Alyy Khan) that he will make her dreams of becoming a star come true, the next sequence begins to pull back the curtains to expose the realities behind the scenes. Though capturing the ordinary by presenting a collage of snapshots of the real workers carrying out the day-to-day tasks that keep the facade of film going, this montage also lovingly hints at the magical. From the prop assistants to the tailors to the caterers, the unsung workers appear before the camera, immersed in their work without a moment to pause, but for once extracted from behind the scenes and put in the spotlight.[2] There is a celebration of the joy and passion that go into making films, the familial bonds that those in the industry create in what is, if not their first, then at least their second home. The complexities of this larger-than-life character only grow as the film unfolds and we see the industry's conniving and manipulative practices, the betrayals and backstabbing that occur, and yet at the same time the immense love and forgiveness that it can hold.

The industry becomes the film's driving character as the human protagonists dream of it, lust after it, live in it, feed it and grapple with it as they struggle to become part of it and yet also, if possible, maintain a part of their own identities. Its power is overwhelming and we see one protagonist, Vikram (Farhan Akhtar), become consumed by it, while Sona in the end must leave it to keep alive a part of herself. The film thus becomes a navigation of the relationships that can be built between the individual and the industry, an intriguing debut for Akhtar as a director who enters this industry with so much of its past in tow and yet will spend a career riding and shaping the tides of its future.

This book celebrates these complicated relationships with one of the world's largest film industries and the way in which Akhtar navigates them to find her own voice. Growing up in a family of Bollywood insiders, Akhtar has seen many changes in the industry, from its being granted official status as an industry in 1998 and its corporatisation, to its global expansion and shifts in social dynamics. Living through these changes, Akhtar has a deep understanding of the past, yet has a keen eye looking forward, taking risks and surveying the industry's new horizons. Though she works in the industry, her cinematic style shows influences beyond the mainstream; in various interviews, she has spoken about the profound influence of her mother Honey Irani's education at the Film and Television Institute of India (FTII) as well as Mira Nair's *Salaam Bombay!* (1988) on her own idea of cinema. At the same time, she also mentions her immense fandom for the Hindi film blockbuster *Sholay* (Ramesh Sippy 1975) (Bollywood Roundtables 2013). Further, her own training reflects a diversity of perspectives from her education in sociology in Mumbai and her cinematic education at New York University to her work as a casting director and an assistant to directors ranging from Mira Nair to Dev Benegal to her brother Farhan Akhtar. Over the course of her career, she has moved from a more 'arthouse' or 'multiplex' genre style of filmmaking to work within a mainstream Bollywood form.[3]

The themes of Akhtar's films after *LBC*, *Zindagi Na Milegi Dobara* (*ZNMD*) (2011), *Dil Dhadakne Do* (*DDD*) (2015) and *Gully Boy* (2019), represent an aspiration for box office success while retaining complexity in the representation of characters and narrative arcs. Her experiments with the short film form, in *Bombay Talkies* (2013), *Lust Stories* (2018) and *Ghost Stories* (2020), and the streaming series *Made in Heaven* (2019), where we find a relatively more subversive interpretation of gender and class than is generally presented in her feature films, also add an interesting thread to this discussion. In the works so far produced by her and Reema Kagti's nascent production company, Tiger

Baby Films,[4] starting with *Lust Stories* and including *Gully Boy* and *Made in Heaven*, one can see the simultaneous continuation of and playing out of new trends as Akhtar takes greater artistic control and begins to cater to a more diverse international audience.

Akhtar also presents a unique study of the creative process. The intriguing themes and portrayals that stand out in her work are shaped by her collaborative writing practice. This includes her long-time co-writer Reema Kagti, her family members Javed Akhtar and Farhan Akhtar, recent collaborators like writer Vijay Maurya on *Gully Boy* or filmmakers like Alankrita Shrivastava and Nitya Mehra on the *Made in Heaven* series. These collaborations are an integral aspect of her film style. Unlike the figure of the male auteur as a solo genius, this is a working style where collaborations are acknowledged and celebrated in interviews and conversations.

Looking at this multifaceted, multimedia oeuvre, we can see how Akhtar is one of the contemporary Indian filmmakers through whom we can understand how and why the big budget mainstream Bollywood film, with its reliance on popular stars, song-and-dance numbers and a melodramatic imagination, continues to remain relevant. At the same time, through her career's evolving trajectory, we see the negotiations of an industry that finds itself in a state of constant reinvention that rely on directors like Akhtar to push it in new directions.

This introduction to the filmmaker Zoya Akhtar examines how she represents a space of intersectionality in the Hindi film industry, as both a high-profile filmmaker of Hindi cinema blockbusters and as an agent of change who pushes and propels the industry to undergo shifts reflecting a twenty-first-century global media market. While looking at her personal context and ties to the industry, we also explore how she has managed to create her own style in her work and how she has taken part in shaping her public image. We will further highlight the development of the director's status in contemporary Bollywood, from her debut difficulties to her most recent film *Gully Boy* being an enormous hit at the Indian box office, and how her current ventures reflect the industry's burgeoning aspirations and changes. Most importantly, we will look at Akhtar as an individual whose development of distinctive thematic and cinematic techniques has given her a voice that allows her not only to survive in this relationship with an industry that at times can be fickle and yet just as much faithful, but to shape it.

FILMY FAMILIES: STANDING ON THE SHOULDERS OF GIANTS

A review of Akhtar's first film, *LBC*, published in the newspaper *The Indian Express*, described Akhtar as 'daughter of Javed, sister of Farhan' (Gupta 2009). Another reviewer wrote about the film, 'Akhtar's script is a bit lengthy but it has the distinct advantage of her father Javed Akhtar's brilliant dialogue' (Mohamed 2009). These two reviews point towards an important context: Akhtar's film family background is one of the defining aspects of her identity that reviewers, film scholars and spectators familiar with the industry often refer to when they engage with her work. In fact, as this book is being written, discourses surrounding the Indian film industry have been rife with questions of nepotism and the unfair advantage that the children of stars receive vis-à-vis people who come from the outside, a theme that was incidentally a part of *LBC*.

However, this aspect of Akhtar's identity also makes her a rewarding case study for understanding contemporary Bollywood. Akhtar's location in the film industry points towards the very specific ways in which Bollywood functions: she is a woman who makes films in what she admits is a 'masculine space', but she also belongs to a film family which eases her access to the industry and to the stars she wants to work with. This is reflective of a trend, as two of the most commercially successful women filmmakers working in mainstream Bollywood, Farah Khan and Meghna Gulzar, also have a film family connection.[5] While Farah Khan's father, Kamran Khan, was a film producer (and she and Akhtar are cousins), Meghna Gulzar is the daughter of veteran film actor Rakhee and veteran poet-lyricist and filmmaker Gulzar. Thus, Akhtar's film family context is not only a personal detail reflecting the caste-class privileges in Indian society, but it is indicative of the ways in which location determines who has access to the opportunity to make big budget commercial films, which in turn is reflected in the film style and the content of films that are made.

Akhtar acknowledges her family as one of the foremost influences in her life, contributing to her love for cinema and her career as a filmmaker (Akhtar 2020). She was born to child actor, screenwriter and director Honey Irani and poet, screenwriter and lyricist Javed Akhtar on 14 October 1972 in Bombay. Her brother Farhan was born two years later. As her mother's career as an actor was winding down and being taken over by her new role as a mother, Akhtar's father's transition into one of the most famous pens in Hindi film history was just beginning. Along with writer Salim Khan, Javed Akhtar formed one half of the duo that would shape not only the 1970s, but much of Bollywood's history up until this day. Salim-Javed, as the duo was affectionately dubbed, were the authors behind *Zanjeer* (Prakash Mehra 1973), *Deewar* (Yash Chopra 1975) and one of, if not the most celebrated Hindi film of all time, *Sholay*. The duo brought the art and celebration of screenwriting to a whole new level as they gained as much recognition for their roles in these classics as the directors did.

After her parents separated, Akhtar's mother Honey Irani began to pursue her own path as a screenwriter and enrolled at the prestigious FTII in Pune. Eventually she too went on to become a successful screenwriter whose work ranged from critically acclaimed films like *Lamhe* (Yash Chopra 1991), lesser-known films like *Aaina* (Deepak Sareen 1993), as well as some of the most successful Hindi films of the last decades, like *Darr* (Yash Chopra 1993), *Kaho naa... Pyaar Hai* (Rakesh Roshan 2000) and *Krrish* (Rakesh Roshan 2006). She also directed *Armaan* in 2003. Curiously, despite Akhtar having grown up with her mother, film scholarship and reviews, like the one quoted at the beginning of this section, often underplay her mother's influence. This is a telling omission that underlines the male-centric nature of film discourse. It also reveals the lack of space and desire to engage with her film family context beyond questions of access to resources. The ways in which her family could have had an influence on her film sensibilities and world view, as she has discussed on several occasions, are not considered both in film scholarship and in film journalism.

While Irani studied the art of film, so did her children, and Akhtar fondly recalls her mother bringing home films by Carlos Saura, Franco Zeffirelli or Costa-Gravas that they would watch together; 'you didn't understand these films but you watched them and if you were bored you passed out but they were there so when you got older you watched them again' (Akhtar 2020). From Akhtar's perspective, her film family background has had a positive impact on her intellectual and creative growth and has contributed to her having an appreciation of the world of cinema ranging from Bollywood to global musicals to arthouse films. At the same time, she grew up in an atmosphere where discussions on the art of cinema were accompanied by discussions on the commerce of cinema and the relevance of the box office (Akhtar 2020). The understanding of these multiple layers of film is significant, as it can be seen in some of the choices that she has made in terms of film style, scale and themes, as the next two sections will explore.

While Akhtar views her family as an empowering facet in her growth, film scholarship has not always viewed this positively in terms of her development as a filmmaker with an independent voice. In fact, Nandana Bose argues that this has had a limiting impact on her agency, stating:

> I contend that such familial dependence limits the creative vision and artistic range of a young, emerging filmmaker who is working very much within her comfort zone and operating within a familial space in which her father, brother, extended family members and childhood friends are the pillars that have supported her burgeoning career (2017, 218).

As the chapters in this book demonstrate, this is an unfair, though repeated, reduction of Akhtar's growing body of work and of her career. A more productive approach would be to treat her as an individual filmmaker in her own right, who is shaped by her familial background, but also has agency over it. This becomes especially important in the context of how her familial background impacts her choice of film style and sensibility as a director, writer and producer, marking continuities with the older Hindi film form as well as explorations into more global trends.

Despite her ties to the industry, in her early years Akhtar often took an independent path, though within the context of the resources and opportunities available to her. While studying literature and sociology at St Xavier's College (Mumbai), she began working as a copywriter and by the time she was twenty-one was assisting Mira Nair in her film *Kama Sutra: A Tale of Love* (1996). After her work on that film and the indie comedy *Bombay Boys* (Kaizad Gustad 1998), Akhtar went to New York University to pursue a diploma in filmmaking. On returning to India, she and Reema Kagti, who would later become her long-time collaborator, became the 'only freelance people' in the industry (Akhtar 2020). She did not want to stick to one single director and then carry forward their style; neither did she want to use dubbed sound like other Hindi films did at that time. She took up work that came mainly from non-industry films that were being produced in India with a mixture of local and foreign crew members. These experiences, combined with her eclectic exposure to local, Hollywood and world cinema from a young age, made an impression on Akhtar and later influenced her style and led to what we can see in her work as a quest to merge these influences, while being aware of the Indian box office demands and Bollywood conventions.

As she set off at an early age to forge her career, her familial connections did help her realise it. By the time she started directing films, for instance, her brother Farhan Akhtar had already established the production company Excel Entertainment with Ritesh Sidhwani, which produced her films. This is in contrast to the uncertainty that many other contemporary filmmakers have faced; a good example is filmmaker Dibakar Banerjee, who signed a three-film deal with the premier production house Yash Raj in 2013, but said in a 2019 interview that he 'hasn't had a film release for five years' (Bollywood Hungama 2019).

In spite of her advantages and connections, Akhtar's initial career was also accompanied by precariousness. Her first film took seven years to make because she could not find a suitable cast for it as the male lead character was an anti-hero, which did not fit with how leading stars of the time wanted to be portrayed.[6] Even though Akhtar had been working in the film industry from a young age, she made her directorial debut relatively late in 2009 when she was thirty-seven years old. By this time her brother Farhan had already made his first film, *Dil Chahta Hai* (*DCH*) (2001), considered a path-breaking film on male friendships, when he was twenty-six. Until her directorial debut, Akhtar had worked as a casting director and assistant director, including on *DCH* and on Reema Kagti's debut film, *Honeymoon Travels Pvt. Ltd* (2007). This is reflective of a trend when it comes to women filmmakers working within big budget Bollywood: Farah Khan worked as a choreographer for more than a decade before she made her directorial debut with *Main Hoon Na* (2004). Meghna Gulzar made her debut film quite early in 2002 but faced criticism for years for not matching up to her lineage. It was only in 2015 when Gulzar made *Talvaar* and later *Raazi* (2018) that she began to be considered a critically and commercially successful director.

LBC was not a hit at the box office and Akhtar's next two films, *ZNMD* and *DDD*, while successful at the box office, placed her in a curious position vis-à-vis film criticism, as she was decried for her sumptuous portrayal of Indian high society. Playing to a crowd that increasingly consume movies in the multiplexes of luxury malls or global audiences, Akhtar is not the first nor the last director to turn her focus to the upper echelon of society, representing an economic experience that most could only dream of. In this focus, however, she has often been singled out and criticised for portraying the rich and 'first world problems' as compared to her contemporary directors, a phenomenon that Ruchi Jaggi and Mudita Mishra explore in their chapter in this volume. It is only her most recent film *Gully Boy*, arguably her most popular work to date, along with the streaming series *Made in Heaven* co-created with Kagti, with which she has become someone whose work is celebrated commercially and critically, marking a shift in her career.

This book includes her family context in a wider reflection of the workings of the contemporary Hindi film industry. The familial link that Bose refers to thus becomes not a damning but rather an intriguing point worth exploring in the context of Akhtar's choice of placing herself very much within Bollywood traditions and mainstream forms of filmmaking, while at the same time creating an independent voice that is changing this tradition from within. Standing on the shoulders of giants, she has seen further and continues to explore new horizons.

THE SHIFTING TIDES OF INDUSTRY: BRIDGING THE GAP

Akhtar made her first film more than a decade after an era that encompassed the 'Bollywoodization' of Indian cinema (Rajadhyaksha 2003) and the emergence of what has been labelled by academics and critics as '"multiplex cinema", "New Bollywood" or "Hatke cinema"' (Jain 2017: 98). These terms indicate that the Hindi film industry of the new millennium has been characterised by a 'stunning multiplicity of genres and styles' (Jain 2017: 99) and an 'eclectic body of films' (Viswamohan 2017: xix) that can often defy easy definitions. In her interview in this book, Akhtar reflects on the use of terms like 'New Bollywood', reminding that Bollywood, like other film industries, has always been in flux, reinventing itself to meet new times and demands (Akhtar 2020).

Though it may be difficult to label this exact moment as that of a 'New Bollywood', Akhtar's career has not only seen but contributed to this eclectic range of films and a shifting tide in the industry, resulting in something new that defies a definition at this point. As Ayesha Viswamohan writes, 'what remains most striking is the way Bollywood is finally re-examining the formula, while retaining its identity, thus bridging the gap between commercial and art-house cinema' (2017: xx). In this context, Akhtar is an excellent example of a filmmaker who has done this over the course of her career, from her features to her short films. She represents a particularly interesting point of intersection not only in terms of the shifting times but as somebody whose work has a place between markets and styles, or as she describes: 'it's industry but it's not industry enough, it's alternative but it's not alternative enough' (Akhtar 2020). In Akhtar's cinema, we find a reflection of the great influences and trends of the industry in the new millennium and her growing position as a bridge between practices, styles and audiences.

As Akhtar was starting her career in the 1990s, working on a mix of Indian independent and internationally produced films made in India, the larger Bombay-based industry was going through changes that would dramatically shape the filmmaking space she would enter. The wave of economic liberalisation that drastically opened up India, starting with Prime Minister P. V. Narasimha Rao's policies in 1991, had a profound impact on the Hindi film industry through several precipitating factors. Acquiring the official status of 'industry' in 1998, the Hindi film industry began to turn from a more fraternal club to a corporatised business atmosphere (as Aakshi Magazine's chapter in this book highlight some of the implications of this change). While this shift signified more money coming in, especially through legal sources, it also led to a more intensified look at the money to be made from abroad. The 1990s Non-Resident Indian (NRI) films, like *Dilwale Dulhania Le Jayenge (DDLJ)* (Aditya Chopra 1995), *Pardes* (Subhash Ghai 1997) and later *Kabhi Khushi Kabhi Gham (K3G)* (Karan Johar 2001), portrayed wealthy families who negotiated between their new residencies abroad and the cultural values of their homeland. This increased focus on Indians living or going abroad, usually surrounded by varying degrees of opulence, was not only a tactic to increase box office revenue, it also reflected the industry's 'drive for global relevance' (Govil 2008: 212).

These cultural shifts had two major effects on Indian cinema. Starting in the 1990s, this led to a coalescence of forms that are now easily identified as 'Bollywood'. Ashish Rajadhyaksha has described this shift in the 1990s as the '"Bollywoodization" of the Indian cinema', noting how films catering to diasporic audiences emphasised the lavish song-and-dance sequences, the family dramas, a preoccupation with 'Indian' cultural values and sumptuous settings that became the immediate image of a Bollywood film and the perfect vehicle to convey the 'export of Indian nationalism itself, now commodified and globalized into a "feel good" version of "our culture"'(2003: 37). The Bollywood industry, he argued, came to represent a culture industry distinct from the older Indian cinema national industry (28–9).

Priya Joshi elaborated on this concept, describing this shift in cinema as 'Bollylite'. This cinema's 'fabrication that heavily pillages formal characteristics from Bollywood cinema while shearing much off that cinema's social substance and political edge' creates a lightened fare that allowed it to travel while also creating a mechanism of survival to confront 'the onslaught of a renewed global machinery with new capital' (Joshi 2015: 93–4). In an era of intensified globalisation, this shift enabled Bollywood not only to survive, but to become a global example of a place 'where popular and mass culture have managed to coexist and even be the same thing' (Joshi 2015: 94).

Sangita Gopal marks a similar phenomenon in what she defines as 'New Bollywood'. Again observing the emphasis of overseas markets, she notes the increased use of branding, which also spurred

> the rise of the star-director, a trend signalled in credits by opening titles like 'A film by director X' or 'A director X film.' Figures like Mani Ratnam, Ram Gopal Varma, Vidhu Vinod Chopra, J. P. Dutta, Raj Kumar Santoshi, and Sanjay Leela Bhansali were widely described in the popular press as 'artists' whose distinctive style and unique vision would help Bollywood straddle the gap between creativity and commerce. But this also functioned as a new legitimacy to popular cinema. (2011: 64)

This bridging of the gap between 'creativity and commerce' took on a whole different meaning as the years went by. The changes in the 1990s set the stage for another shift in style heralded in as the multiplex, first inaugurated in 1997, made new audiences available. The audience was undergoing its own transformation as a 'new middle class' began to grow.[7] This brought the development of modern shopping malls and, with it, India's shift from single-screen cinemas to multiplex theatres located in these middle-class spaces in cities. The large, single-screen cinemas that had once been the mainstay theatres represented a wider access to the cinema primarily because of the lower ticket price. This meant that spectators from across different classes could be the audience of the Hindi film. The single-screen theatre, showing only one film at a time, also meant that they tended to prefer screening blockbusters that would draw the largest audience possible. With the growth of shopping malls and multiplex theatres that could screen several films at once, film distributors gained access to smaller, wealthier audiences with their own tastes. As Tejaswini Ganti writes, the multiplex became a 'metonym for a certain type of film, as well as a certain type of audience, which poses far fewer creative constraints on filmmakers than audiences who frequent the traditional single-screen theaters' (2012: 145). With this change in viewing practices, screenings and content were increasingly shifted away from catering to the 'masses' to instead intriguing the burgeoning middle class, with their global consumer tastes becoming an 'elite culture' (Biswas 2013: 238). This shift in screening practices allowed for films of commerce (such as 'Bollywood' or 'Bollylite' films), indie films, as well as films marrying the two styles, which represented a new kind of middle ground (different from the state-funded parallel cinema movement of the 1970s and 1980s), to flourish.[8]

While commercial success was still important, different types of films began to appear on the screen. The early waves of this change were seen in Ram Gopal Varma's *Satya* (1998) as well as Nagesh Kukunoor's 1998 film *Hyderabad Blues*, which is said to have started 'the "indie" movement in Hindi cinema' (Viswamohan 2017: xxi). This was later followed by filmmakers like Anurag Kashyap (who had been the scriptwriter of *Satya*), who brought a grittier picture of India to the screen through films like *Black Friday* (2004), *Dev D* (2009) and *Gangs of Wasseypur* (2012). During this period, Vishal Bhardwaj made his first critically acclaimed adaptations of Shakespeare with *Maqbool* (2003) and *Omkara* (2006), and Dibakar Banerjee realised socially critical yet popular and critically acclaimed (winning National Film Awards) works such as *Khosla ka Ghosla* (2006), *Oye Lucky! Lucky Oye!* (2008) and the controversial *LSD: Love, Sex Aur Dhokha* (2010). Other directors like Onir and Shonali Bose continued to work within an 'indie' space, often touching on more serious subjects, such as homosexuality or state complicity in violence. Together, these directors contributed to what has often been termed the 'multiplex film', defined as a 'unique, low budget, non formulaic genre' (Gopal 2011: 125).

On the other hand, there were more big budget films like *Lagaan* (Ashutosh Gowariker 2001) that were experimenting with the mentioned gap between commerce and creativity. Farhan Akhtar's debut *DCH* was also released at this time, supported by his own production company Excel Entertainment, and was heralded for celebrating this new class of Indian who was the multiplex target. Reema Kagti, Zoya Akhtar's writing and producing partner, came onto the scene with her debut *Honeymoon Travels Pvt. Ltd.* which, through a quirky cast of characters on an organised honeymoon group trip, weaved in stories about homosexuality, ageism and gender double standards. As the years have gone by, the lines between many of these filmmakers, some more 'indie' than others, have constantly blurred. The 'indie' filmmakers, for instance, have experimented with different budgets and storylines; Kashyap has worked on the big budget *Bombay Velvet* (2015) while Banerjee signed a three-film deal with Yash Raj Films in 2013. Kagti recently wrote and directed *Gold* (2018) starring Akshay Kumar, about India's quest for Olympic glory, a departure from her debut film in tone and style. This blurring of boundaries is reflective of the range of cinematic styles of contemporary filmmakers working from within the Hindi film industry.

Many of these directors have been highlighted together in recent books such as *Brave New Bollywood: In Conversation with Contemporary Hindi Filmmakers* (Kumar and Chaturvedi 2015) and *Behind the Scenes: Contemporary Bollywood Directors and their Cinema* (Viswamohan and John 2017), both of which feature chapters on Akhtar. While the latter highlights directors working at many different intersections of the industry, the former, with its emphasis on some type of 'New Bollywood', brings to the fore how, unlike the stereotypical understanding of 'Bollywood' as being composed only of song-and-dance and glamour, contemporary Bollywood is a coming together of a diverse set of filmmakers experimenting with different styles, genre, politics and form.

Akhtar also bridges these two tendencies, while still upholding the continuation of some conventions associated with big budget Bollywood. Viswamohan writes, for instance, that the directors who are 'altering' Bollywood 'go easy on melodrama glamour and gloss' (xix). Akhtar too leaves out the melodrama, but uses glamour and gloss in her feature films if the theme demands it, a characteristic for which she has often faced criticism. What that criticism misses, though, is the range of themes and complex characterisation she touches on, masked by that glamour. Vijeta Kumar's chapter in this book, for instance, focuses on the recurring 'self-made' characters across Akhtar's films to argue that unlike most Bollywood films, the notion is made to confront social realities of class, caste and gender in Akhtar's work, while analyses of her representation of gender in the chapters by Amber Shields and Sharanya reveal her challenging gender stereotypes in subtle yet profound ways. In this, Akhtar is one of the directors who is 're-examin[ing] the formula and are balancing box office with more innovative films' (Vishwamohan 2017: xix).

It is in this moment of industrial shifts – most recently impacted by the rise of streaming services that have become not only further global showcases of these films but also a platform for many of these directors (such as Akhtar, Kagti and Kashyap, among others) to make their mark on long-form series – that Akhtar finds herself not only navigating but shifting the tide. As she does so, she bridges styles and sensibilities. This is captured in an anecdote narrated by the actors Ranveer Singh, Anil Kapoor and Priyanka Chopra about their work on *DDD*. Singh and Kapoor, who are known to have predominantly worked in mainstream big budget melodramas, explained how their acting style on that film was a mix of what they called 'single screen' and 'multi' (multiplex). The former refers to a more melodramatic style of acting that Bollywood has been known for; the latter, referencing the 'multiplex genre' discussed in this section, is a subtler, realist style. For Akhtar's film, they were often reminded that they had to be more 'multi' than 'single screen'. At the same time, during the shooting of the dance sequence *Gallan Goodiyan*, they were asked to change their style as Akhtar found a missing element in their performance: the 'single screen' style (Film Companion 2015). While narrated as a joke, this telling distinction indicates the stylistic bridging that is characteristic of Akhtar's feature films: she is neither completely multiplex nor only single screen and as such creates a new style that is distinctly her own.

BEHIND THE GLITZ AND GLAMOUR: ZOYA AKHTAR'S STYLE AND VOICE

A radical impact of the multiplex on Indian cinema was the dismantling of the notion of the 'pan-India' film. Unlike the earlier 'national blockbusters' that 'sought to win as large an audience as possible', the target audience of the multiplex genre of films was specific: 'urban, globalized, middle class' (Gopal 2011: 125). The form of the earlier films, variously called Bombay cinema, Hindi cinema or popular Hindi cinema, was heterogeneous, reflected in the *social* and *masala* films.[9] In this context, Akhtar's explanation for why she added a song at the end of her second feature film, *ZNMD*, is revelatory, for it shows the importance of the audience in her filmmaking. At the end of their feedback sessions with diverse viewing groups, Akhtar realised that the audience did not understand the original abstract, poetic ending where the three protagonists are running with bulls in Pamplona, accompanied by a voiceover about the importance of facing one's fears instead of hiding from them. Most of the audience wondered if the protagonists had died. To avoid the misunderstanding, Akhtar decided to add the song '*Suraj ki Bahon Main*' during the final credit sequence. Here not only does the audience see that the protagonists have survived, but all the romantic plots are neatly resolved: one couple is getting married, one couple has broken up and one couple has been newly formed.

Akhtar's awareness of the commercial side of the film industry could be traced to her formative years where, as discussed in the section on family, both commerce and art were considered equally important when discussing a film. At the same time, she knew what she wanted to do from an early working age, as reflected in her decisions not to work with a single director or dubbed sound, for example. In her work, we see attempts at reconciling both these aspects: of knowing her voice, but also adapting it so that it can be understood by as large an audience as possible, both in India and globally, a reach amplified by streaming services. As she says: 'you want the whole world to watch your movie' (Akhtar 2020).

From the perspective of her film style, this desire is reflected in her films being situated within many of the conventions of Bollywood, while also reworking them from within. While her style continues to develop as she matures as a filmmaker, an interesting aspect of Akhtar's journey from *LBC* to *Gully Boy* is the relationship of her films to the conventions associated with the earlier Hindi film form. With each of her feature films, she moves further away from a 'multiplex film' to a film that has more 'national' (and international) aspirations, which is often reflected in the themes of her films, like male friendships, Indian family and class conflict. Though her feature films are far from melodramatic in form, they do not follow a strictly realist style of narration and include big stars like Hrithik Roshan, Ranveer Singh, Priyanka Chopra and Alia Bhatt, as well as the more popular actors from among those who started their careers in alternative or multiplex cinema, like Kalki Koechlin, Abhay Deol and Farhan Akhtar. Her short films in *Bombay Talkies*, *Lust Stories* and *Ghost Stories*, on the other hand, are closer to the multiplex film genre in their exploration of sexuality and gender, as well as their more realist style of filmmaking and choice of actors. The chapters in this book explore questions of film style from the perspective of Akhtar's scriptwriting style and the representation of gender and sexuality across her work, while also locating the themes of her films in the context of existing tropes of Hindi cinema.

At the same time, the perspectives here also question how Akhtar is at times breaking from the Hindi film industry, or at least working within its more globalised arm. The impact of her early exposure to global cinema, as well as her formative working years spent with international crews and going to film school abroad, can clearly be seen in her work, especially that which is showcased on international streaming platforms. Even Akhtar's feature films, while sitting more clearly in the style of the Hindi film industry, have taken on a more international scope that also aligns with the increased recognition of Hindi films worldwide. For example, her film *Gully Boy* more closely resembled the music (and particularly hip-hop) biopic that has been extremely popular in mainstream American cinema. The film went on to premiere at the Berlinale Film Festival, signalling that while this film may be the product of the Hindi film industry, this is a global industry with globally recognised stars catering to audiences across the world.

Working within the mainstream Hindi film industry as it continues to reimagine its place locally and globally, while also experimenting with short films and streaming series, Akhtar has worked to create a unique voice in film and media. Given the gendered dynamics of society, and the world, however, many of these pursuits have been framed in terms of what Akhtar has done as a 'woman filmmaker'. As discussions about the gender discrepancies, discrimination and pay gaps – not only in the Hindi film industry, but other film industries worldwide as well – are prominently featured in the media, this effort to centre gender when talking about filmmaking accomplishments has increased. Akhtar belongs to a generation of women filmmakers, many of whom view the tag of being called a 'woman filmmaker' as a burden or an inconvenience. At different times in history, and according to their politics, location, privilege and industrial context, women filmmakers have had a diverse range of responses to this tag and the expectations it brings. In the 1970s and 1980s, parallel filmmaker[10] Sai

Paranjpye noted how because of her gender 'I have been accused of ignoring the woman's condition in my movies' (quoted in Gopal 2019: 58) and rejected the limitations of this descriptor. The contemporary actor and filmmaker Nandita Das, who makes independent films, however recently said in an interview that she has now come to 'own the identity' (Goyal 2020). For others like Akhtar, it is an outdated tag that should become irrelevant with more women working in the industry. In our interview with her, Akhtar explained how her gender shapes her filmmaking by saying that 'my gender is my gaze', while also discussing how limiting the tag 'woman filmmaker' is: 'why not call someone a male editor then?' (2020).

Akhtar's defiance of being boxed in by labels others have tried to create for her, from 'woman filmmaker' to 'Bollywood elite/insider' to 'daughter of Javed, sister of Farhan', is reflected in her quest to find new ways to assert her own voice in the industry and, while doing so, contribute to its development. It is these intersections and creative defiances and the art born from them that we examine in this book, as we look to contribute to the understanding of not only what she has made, but the impact her work is leaving on Bollywood.

Beginning with a section placing her work within the context of the Mumbai film industry and film form, the first four chapters in this collection interpret her films in their industrial context. Aakshi Magazine's chapter focuses on Akhtar's first film, *LBC*, to argue that even her least Bollywood-style film has traces of cinephilia towards the form, while also having a unique empathetic gaze that captures the transition towards corporatisation by framing it as a loss. Her chapter also explores the gendered lens of the film in its representation of its female protagonist, an idea that is further explored in the third section of the book. Further underscoring twentieth-century changes in the industry, Sangita Gopal argues that Akhtar's work, particularly her film *Gully Boy*, 'inaugurate the project of relocating Bollywood' by capturing and practising the industry's shift in forming new relationships with other popular media and entertainment in India, particularly the music industry. Amber Shields also looks at how Akhtar's work represents industrial shifts by examining the possibilities being explored in India by filmmakers through the short film format, and how Akhtar uses this distinct form and method of distribution to push her work as a filmmaker. Finally, Vyoma Jha's chapter wraps up this section by examining the personal and industrial influences that Zoya Akhtar has had as a scriptwriter. In focusing on this often overlooked but essential aspect of Akhtar's art, Jha argues that Akhtar has 'created a unique individual style' of writing while working as a collaborator with Kagti, making them a distinct female writing duo in the Hindi film industry.[11] Akhtar's writing style includes the recurring use of an ensemble of complex characters that serve to transform niche stories and settings into mainstream audience fare.

Another aspect that makes Akhtar's writing, as well as her direction, stand out is her rewriting of the preoccupations of the popular Hindi films of an earlier time period. The chapters in the second section delve into how Akhtar reworks Bollywood themes as she reshapes the mainstream. In her chapter on *DDD*, Debnita Chakrabarti shows how the film reworks the family film of the 1990s, associated with films like *DDLJ* and *Hum Aapke Hain Koun* (Sooraj R. Barjatya 1994), to address the foundational fault lines of the Indian family by challenging accepted social and gender norms. Likewise, Kamayani Sharma's chapter explores how the two erstwhile recurring cinematic figures of the *shayar* (poet) and the *tapori* (urban vagabond) come together in a new era to reflect the current politics of class, city and neoliberal logic through the figure of *Gully Boy*'s male protagonist Murad (Ranveer Singh). In contrast, Iqra Shagufta Cheema's chapter places the representation of homosexuality in *Made in Heaven* as disruptive of Indian popular and independent cinema's invisible though long-standing engagement with portraying homosexuality. The representation of Karan Mehra (Arjun Mathur) stands out, she argues, as it is 'parallelized with heterosexual portrayals of love' and Akhtar's work on the series helps usher in a more multidimensional engagement with homosexuality.

As themes are being reworked, so are the cinematic and societal gender roles that are key elements of them. The next section explores the complex gender politics of Akhtar's films and streaming series in their representation of men, women, family and romance. Amber Shields argues that the male protagonists across works like *ZNMD*, *DDD*, *Gully Boy* and *Made in Heaven* demonstrate a vulnerability that challenges the existing representation of masculinity in mainstream Hindi cinema and opens a space to explore the new masculine identities being shaped in neoliberal India. In Sharanya's chapter, the representation of women at work is presented as a site to examine the complex gendered politics of women's work and leisure to ask, 'how does Akhtar's gaze re-inscribe or resist a patriarchal co-option of women's labour in work and leisure?'. Vijeta Kumar's chapter looks at how the ideas of 'self-made' and 'self-respect' play out across different social lines, especially gender, ultimately pointing to how Akhtar captures a unique subset of women and lets us see how they make decisions on how they want to balance both.

Just as the characters in her films face certain gender expectations, so does Akhtar as a director. Akhtar has often faced criticism for not having the 'right' voice that others expect of her, being told that her films are not female-centred enough, are too focused on the rich, are too commercial, are too influenced by her family and industry background, etc. Akhtar continues to be told, perhaps more so than most of her contemporary (male) directors, what her voice should or should not be. Ruchi Jaggi and Mudita Mishra's chapter focuses on this aspect through a study that critically examines reviewers' responses to Akhtar and interviews film critics to understand their changing perception of Akhtar's films. In this, they argue that Akhtar and her work has been more often unfairly discounted by cultural influencers who have overlooked the significance of her offerings. Despite the critiques, Akhtar has managed to shape her own course and find her own voice, and thus this volume ends by giving Akhtar the final word in an interview exclusively for this book.

Still in the midst of her growing career as a mediamaker and 'aesthetic producer', this book contributes to the study of Akhtar's work, examining it more closely in order to understand this moment in popular Hindi film and the new directions it will take in the future. With the commercial success of her latest film *Gully Boy*, Akhtar's career trajectory has been moving closer to the mainstream, while also changing it from within, making her a fascinating figure to understand the continuities and discontinuities of the Bollywood film form and how it reinvents itself constantly.

NOTES

1. A note on style: The longer names of Hindi films often result in the common practice of shortening these titles to their initials. We will be following that practice in this book.
2. Farah Khan, another director who grew up in the industry, also offers a celebration of the people who make films possible, albeit in a more playful way that avoids revealing the hard work itself. The thematic ending credits of *Om Shanti Om*, for example, feature members of the film team, from accountants to costume designers, walking a red carpet, while *Main Hoon Na* (2004) shows the team frolicking together at an end-of-year school fair and *Happy New Year* (2014) shows different departments competing in a mock dance competition.
3. A note on terminology: In recent times, the word 'Bollywood' has become an increasingly popular term in international use to refer to 'Indian cinema'. We and the authors in this volume use the term to refer to a very specific strain of Indian cinema: post-1990s big budget, mainstream films in the Hindi language produced by the Bombay/Hindi film industry (which are also terms we use interchangeably to reflect these films). While on closer examination the term 'Bollywood' also carries with it specific thematic and stylistic choices that do not necessarily define all films produced by this industry, the term has become so pervasive that we have opted to use it, trying also to distinguish it clearly from films that might not meet these understandings with different terminology.
4. Honey Irani, Akhtar's mother, is also a partner in the company.
5. These are not the only contemporary female directors working in the industry, but they are by far some of the biggest who can now consistently command big budget, star-studded films. Other directors like Zoya Akhtar's artistic partner Reema Kagti, Ashwiny Iyer Tiwari, Gauri Shinde, Shonali Bose and Alankrita Shrivastava have also often enjoyed increasing mainstream success.
6. The role was eventually taken on by her brother Farhan who had only acted in one film and whose acting career has been defined by a willingness to take on offbeat and complex roles.
7. See Dwyer 2000 for a more in-depth look at this phenomenon.
8. The Indian Parallel cinema movement (also called New Indian Cinema/Wave) of the 1970s and 1980s was associated with funding from the government bodies the Film

Finance Corporation and its successor the National Film Development Corporation. It encompassed the work of a diverse range of filmmakers who defined themselves in opposition to the mainstream Indian film industry, including critically acclaimed directors like Satyajit Ray, Ritwik Ghatak, Mrinal Sen, Mani Kaul, Shyam Benegal and Saeed Mirza. Owing to a host of complex factors, including the lack of viable screening spaces, these films never gained the kind of mainstream popularity that the new indie directors of the late 1990s–2000s did (see Rajadhyaksha and Willemen 1998: 165).
9. The social is an 'umbrella genre' that refers to 'melodrama with a 20th century setting, rehearsing a variety of "social" issues' (Rajadhyaksha and Willemen 1998: 219). Film scholars argue that it dominated the 'classic' period of Indian cinema in the 1950s and 1960s. This was followed by the period of the *masala* (spice) film of the 1970s which, like its name, was a coming together of elements like romance, comedy, action, melodrama, song-and-dance and often multiple stars. The *masala* film could be viewed as an 'entertainment-driven version of the social film' and its mixing of various components gave it a popular appeal as it had something in it for everyone (see Gopal 2011: 24).
10. The term 'parallel filmmaker' refers to the Indian Parallel cinema movement (see note 8 above).
11. The recent collaboration between filmmaker Tanuja Chandra and writer Gazal Dhaliwal on the film *Qarib Qarib Single* (2017) is another emerging female filmmaker–writer duo that comes to mind. Also see Anubha Yadav's recent book *Scripting Bollywood Candid Conversations with Women Who Write Hindi Cinema* (Women Unlimited 2021).

WORKS CITED

Biswas, Moinak (2013), 'Bodies in syncopation', in Meheli Sen and Anustup Basu (eds), *Figurations in Indian Film*, New York: Palgrave Macmillan, pp. 236–52.

Bollywood Hungama (2019), '*Ghost Stories* is my most SATISFYING experience: Anurag Kashyap', *Bollywood Hungama*, Video, 11:35. Available at <https://www.youtube.com/watch?v=oGkRRPcRfrY&t=183s>

Bollywood Roundtables (2013), '"Bombay Talkies" directors discuss cinema', *CNN IBN*, 27 April 2013. Video, 18:42. Available at <https://www.news18.com/videos/india/bollywood-roundtables-2013-show-605692.html>

Bose, Nandana (2017), 'Globalization, reflexivity and genre in Zoya Akhtar's films', in Ayesha Mohan Iqbal Viswamohan and Vimal Mohan (eds), *Behind the Scenes: Contemporary Bollywood Directors and Their Cinema*, New Delhi: Sage, pp. 215–26.

Chaturvedi, Preeti and Nirmal Kumar (2015), *Brave New Bollywood: In Conversation with Contemporary Hindi Filmmakers*, New Delhi: Sage.

Dwyer, Rachel (2000), *All You Want is Money, All You Need is Love: Sex and Romance in Modern India*, London: Cassell.

Film Companion (2015), 'Team Dil Dhadakne Do. FC ADDA'. Interview by Anupama Chopra, *Film Companion*, 1 June 2015. Video, 23:55. Available at <https://www.youtube.com/watch?v=LwIEw_yI7tk&t=1192s>

Iqbal Viswamohan, Aysha (2017), 'Introduction', in Ayesha Mohan Iqbal Viswamohan and Vimal Mohan (eds), *Behind the Scenes: Contemporary Bollywood Directors and Their Cinema*, New Delhi: Sage, pp. xvii–xxviii.

Ganti, Tejaswini (2012), *Producing Bollywood: Inside the contemporary Hindi film industry*, Durham, NC: Duke University Press.

Gopal, Sangita (2019), 'Media meddlers: Feminism, television and gendered media work in India', *Feminist Media Histories*, 5: 1, 39–62.
—— (2011), *Conjugations: Marriage and Form in New Bollywood Cinema*, Chicago: University of Chicago Press.
Govil, Nitin (2008), 'Bollywood and the frictions of global mobility', in Rajinder Dudrah and Jigna Desai (ed.), *The Bollywood Reader*, Maidenhead: Open University Press, pp. 201–15.
Goyal, Divya (2020), 'I have started to own the woman-director identity: Nandita Das', *The Indian Express*, 16 February 2020. Available at <https://indianexpress.com/article/lifestyle/books/nandita-das-saadat-hasan-manto-film-nawazuddin-siddiqui-book-6270095/>
Gupta, Shubhra (2009), 'Movie review: *Luck by Chance*', *The Indian Express*, 30 January 2009. Available at <http://archive.indianexpress.com/news/movie-review-luck-by-chance/417117/>
Jain, Anuja (2017), '*Love Sex Aur Dhoka*: A new morphology of contemporary Bombay cinema', *Screen*, 58: 1, Spring 2017, 98–106. Available at <https://doi.org/10.1093/screen/hjx010>
Joshi, Priya (2015), *Bollywood's India: A Public Fantasy*, New York: Columbia University Press.
Mohamed, Khalid (2009), 'Review: *Luck by Chance*', *Hindustan Times*, 30 January 2009. Available at <https://www.hindustantimes.com/movie-reviews/review-luck-by-chance/story-WwQIxior8xhkMoCcAfmmjM.html>
Rajadhyaksha, Ashish and Paul Willemen (1998), *Encyclopaedia of Indian Cinema*, New Delhi: Oxford University Press.
Rajadhyaksha, Ashish (2003), 'The "Bollywoodization" of the Indian cinema: Cultural nationalism in a global arena', *Inter-Asia Cultural Studies*, 4: 1, 25–39.

PART I

Growing up Industry

CHAPTER I

Loving but Critical: The Empathetic Gaze of *Luck by Chance*

Aakshi Magazine

In the opening sequence of *Luck by Chance* (2009), Zoya Akhtar's debut film, we are witness to a conversation between the film's female protagonist, actress Sona Mishra (Konkona Sen Sharma), and film producer Satish Choudhury (Alyy Khan). He is the one doing all the talking while she is sitting in front of him, listening closely. This appears like a professional meeting as he mentions artists, screen tests and his production company Pinky Productions. She should keep meeting him, he says, so that they can understand each other; the importance of spending time together is emphasised by asking her if she understands what he means. As he says this, the camera closes in first on his face, and then on Sona, who shows a hint of doubt before she nods and smiles.

Throughout the film, various characters talk about this 'special' relationship that Sona shares with Choudhury: some of her co-workers gossip about it behind her back, wondering who the exploiter in their relationship is. The most direct reference, however, is first made during a date with her boyfriend, Vikram (Farhan Akhtar), as he comments that she must share a special relationship with Choudhury as she seems to be relying solely on him to make her into a big Hindi film star. Only when Sona replies that he is married, has kids and that she has no complaints does it get confirmed that she is sleeping with him in return for his promise that he will give her a big break. This is the infamous 'casting couch' of Bollywood but the film does not dwell on this moment; neither do the characters. Its significance, in fact, is underplayed. In response to her 'confession', Vikram recites a couplet about success and failure being choices and follows this up with a joke that lightens the mood.

This representation of the casting couch is unusual when compared to the sleazy and scandalous tone of the discourse around it in film magazines and film gossip. Its almost casual, non-judgemental representation of a woman's experience of the film industry would have been revelatory in the 2000s when it was only ever spoken about, reported on and, in some rare instances, represented on the Hindi film screen (*Fashion* [Madhur Bhandarkar 2008]; *Heroine* [Madhur Bhandarkar 2012]) as catastrophic for the lives of the women involved. It is only in recent times with discussions on #MeToo that conversations around the casting couch have begun to move away from a focus on women as 'victims' to discussing the men as the problem. Though a brief moment, its disruption of the dominant narrative is significant.

In this chapter, my focus is on interrogating Akhtar's often subversive take on some key themes: the Bombay film industry, the popular Hindi film form, romance and success. Akhtar's critically appreciated but otherwise least commercially successful film took seven years to start shooting because no leading male actor wanted to play the role of a protagonist who appeared morally questionable. Since its release, *LBC* has been viewed by critics as an aberration in Akhtar's career, for her next two films were focused on the rich and upwardly mobile and had a bigger scale. However, as the chapter will show, the film also works within certain Bollywood conventions like big stars and song-and-dance sequences and therefore retains a connection to this form, suggesting continuities between its style and that of Akhtar's later films. The film thus provides a glimpse into Akhtar's later career trajectory as it shows her connection to the industry through which she traces her history.

OUTSIDERS AND INSIDERS: CINEPHILIA VS FILMMAKING

Set in the 2000s, *LBC* portrays two worlds: one is the incestuous, closely knit Bombay film industry where everyone is related to everyone, and the other is of 'outsiders' like Sona and Vikram, who are waiting for their big break into this industry. While Vikram, through a mix of his charm, manipulation and luck, manages to find success by landing a lead role opposite the star-kid Nikki Walia (Isha Sharvani), Sona is not successful in becoming a film star, and becomes a TV star instead. In tracing their two journeys, the film shows different sides of the experience of the struggling artist and the nuances of the established industry.

As part of the second generation of her family to work in the Bombay film industry, in real life Akhtar belongs to the former world. Due to the film's casting choices, the presence of Bollywood stars and superstars, and her own location in the film industry, film criticism as well as academic scholarship has focused on the film's self-reflexivity. Nandana Bose, for instance, writes that *LBC* is a 'self-reflexive, satiric meta-film, on the chaotic and idiosyncratic Bombay film industry' (2017: 219). At the time of its release in 2009, film critic Shubhra Gupta called it 'the latest in the line of Bollywood-looking-at-Bollywood ensembles'.

The self-reflexive tone of the film makes it representative of a trend in early 2000s Bollywood, which Bhaskar Sarkar called a film industry representing itself 'obsessively' (2013: 205). He argues that while self-reflection is not entirely new in Indian cinema's history, with films like *Kaagaz Ke Phool* (Guru Dutt 1959) and *Guddi* (Hrishikesh Mukherjee 1971) among others, it is in recent years that an emphasis on its own working 'has emerged as one of the most salient and popular plot ingredients' (206). Referring to films like *Om Shanti Om* (Farah Khan 2007), *Billu* (Priyadarshan 2009), *I Hate Luv Storys* (Punit Malhotra 2010) and *LBC*, Sarkar interprets this self-representation as 'Bollywood being engaged in the consolidation of a "Bollywood model" at the heart of global cinema' (206). He also adds a series of films made by Ram Gopal Varma through the 1990s and early 2000s like *Rangeela* (1995), *Mast* (1999) and *Naach* (2004) to this list, arguing that these contributed to consolidating a 'Bollywood genre' (208).

A closer look at these films reveals a considerable difference in the representation of the film industry in the 1990s 'Bollywood genre' and the 2000s 'Bollywood-on-Bollywood' films. A useful framework for viewing this difference comes from their relationship to their love for film vs their love for the industry and its people. Here I am using Lalitha Gopalan's comment about the narrative resolution of the 1995 film *Rangeela*, which she interprets as favouring 'cinephilia over film-making' (2002: 1). In the film's romantic union, the film's heroine Mili (Urmila Matondkar) chooses the local ticket tout and *tapori* (urban vagabond) figure Munna (Aamir Khan) over the Bollywood superstar Kamal (Jackie Shroff). In Gopalan's interpretation, the film's resolution indicates that the characters' 'love for film' guides their love story. While her larger argument is about film scholarship and cinephilia, I am using her comment to locate the specificity of *LBC*, whose relationship to Bollywood reflects a tension between these two loves. Its cinephilia is not just for the film form but for the film industry itself. It visualises the industry's history through well-sketched, nuanced characters who live out its clichés and make them work.

This emphasis on the industry is what the 2000s films like *Om Shanti Om* and *LBC* have in common: these are films made, at a particular time in Bollywood history, by second-generation filmmakers who, as filmmaker Tigmanshu Dhulia observes, 'grew up in the Hindi film industry' and 'had not seen India; they had only seen Bombay' (quoted in Tejaswini Ganti 2019: 127). The films reflect their insider knowledge, negotiating with a filmmaking tradition that comes to them as a legacy (though it might be fraught as in the case of *Om Shanti Om* director Farah Khan whose producer-father Kamran Khan lost all his money in the industry when she was a child). Their insider view often leads to their attempts at a balancing act between their love for this world and their observations about its inequities (*Om Shanti Om*; *LBC*), justifying the conventions considered ridiculous (*I Hate Luv Storys*), or in some cases, simply celebrating them (the song '*Phir Milenge Chalte Chalte*' in *Rab Ne Bana Di Jodi* [Aditya Chopra 2008]).

Despite this distinction, there is one trope that *LBC* does share with 'Bollywood genre' films like *Rangeela*, *Mast* and others: the film's protagonists Vikram and Sona are outsiders to the film industry. It takes this trope to view the film world as unfairly divided between them and the rest, an aspect of the film that even prompted some recent interpretations of it being ahead of its time as a 'film that called out nepotism', referencing the recent controversy in India around that term (Chopra 2020).[1]

In fact, the film's comment on the industry is an intriguing point resulting in a diverse set of readings. While Anne Ciecko finds in the film an 'ultimately bleak view of the foibles of the film industry' which offers 'little hope of entry for the uninitiated' (2016: 33), film reviews have used phrases like 'soft-toned', 'jibes are gentle' (Kazmi 2009) and 'beguiling' (Chopra 2014) for it. The diverse and new readings of the film reflect the complexity of *LBC*'s world view: it is not as direct as a satire nor is it a parody. Most reviews and academic interpretations of the film emphasise that the film represents both love of as well as a critical distance from the world it represents.[2] Stylistically too the film balances this attachment to and distance from the film world, as it appears neither mainstream Bollywood nor completely the kind of style that was being seen in more independent and smaller budget films made in the same year like *Dev D* (Anurag Kashyap), *Sankat City* (Pankaj Advani) or *Firaaq* (Nandita Das). The rest of this chapter will explore the complexity of the film's narrative, which balances its critical representation of the Hindi film industry, including its gendered dimensions, with its love for that world.

CRITIQUE OR TRIBUTE? *LBC*'S VIEW OF THE BOMBAY FILM INDUSTRY

Vikram and Sona's aspirations are not just to become actors; both specifically aspire to be mainstream Hindi film stars. Integral to the film's story is its wide-ranging representation of the mainstream Bombay film industry of that time, in the midst of the shift towards corporatisation. As mentioned earlier, while Akhtar is an insider to the film industry, the protagonists of her film are two outsiders. In this section, I focus on the film's interpretation of the film industry, balancing the insider–outsider dynamic that comes from Akhtar's own location within it. The film is empathetic towards all its characters, both insiders and outsiders, but it also recognises the inherent insularity of the film industry. This nuanced relationship to an industry in the middle of a great shift makes it a sensitive chronicle of Bollywood.

Beginning with a beautiful opening credits song that makes visible the people working on a film set whose work we don't usually view as 'craft', the film envisions the industry through a range of characters. Its ensemble of characters includes the old-world producer-director Romy Rolly (Rishi Kapoor), the star daughter Nikki Walia and yesteryear superstar-turned-heroine's mummy Nina Walia (Dimple Kapadia). Others are the producer's less talented brother Ranjit Rolly (Sanjay Kapoor), Rolly's wife Minty (Juhi Chawla), her earnest butt-of-all-jokes sister Pinky (Sheeba Chaddha) and the B-grade producer brother-in-law Satish Choudhury. Each of these characters has a well-etched backstory, of which glimpses are revealed through the film's dialogue, contributing to an empathetic perspective towards them. While the Bombay film industry is usually viewed as a highly male-dominated space, and it does come across as such in the film too, the film often keeps its focus on the women. Parallel to Vikram's lucky break in the big budget film, for instance, is the story arc about an accidental exchange of his portfolio photographs between Sona and Pinky. As his dream takes off, Sona's gets shattered, for she is told that the break she is waiting for will not happen. Pinky, on the other hand, often feels left out in her family and the fact that she played a role in Vikram's break is something she later quietly takes pride in.

Sona and Nikki, who occupy two extreme locations in their relationship to the industry, are both represented with a degree of non-judgement. Sona's is a significant point of view in the film. The film begins with her, and the first time we catch a glimpse of Bollywood is also through her as she is watching the launch of the production of Nikki's film, the parodically titled *Dil Ki Aag* (*The Heart's Fire*), on television. The television segment highlights the incestuous nature of the film industry, introducing everyone through their relationship to each other – 'Rommy's brother', 'Neena Walia's daughter', 'Rolly's protégé'. It ends with Nikki's television interview about wanting to be a vet and then changing her mind when approached by the producer to become an actress because 'why not'. This is immediately followed by a shot of Sona mimicking her tone. The difference is stark: while Sona has to struggle for years just for minor nameless roles like 'dead sister's friend', Nikki does not even need to be ambitious in order to land the lead role opposite the reigning star. The film employs this contrast often. Sona is handed an ungainly black dress for her unnamed character, but Nikki is spoiled for choice with a range of designer wear at her disposal. At a later crucial and poignant moment when Sona tells Choudhury that she has talent and can act, his reply is a jarring comment on what the industry expects out of its heroines: 'who wants that'.

The awareness of this stark difference often leads to a mocking tone towards Nikki. There are occasional scenes that evoke laughter at her expense, like the one where she cannot pronounce the Hindustani word *khoon* (murder) during rehearsal, or the running joke between Sona and Vikram about her pink 'cake' room and her love for her stuffed animal 'doggy'. As the film progresses, however, Nikki becomes a more layered character, who has a complex relationship with her mother. This is especially evident towards the end, in her confrontation with Vikram after the publication of the gossip story about their relationship. As Vikram denies his relationship with Sona, and mocks Nikki's ability to act, Nikki reacts strongly, her face indicating he has crossed a line. That small moment, when she stands up for herself, is a hint towards her inner world that could have otherwise easily been lost in a unidimensional representation of the character as a childish spoiled brat. This reflects a writing style that pays attention to developing even seemingly minor characters in the ensemble.[3]

At the same time, her confrontation with her mother Nina that follows this sequence puts the latter's choices in context. After an initial ugly outburst at the magazine editor who published the story about Nikki and Vikram's relationship, Nina soon changes her tone when the public have a positive reaction to this relationship. She encourages Nikki to patch things up with Vikram despite his cheating on her, prompting Nikki to disappointingly comment that she does not understand her mother. Nina's response indicates that the script does: Nikki has the privilege to make choices which Nina, who grew up in *chawls* (tenements) and worked as a child star doing favours for producers, did not have. This reflects not only Akhtar's approach of writing characters with a degree of detail and attention but also of having a non-judgemental perspective towards contrasting motivations. In doing this, the film avoids easy stereotypes and does not restrict its female characters, including that of Nina, to the limiting binaries that popular Hindi cinema is known for. Sona and Nikki are on opposing ends of the film family privilege spectrum but they are not pitted against each other. The film does not take either of their sides, and in doing that, ends up taking both their sides.

In fact, the film industry is not represented as one that is singularly prosperous and thriving. It has insecurity and failure as exemplified through the character of Choudhury, who makes B-grade films and aspires to be more successful like Rolly. He approaches Rolly several times with ideas and tags along on Rolly's productions to be close to the action. The insecurity is also evident in the changing relationship of the superstar Zafar Khan (Hrithik Roshan) to his one-time mentor Romy Rolly and to his own stardom. Zafar's confidence and cockiness in the initial scenes begin to change towards the end with the rise of the new male star on the block, Vikram, who takes over the role that Zafar dropped. The suggestion of his eventual unease about Vikram evokes the insecurities of male stardom. As Karan Johar (playing himself) quotes trivia about how every new male star without family connections was born because an established star refused a film, even a superstar like Zafar has to contend with the possibility that he might be replaceable. The nuances of these changing equations indicate that apart from the insider–outsider difference, *LBC* complicates the view of the inside.

The inside that *LBC* captures is complicated especially as the film shows the industry moving towards corporatisation in the early 2000s, leading to a change from individual and film family 'banners' to the entry of new production companies called 'corporates'. Some of these included UTV, Percept Picture Companies and Sahara One (Ganti 2012: 268). The eventual result of this change would mean that 'filmmaking became more systematized, with written contracts, prompt payments, film insurance, completion bonds, and the use of both executive and line producers' (Ganti 2012: 268). The film captures these developments in the sequences between Rolly and Choudhury and two corporate heads, who talk about bringing a 'change' in the industry culture by introducing more standardised practices. In contrast to their self-professed (though inconsistent) professionalism, Rolly is guided by emotion, the need for *izzat* (respect), making him willing to change scripts as and when his lead star demands. At the same time, he is a shrewd businessman who makes sure he saves money when deciding the pay for the new actor Vikram. While the character represents, as Ashwin Punathambekar calls him, a 'filmic exemplar for Bollywood in a phase of transition', it also reflects the specific way in which the transition is framed in the film (2013: 51).

In the film's interpretation, this transition is viewed from the perspective of an emotional landscape that is being eroded with this change. Rolly is used to a style of filmmaking that revolves around the male star and places less emphasis on the script or other production factors. If, for example, the film's male star feels his role is too negative, Rolly agrees to change it, disregarding script or continuity. This corroborates what many film stars have said about the working style of the 1990s, such as actress Raveena Tandon, who said in an interview that they worked without a script and the dialogues would often be written before the scene (Rammohan 2018). Zafar feels tied down by the loyalty Rolly expects out of him just because he gave him his break, compelling him to act in the film being made by Rolly's failed actor-turned-director brother even though he has no interest in working on that project. Perhaps he has started finding Rolly's kind of films devoid of logic now that he has moved on to the more serious fare of Mani Ratnam, or to Karan Johar's more popular Bollywood style, for whose film he finally leaves Rolly's film. Zafar's impatience with Rolly is a product of the changing 'multiplex' sensibilities that are even referenced in the film in the sequence where Minty comments on the decision of casting Vikram in their film.

Unlike Zafar's attitude towards him, the film is affectionate towards Rolly. The casting of yesteryear superstar Rishi Kapoor plays a role in contributing to this warmth. Like Nikki, he too is often playing for laughs, but the script understands where he comes from. At one point, fed up with Zafar's evasiveness, he breaks down in front of Minty, sobbing that he is done chasing youngsters the age of his children for 'dates'. His dialogue is a comment about his place in the new professional world of Bollywood filmmaking: 'Today's generation is ill-mannered. There was a time when I used to feel happy making films. Today there is no fun in it . . . After working here for so many years no one respects me anymore . . .'. The words *tameez*, *mazza* and *izzat* – cultured, fun and respect – that are used in the original Hindustani dialogue are crucial in this scene because they reflect the very peculiar coexistence of a business-cum-fraternal, modern but feudal model of working that characterises this tradition of filmmaking. It also becomes another moment highlighting the insecurities of the industry, for even Rolly faces insecurities in a moment of change. In a recent interview, actress Sushmita Sen said that she 'misses the intimacy of the 1990s' because contemporary industry is 'a full-blown business . . . I miss the human connect' (Sen 2020). Rolly is a personification of this observation. He is a well-established director-producer whose style of working will eventually grow irrelevant.

At the end of *LBC*, though, he remains relevant as his film is a box office hit. This fits the time period the film was made in, for by 2005, as Ganti notes, the initial excitement about corporates changing Indian cinema had come under doubt, with many of the corporate-produced films not faring well at the box office. The blockbusters of the time like *Veer-Zara* (Yash Chopra 2004), *Munna Bhai M.B.B.S* (Rajkumar Hirani 2003), *Chak De! India* (Shimit Amin 2007), *Dhoom* (Sanjay Gadhvi 2004) and *Kal Ho Na Ho* (Nikhil Advani 2003) continued to be made by producers and banners like Yashraj Films, Dharma Productions and Vinod Chopra Films, who had experience in the business, often being second-generation industry professionals (2012: 273).

The long-lasting impact of the corporates, however, was in reshaping even the existing banners and 'changing the overall and everyday work culture of the industry' (278). Ganti argues that the term 'corporate' represented a 'new way of being in the world', with even the traditional family businesses like Yashraj transforming and becoming a 'corporately organized body' (266). Rolly represents the opposite of this 'new way', though he remains a shrewd businessman who understands these changes, as is evident in his meeting with the corporate company where he talks in their language. The film views the 'unprofessionalism' of the pre-corporate era from the perspective of those who perpetuate it. Eventually the transition might have meant better filmmaking conditions and technically sound films but viewing it from the perspective of people who were invested in the earlier system, it could be framed as a loss. Not only does this reflect another example of *LBC*'s empathetic world view, it could be argued that the emphasis on loss is also indicative of Akhtar's insider status and location, reflecting the film's cinephilic relationship to not just the popular film form, but the industry itself. At the same time, it also recognises the unfairness of the existing system. What the film represents, then, is a nostalgia that does not rush forward to the promises of a corporate future. It is never just a tribute or only a critique. It is both.

NOT A 'SONGLESS' BOLLYWOOD FILM: CINEPHILIA AT WORK

Its empathy towards Rolly notwithstanding, *LBC* itself is not the kind of film that Rolly would make. It does not follow the formal style and conventions that one associates with classic pre-corporatisation Bollywood that he represents. At the same time, the film is not completely unmoored from the form either, and another site to understand the film's relationship to the industry and the film form it produces is its own form and style of filmmaking. As the examples in this section will demonstrate, in *LBC*'s engagement with the conventions of the song-and-dance sequence and with stardom we find traces of the film's cinephilia towards Bollywood. This indicates that even in what is considered Akhtar's least Bollywood-style film, she still stayed within the conventions associated with it.

I focus on the two songs that are being shot in *Dil Ki Aag*, the film being made in the film: '*Baawre*' and '*Pyaar Ki Dastaan*', both of which make use of lip-sync singing. The existence of the film-within-the-film gives Akhtar the space to unironically explore one of the most well-known conventions of the popular Hindi film: the lip-synced song-and-dance sequence using playback singers. This contrasts with the trend of using the song-and-dance number as 'the locus of the most self-conscious and intense negotiations' (Sarkar 2013: 211). The function of the two songs is the opposite of the self-reflexive songs that resemble, as Sarkar calls them, the 'air quotes of common parlance' (211). None of Akhtar's films up until this point have used the song in such a manner. At the same time, the film also has another type of song sequence: the songs that are a part of the diegetic world of *LBC*, which are mostly picturised without a lip-sync. The presence of these two different types of songs in the film is both a continuation of tradition, but also an intervention in it of the Hollywood-style, realist idea of the song: you don't lip-sync unless it's a performance or, in this case, a self-professed film song. This dual existence of the song is often seen in all of Akhtar's feature films to date.

Snippets of '*Baawre*' are repeated throughout the film, through the various stages of its making – the first time it is being rehearsed by the choreographer and the dancers, and later one short sequence from it is shown in the film theatre, this time picturised on Vikram. In between we also see the full song picturised on Zafar and Nikki (with Sona in a brief appearance as 'dead sister's friend' sitting next to Nikki). Through these three sequences, the film captures different aspects of the Hindi film song – behind the scenes, reception in the theatres and the joy of the lip-synched song sequence. The song, choreographed by Vaibhavi Merchant, was filmed in Mumbai's Film City on a set that resembled a circus. Akhtar wanted the song to be 'chaotic' as it was 'a metaphor for how the film industry works' (Sharma 2019). The lyrics, written by Javed Akhtar, repeatedly use the word *baawre* as a play on someone who has lost their senses. Along with the lyrics, the fast-paced tempo of the song and the dance sequence emphasise the chaotic and all-consuming nature of the work in the industry: '*Main tan haara, Main man haara, Main jaan haara . . . Main sab haara*' ('I lost my body, I lost my mind, I lost my life . . . I lost everything').

Interestingly, the picturisation of the song is often discussed in the film much before we see it. Right before the song, the director Ranjit is explaining the sequence of the song's picturisation. His description is portrayed in a humorous light for he comes across as someone who, while an eager fan boy, is completely naive in his field. In an earlier scene, the same song had been the source of an argument between Zafar and Ranjit, as Zafar finds the placement of the song illogical. In contrast to these two instances, when we actually watch the song, it is shot beautifully in a spectacle mode, often using a direct address that builds on Roshan's stardom. If the film was following a realist style, the song would have been amateurish in keeping with Rolly's explanation of it. In the song, however, we catch a glimpse of Akhtar's adoring gaze towards it; it is a song from Akhtar's film, not from Ranjit's. This reflects the film's cinephilia for the Bollywood form, specifically the song-and-dance sequence. Likewise, the third time we see the song in the cinema theatre after its release, Vikram is watching his song with a sense of pride as well as the audience dancing to it, the latter capturing the single-screen experience that is so particular to popular Indian cinema across languages.

A similar respectful attitude towards the tradition of the romantic duet song is displayed in Akhtar's use of the song '*Pyaar Ki Dastaan*'. Picturised on Nikki and Vikram as they shoot the song for their film, the song is as much a part of *LBC* as it is of the former. Akhtar's specific brief to the song's choreographer Rajeev Surti was not to make it 'funny' (Movies 2009). This is significant for it tells us that it is a song in the tradition of classic romantic duet songs; it is not mimicking it nor is it an ironic tongue-in-cheek engagement with it. It is only towards the song's end that it briefly shows the behind the scenes. This serves a diegetic purpose: it shows Nikki's feelings towards Vikram and also makes the choreographer – who is Sona's friend – suspect their impending love affair. This would eventually lead to Sona and Vikram's break-up.

The use of songs in this manner recalls a comment made by Ian Garwood in his exploration of three other 'songless' Bollywood films in the 2000s, as he finds that the films are unable to completely escape the song-and-dance sequence and instead 'contain traces of the form they are ostensibly eschewing' (2006: 173). Interestingly, *LBC*'s relationship to another convention – stardom – is also on similar lines. While the hero and heroine of the film are Konkona Sen Sharma and Farhan Akhtar, both of whom were not big stars, the film has a range of Bollywood stars who play themselves in small cameo roles. This includes superstars like Shah Rukh Khan and Aamir Khan. This too could be viewed as a surrogate strategy for including Bollywood stars while not including them.

However, the casting does not lend itself to a definitive interpretation. Apart from reflecting Akhtar's insider status and access, the casting choices are a curious mix of being self-reflexive but perpetuating the same insidious system that in the film Vikram and especially Sona find difficult to break into. The three prominent characters are played by second- or third-generation film actors who belong to film families. Apart from Farhan Akhtar, who is Akhtar's brother and a filmmaker himself, Konkona Sen Sharma who plays Sona is the daughter of former actor and renowned arthouse filmmaker Aparna Sen. Romy Rolly is Rishi Kapoor, the son of Raj Kapoor and grandson of Prithviraj Kapoor, whose relationship, in turn, connects him to other Kapoor family members who are also prominent in the industry (some of whom, like his son Ranbir Kapoor and niece Kareena Kapoor, also appear in cameo roles in the film).

Some of the other casting is self-reflexive: Rolly's failed-actor-turned-director brother Ranjit Rolly is Sanjay Kapoor, who in real life is the less successful brother of the actor Anil Kapoor; both belong to the 'lesser' Kapoor family compared to the Raj Kapoor dynasty. Superstar Zafar Khan is played by superstar Hrithik Roshan (son of actor turned director Rakesh Roshan) and yesteryear star Nina Walia is played by yesteryear star Dimple Kapadia (whose daughters Twinkle and Rinki Khanna, who she had with film superstar Rajesh Khanna, were film stars too). These casting choices work as a nod towards the cinephile. Fans would understand their gravity and place them in the context of popular Hindi cinema.

At the same time, the film's use of real-life film stars is strikingly different from a similar use of stars in the song '*Deewangi Deewangi*' in *Om Shanti Om*. While in the latter the stars appear for silent nods towards the screen as they enter one by one into an industry party, *LBC* casts stars in roles where they play themselves but do not exert stardom. As such, its gaze becomes fascinating and perhaps confusing, for one is not sure who the joke is on and whether the joke is consistent. The best example of this is the sequence in which Shah Rukh Khan, playing himself, accidentally meets Vikram at a restaurant. Khan offers him advice to deal with the uncertainties of stardom. As I will discuss in the next section in regard to the penultimate sequence between Sona and Vikram, this advice turns on its head and could even be interpreted as a comment on the inherent self-centred nature of stardom when seen through Sona's perspective.

SONA AND VIKRAM: *LBC*'S COUPLE-FORM

Arguing that the couple-form has 'critical value as an analytic category' in classic as well as contemporary Hindi cinema, Sangita Gopal identifies a distinct change post-1991 with the emergence of a 'post-nuptial couple-form that replaced the standard Hindi film romance duo' (2011: 2–4). The most striking aspect of this change was that 'the couple's right to be – once a source of conflict – is no longer in question' (2). Vikram and Sona fit into these categories in as much as their 'right to be' is not questioned because of societal norms or family pressure. Like other love stories in contemporary cinema of that time like *Love Aaj Kal* (Imtiaz Ali 2009), *Shuddh Desi Romance* (Maneesh Sharma 2013) and *Yeh Jawaani Hai Deewani* (Ayan Mukherji 2013), among others, the source of conflict is not external to the couple. The departure lies in how this personal conflict leads in the film to a gradual decomposition of the couple rather than of them coming together. Their evolution lies not in staying together, but rather in staying apart.

The first few times Vikram and Sona meet, the differences between them are apparent. While Vikram is new to the city, Sona has been in Mumbai for a longer time. She has done the rounds and is already a few films old. Her body language is of someone well-versed with the ways of the city and of the industry. Another difference that places Vikram at an advantage is of where they come from: Vikram Singh is from a business family in Delhi with extended family in Mumbai, which ensures that he has a place to live and does not have to do small roles for money; Sona Mishra, as we get to know towards the end, ran away from small-town Kanpur without parental support or approval and must work to maintain herself in her one-room flat.

As they start spending time together, a shared camaraderie emerges between them. Their romance has an unusual progression: it is always aware of their larger context, that of the Bombay film industry. This is reflected in the conversations they have which bring them closer; these are about the struggle, the film industry, about the film that has to start or the film that got shelved, and even about Sona's equation with Satish Choudhary. Their friendships too are formed, broken and mended with a change in career graph. Vikram's friends are a theatre actor and a struggling assistant director. Sona's friends are a junior choreographer and a film magazine's cub reporter. This becomes a comment on the life of the struggling artist in the film industry, for it engulfs those within it. Everything in their lives and those of their friends revolves around it. Sona and Vikram, therefore, are both ambitious about something other than each other. This ultimately interferes with their relationship, as *LBC* recognises that for both their ambition is the more central aspect of their lives.

In its eventual resolution, the emphasis on the all-consuming ambition also becomes a critique of heterosexual coupledom, modelled in the film on the prototype of the male star and his star-wife. This couple-form is not able to survive the ambitions of both. In one of the most radical subversions of Hindi cinema romance, *LBC* overturns the convention of the 'late realisation' wherein characters often make amends towards the film's end to confess love, realise mistakes and find a resolution. Seemingly subscribing to this convention, it is towards the end, after his film is a success, that Vikram realises his mistake in breaking up with Sona. After his quick success as a film star, he had refused to acknowledge her, cheated on her and accused her of trying to gain profit from their relationship by spreading gossip in a film magazine. As alluded to in the previous section, at the first pangs of loneliness Vikram encounters Shah Rukh Khan, who advises him that since stardom can drive you 'insane', he should keep those people close to him who knew him when he was not successful. Only they will speak the truth to him. This advice reminds Vikram of Sona, whose reporter friend has just told him that she did not leak gossip about him. This revelation, coupled with Khan's friendly advice, leads him to land up on the set of the television serial where Sona is working, hoping to mend things with her. For spectators of Hindi cinema, this is a usual moment to expect a reconciliation between the two because that is how romance was represented at that time (and still is). The sequence that follows, however, is unexpected.

Figure 1.1 The final conversation: Sona and Vikram.

Vikram apologises to Sona, for he cannot forget that she supported him and believed in him when no one else did. He needs an 'anchor' and 'support' like her. During his monologue, the camera often stays on Sona, her expression not decipherable until she speaks. Finally, she sighs and explains how she has understood he really is this 'selfish'. She had been listening to him closely and everything he said was only about him: 'Where am I in it?' she asks. The sequence is remarkable in multiple ways; I will focus here on its implications for Hindi cinema's couple-form. Not only does Sona's perspective indicate that their relationship is unequal, it tells us that staying together is not good for her. It may or may not be the best choice for Vikram, but the resolution of the sequence focuses on her. It is in recognising that both need different things for self realisation that *LBC* marks a rupture in cinematic representation of romance.

This becomes clearer when we focus on Sona's use of the word 'selfish' to describe what sounds like a very conventional declaration of romance on Vikram's part. Akhtar has mentioned in interviews that both the characters learn something from each other. A closer look, however, tells us that we don't really know what Vikram learns from Sona. Sona learns the value of defining her own success from Vikram's confidence. In an earlier sequence, she is shown staring at the refrigerator she has won only because Vikram had the confidence to fill out the form and enter her in a competition for it. That sequence indicates that she has had an epiphany but does not reveal in words exactly what that is. It is only in the final monologue that we get to know her version. In contrast, we do not know what Vikram learns from her; the apology just tells us he needs a support system in his life to deal with the vagaries of stardom. It is in this imbalance of perspectives that we find an indication of a female gaze that foregrounds Sona's inner world over Vikram's.

In the aftermath of the sequence, for the last few minutes of the film, it is Sona's journey that the film narrates. For the first time during the entire film, we are told her background: where she came from, what she thinks, what her work means to her, all of which contextualises that first scene where she had landed up in a producer's office hoping for a breakthrough. Unlike Vikram, who could afford to train at an acting school, Sona just landed in Bombay. The stakes were much higher for her all along.

Sona and Vikram's story then, is not just a couple's story, but also the story of two different kinds of experience of the struggling actor in the Bombay film industry. Just like the film nuances the representation of the industry insider, the outsider too is not only of one type. Both their career trajectories follow a pattern that is shaped by their respective gender and class positions. It is Sona who sleeps with a producer, it is she who is told that she is not good-looking enough to be a leading film star. Vikram's romantic declaration is also gendered, for it is geared towards the existing template of Bollywood star-couple relationships of that time, into which he expects Sona to fit. Sona's monologue at the end, however, reveals that both have found different approaches to work and success.

As she narrates her perspective, we see her walking on the road along with many other women belonging to different classes and occupations. While Sona is not a film star, she is doing what she loves doing (acting) and says that she has decided to be happy. She reflects on Vikram's dialogue about success and failure being choices, saying that she has learned its meaning only now. It is at this point that we get to know that she has made Vikram's philosophy her own – unlike him, she has also learned to be content. The film ends on a long one-shot sequence where Sona looks out of a taxi window after having told the driver that she wants to go to 'film city'. Like the ending of many of Akhtar's other films, her story too does not have a conclusive resolution. Though Vikram is the successful film actor, we are left with our eyes on her, while a philosophical song about a traveller on a journey plays on the soundtrack. Vikram is only a face on a billboard in the background.

CONCLUSION

While it received a positive critical reception when it was released in 2009, *LBC* did not do well at the box office. The top five box office successes of that year were: *3 Idiots* (Rajkumar Hirani), *Love Aaj Kal* (Imtiaz Ali), *Ajab Prem Ki Ghazab Kahani* (Rajkumar Santoshi), *Wanted* (Prabhu Deva) and *De Dana Dan* (Priyadarshan) (Box Office India 2009). All these films, except *Love Aaj Kal*, were driven largely by male star power and told stories centred on them. In contrast, the key themes of *LBC* – its empathetic world view towards the film industry, its emphasis on Sona and its play with the conventions of coupledom in Hindi cinema – made it a misfit within the largely masculine sensibilities of the box office of that time.

In an interview with journalist Anuradha Sen Gupta telecast in 2011 after the release of her film *Zindagi Na Milegi Dobara*, Akhtar underplayed the film's emphasis on representing a female experience (Akhtar 2011). Sen Gupta began a question on *ZNMD* by mentioning that *LBC* has a 'female protagonist', to which Akhtar responded by saying, 'I don't agree that *LBC* was a female film . . . It's a movie about a couple.' Sen Gupta pressed further, 'but don't you think . . . the female was the protagonist in the film?', to which Akhtar responded that it was a love story that had two protagonists. The discussion ended with Akhtar explaining that out of the two her favourite is actually Vikram: 'I identify with her but I . . . admire him . . . I see how he works and I see his charm . . . So I don't particularly see it as a female protagonist film. Not that there is a problem with a female protagonist film' (Akhtar 2011).

While Akhtar is reluctant towards a reading that emphasises the film as being centred around a female protagonist, though recognising in the same interview that she could never write female characters who are 'props', the gender politics of the film, as argued especially in the last section of this chapter, indicate otherwise. Akhtar is also sceptical of being identified as a 'woman filmmaker', even as she says her gaze is her gender (see interview in this book). As her fellow filmmaker Farah Khan also shares similar views,[4] perhaps this is one of the many contradictions of being successful women filmmakers in masculine and sexist industries where women filmmakers often underplay and even deny the gender dimensions of their work.

NOTES

1. The discussion around 'nepotism' in contemporary Hindi film discourse started in 2017 with a stray comment made by actor Kangana Ranaut on filmmaker Karan Johar's famous chat show, *Koffee with Karan*. Accusing Johar of not giving outsiders like her a chance, her comment soon became a full-blown controversy. Since then the discussion on the unfair advantage for star kids has been a constant in the mainstream discourse.
2. Film critic Khalid Mohamed wrote that the film is a 'valentine as well as a poison pen letter to . . . Bollywood' (2009). Aswin Punathambekar has called it both 'loving and critical' (2013: 51).
3. While discussing her ensemble style of writing and directing, Akhtar has mentioned Nikki as one of the complex supporting characters she loves (Akhtar 2020).
4. In an interview, Farah Khan says that she 'rejected the tag of "woman filmmaker" right from the start' (PTI 2019).

WORKS CITED

Akhtar, Zoya (2011), 'Beautiful people – with Zoya Akhtar'. Interview by Anuradha Sengupta, *CNN-IBN*, 16 July 2011.
Bose, Nandana (2017), 'Globalization, reflexivity and genre in Zoya Akhtar's films', in Ayesha Mohan Iqbal Viswamohan and Vimal Mohan (eds), *Behind the Scenes: Contemporary Bollywood Directors and Their Cinema*, New Delhi: Sage, pp. 215–26.
Box Office India (2009), 'Top hits 2009', <https://boxofficeindia.com/years.php?year=2009&pageId=4> (last accessed 10 July 2020).
Chopra, Anupama (2020), 'Anupama Chopra recommends 40 films to binge during the lockdown', *Film Companion*, 9 May 2020, <https://www.filmcompanion.in/features/bollywood-features/anupama-chopra-reccomends-40-movies-to-binge-during-lockdown/>
— (2014), 'Luck by Chance', *NDTV*, 7 March 2014.
Ciecko, Anne (2016), 'Reflexive global Bollywood and metacinematic gender politics in *Om Shanti Om* (2007), *Luck by Chance* (2008) and *Dhobhi Ghat* (2010)', *Diogenes*, 62: 1, pp. 24–37.
Ganti, Tejaswini (2012), *Producing Bollywood: Inside the Contemporary Hindi Film Industry*, Durham, NC: Duke University Press.
— 2016, '"No one thinks in Hindi here": Language hierarchies in Bollywood', in Michael Kurtin and Kevin Sanson (eds), *Precarious Creativity Global Media, Local Labor*, California: University of California Press, pp.118–31.

Garwood, Ian (2006), 'The songless Bollywood film', *South Asian Popular Culture*, 4: 2, pp. 169–83.
Gopal, Sangita (2011), *Conjugations: Marriage and Form in New Bollywood Cinema*, Chicago: University of Chicago Press.
Gopalan, Lalitha (2002), 'Introduction: "Hum Aapke hai Koun?" – Cinephilia and Indian films', in *Cinema of Interruptions: Action Genres in Contemporary Indian Cinema*, London: British Film Institute, pp. 1–33.
Gupta, Shubhra (2009), 'Movie review: *Luck by Chance*', *The Indian Express*, 30 January 2009, <http://archive.indianexpress.com/news/movie-review-luck-by-chance/417117/>
Gupta, Trisha (2015), 'The heart of the matter', *Mumbai Mirror*, 8 June 2015.
Kazmi, Nikhat (2009), '*Luck by Chance* movie review', *Times of India*, 30 January 2009, <https://timesofindia.indiatimes.com/entertainment/hindi/movie-reviews/luck-by-chance/movie-review/4050572.cms>
Movies, Excel (2009), 'The making of *Pyaar ki Dastaan* – Song from *Luck by Chance*', 17 August 2009. Video, 9:57.
Mohamed, Khalid (2009), 'Review: *Luck by Chance*', *Hindustan Times*, 30 January 2009, <https://www.hindustantimes.com/movie-reviews/review-luck-by-chance/story-WwQIxior8xhkMoCcAfmmjM.html>
PTI (2019), 'Directing films not a gender-specific job: Farah Khan', *The Week*, 29 November 2019, <https://www.theweek.in/news/entertainment/2019/11/29/directing-films-not-gender-specific-job-farah-khan.html>
Punathambekar, Aswin (2013), 'Staging Bollywood industry identity in an era of reform', in *From Bombay to Bollywood: The Making of a Global Media Industry*, New York and London: New York University Press, pp. 51–79.
Sarkar, Bhaskar (2017), 'Metafiguring Bollywood: Brecht after *Om Shanti Om*', in Meheli Sen and Anustup Basu (eds), *Figurations in Indian Film*, London: Palgrave Macmillan, pp. 205–35.
Sen, Sushmita (2020), 'Sushmita Sen interview with Anupama Chopra', *Film Companion*, 9 June 2020 <https://www.youtube.com/watch?v=El16rAx9Trs&t=786s>
Sharma, Sanjukta (2019), 'Nailing a song like Zoya Akhtar', *Live Mint*, 15 February 2019, <https://www.livemint.com/mint-lounge/features/nailing-a-song-like-zoya-akhtar-1550212211204.html>

CHAPTER 2

Relocating Bollywood: *Gully Boy* and the Worlds of Hip-hop

Sangita Gopal

Luck by Chance (2009), Zoya Akhtar's debut film and a commercial flop, is not the first film made about the Mumbai film industry. Nor is it the first to reveal its dark underside roiled by opportunism, hypocrisy and an insider culture indifferent to genuine artistry and fresh talent. As is to be expected in the 'movies about the movie business' subgenre, disenchantment is a predominant narrative and affective payoff. Both protagonists, the one who makes it (Vikram [Farhan Akhtar]) and the one who supposedly does not (Sona [Konkona Sen Sharma]), learn, along with the audience, that talent and ability have very little to do with success. It is all a matter of connections and contingencies or, in other words, luck, by chance. Yet this might have been one of the first films in the *abhinetri* film genre,[1] ranging in the Bollywood context from *Actress* (Balwant Bhatt 1934), *Kaagaz ke Phool* (Guru Dutt 1959), *Guddi* (Hrishikesh Mukherjee 1971), *Hero Hiralal* (Ketan Mehta 1988), *Rangeela* (Ram Gopal Varma 1995) to *Main Madhuri Dixit Banna Chahti Hoon* (Chandan Arora 2003), to suggest that a career in mass entertainment is possible even after your dreams of becoming a movie star have died. *LBC*'s remarkable closing sequence belongs to Sona, who takes her feckless lover Vikram's words that one chooses one's successes and failures to heart. Rather than regret that she could not become a film star, she takes pride in the fact that she became a working actress in television soaps, earning a good living. Sona ends up as an independent professional woman in a big city with a growing fandom of her own, a rising star in a career that may even reconcile her one day to her middle-class estranged parents, for they see her each night on their television screens in the provincial town that Sona left behind. In granting to her protagonist Sona a new life in television, Akhtar inaugurates the project of relocating Bollywood; a process that comes to a successful close with her most recent film *Gully Boy* (2019), a film that, I suggest, captures a new phase in Bollywood's relationship to other circuits of entertainment in contemporary India, pre-eminently popular music.

Gully Boy, again, is not the first Bollywood film to be made about a popular musical genre, nor is it the first to focus on the life of a singer who rises, or fails to rise, from rags to riches. From *Street Singer* (Phani Majumdar 1938) to *Baiju Bawra* (Vijay Bhatt 1952) through *Anuradha* (Hrishikesh Mukherjee 1960), *Abhimaan* (Hrishikesh Mukherjee 1973), *Saaz* (Sai Paranjpye 1998), *Rock On!* (Abhishek Kapoor 2008), *Rockstar* (Imtiaz Ali 2011) and *Secret Superstar* (Advait Chandan 2017), Hindi cinema has repeatedly made films about music and musicians, but they have always had fictional (or in the case of *Baiju Bawra*, historical) characters and have referred to music in general terms rather than a particular genre and/or scene. Though the storylines of *Abhimaan* and *Saaz* bear some resemblance to the relationship between musicians Pandit Ravi Shankar and Annapurna Devi in the former case and the famed Indian playback singers Asha Bhosle and Lata Mangeshkar in the latter, they are far from legitimate biopics.

However, *Gully Boy* is an authorised biography of a kind – while not about specific artists, it does tell the story of a particular music scene: the lifeworld of *gully* rap. Akhtar decided to make a film about this phenomenon because of its autonomy and distance from the musical world of Hindi cinema. As her music director states, 'before entering Bollywood, the Mumbai rappers were already famous, drawing crowds of 15–20,000 per show. This film will live or die because of the legitimacy of what it is representing. It does not need Bollywood's approval because it already has approval' (Ghosh 2019). As a fictionalised account of the rise of the *gully* rap scene and its stars, *Gully Boy* breaks new ground in Bollywood's genealogy of the 'music' film. Faintly recalling *8 Mile* (Curtis Hanson 2002), a fictional account of a white rapper in Detroit starring and containing autobiographical elements of real-life rapper Eminem, *Gully Boy*'s protagonist Murad (Ranveer Singh) is also fictional but has elements of his musical biography borrowed from the lives of hip-hop artists Divine and Naezy. Not only was the film inspired by the phenomenon of *gully* rap, but Divine and Naezy participated in the film's music, contributed to the lyrics (assisted by Zoya Akhtar's father Javed Akhtar) and authenticated, as such, the film's depiction of *gully* rap. As Naezy put it, 'Zoya ma'am and our worlds are poles apart. I helped her find and talk to the rappers in our gullies, then with the lyrics, the script and dialogue' (Ghosh 2019). Multiple rappers, such as MC Altaf, MC TodFod, 100 RBH, Maharya, Noxious D, Blitz, Desi Ma, Ace of Mumbai's Finest, Sofia Thenmozhi Ashraf and Kaam Bhaari, lend their voices to the mammoth eighteen-song soundtrack which took four years to assemble and involves fifty-four contributors, from rappers to deejays to music producers and beatboxers from all across India.

From *LBC* through *Zindagi Na Milegi Dobara* (2011) to *Dil Dhadakne Do* (2015), Zoya Akhtar has been meditating on what happens to a popular cinema when its address (and audience) shifts from the 'masses to the classes', and her approach until *Gully Boy* has been to anatomise through satire and humour Bollywood's aspirational aesthetic and consumerist drives. Having lost its place as *the* demotic medium par excellence, Bollywood in the last three decades has been engaged in a radical process of reorganisation at narrative, stylistic and industrial scales, and *Gully Boy*, I will argue, processes these changes, marking a new and less self-reflexive turn in Akhtar's filmography. Focusing on the film's staging of hip-hop as an autonomous entertainment order not only through the narrative staging of rap battles and other moments of 'musicking', but also through its elaboration of a world of music that does not originate in or get absorbed by the cinema but rather is the object of its representation, I will show how with *Gully Boy*, Akhtar demonstrates that the subject of Bollywood cinema is no longer itself. The first section of the chapter briefly examines the reflexive turn in Bollywood that not only succeeds in rebranding Hindi popular cinema as a global product but relocates cinema from *the* dominant form of mass entertainment to one among other options in a diverse media ecology. In the second section I explore the emergence of hip-hop in India, particularly *gully* rap, to suggest that this musical idiom and its attendant habitats now express populist perspectives that had once been the province of Bollywood cinema. The concluding section turns to *Gully Boy* and its staging of *gully* rap cultures to show how the worlds evoked by this film document a sovereign zone of entertainment hitherto uncolonised by the film industry while suggesting that Bollywood, which once arguably incorporated the perspectives of the disenfranchised, is now only capable of making a film *about* them.

REFLECTING BOLLYWOOD

Akhtar began her film career at a time when Bollywood cinema was being radically restructured by the economic and cultural forces of globalisation (Rajadhyaksha 2010). Not only did the industry seek and find global markets, it was beginning to organise itself into media conglomerates that were attempting to consolidate production and distribution and, subsequently, exhibition. Likewise, the film product witnessed hitherto unprecedented levels of diversification, from blockbusters through genre films to 'indie' fare. Further, the emergence of the multiplex, located in larger metropolitan areas, as the main exhibition platform meant that filmgoing was now mainly an urban and middle-class entertainment form (Athique 2010; Kumar 2019). By the time Akhtar entered the Hindi film industry, cinema, though highly capitalised, had lost its hegemonic position as *the* form of public culture, for even though it was still the dominant revenue maker, it now competed for attention with other modes of leisure such as television, live music, new media and mobile entertainment. Though scholars tend to mark economic liberalisation of the early 1990s as the impetus for these changes, I contend that this periodisation overstates the importance of the 1990s. We need to take another look at the 1970s and 1980s as that interregnum when many of these transformations were set in motion, especially with regard to the steady but sure emergence of television as the pre-eminent domain of the popular, a historical understanding that Akhtar clearly has, as indicated by the ending of *LBC*. Falling theatrical attendance and revenues throughout these decades, the competition from the widespread adoption of entertainment programming on state-owned television, piracy via new technologies like video and a series of fiscal crises within the industry, as well as threats from the state-funded New Cinema, meant that popular cinema post-1970s had to completely rethink its product, audience and social life.

In what I call modernity's 'second coming', the relationship between the Indian state and the popular film industry was recalibrated. To back up a little, the colonial state was alert to popular cinema's mobilising power and regulated it through censorship and levies. It also sought, somewhat lethargically, to promote non-fiction genres like documentary and the short in the 'cinéma-vérité' style but there was nothing resembling state-sponsored cinema in colonial India. The postcolonial state inherited this realist disposition. It was therefore critical of the unruly propensities of popular cinema, its lack of a disciplining frame and its refusal to self-reflect. The state championed, instead, a 'good cinema' that would represent the newly decolonised nation in the post-1945 art film market populated by the various national cinemas of Italy, France, Japan and Brazil. To promote such an alternative cinema, it set up funding initiatives such as the Film Finance Corporation and training and film preservation centres such as the Film and Television Institute of India and the National Film Archives. It encouraged regional film production and film appreciation clubs to cultivate public taste (Majumdar 2016). By the 1970s, the state had somewhat succeeded in installing an alternative 'frame', also known as Parallel Cinema or Indian New Wave Cinema.

The limited commercial success of these state-sponsored films among India's growing urban middle classes activated a phase of self-scrutiny in the popular film industry. At the precise juncture that the industry initiated a project of reform and rationalisation, especially in the production sector, films became self-reflexive. In several movies from this era we witness repeated visual and aural references to the technological apparatus of production and exhibition as well as thematic explorations of the birth of this new cinema. The word Bollywood, as I have shown elsewhere, now gained currency as a pejorative descriptor for Hindi cinema to mark its derivative status in relation to Hollywood (Gopal 2011; Prasad 2003). Self-reflexivity in this period was a taxonomic exercise meant to distinguish one kind of cinema from another. Onscreen representations of the celluloid apparatus legitimated the new cinema as *autonomous media* while alluding to the kind of cinema that it is not. Thus, in films like *Guddi* (Hrishikesh Mukherjee 1971), *Bhumika* (Shyam Benegal 1977) and *Khamosh* (Vidhu Vinod Chopra 1985), the case for a realist cinema was made by referencing the messy excesses of the Bollywood film and characterising it as illusory, underdeveloped and degraded. Akhtar's view of Bollywood in *LBC*, though more loving, does not shy away from revealing the shallowness and nepotism of the industry. The collective audience makes way for a spectator, usually young and female or working class and male, whose viewing habits are reformed in the course of the film. By recognising cinema as mediation, this once naïve spectator accesses modern, bourgeois subjectivity. In this 'second coming', popular cinema no longer presents the modern as sensation/seduction, but rather represents and reflects on modernity as a transformative process. For the first time, the aesthetic agendas of the state and the popular cinema, so long at odds, begin to approach each other as cinema's addressee shifts from the national public to an urban and consumerist middle-class subject.

The 1990s merely accelerated this process as the Hindi film industry received formal recognition from the Indian state and accessed bank finance. Self-reflexivity now resulted in a tendency to codify and package the conventions of Hindi popular cinema into a brand, Bollywood, and sell it in global markets. This is seen in the blockbusters of the 1990s from *Dilwale Dulhaniya Le Jayenge* (Aditya Chopra 1995) to *Kuch Kuch Hota Hai* (Karan Johar 1998) to *Devdas* (Sanjay Leela Bhansali 2002) that were marketing India abroad even as what counts as Hindi popular cinema was being reconstituted by an emergence of genres and multiplexes. By inserting the compulsion to self-reflect in contemporary cinema in this wider arc, we are in a better position to assess the historiographic significance of this drive. It is through this process of self-reflection that Bollywood cinema engages in refashioning itself into something else.

Akhtar's debut film, as we have seen above, participated in this self-reflexive register even more overtly and though a cult favourite, *LBC* failed at the box office. In subsequent films, her approach to reforming Bollywood film form became more stylistically focused on believable milieus, tight plotting and nuanced characterisation, a strategy that paid off at the box office. Thus, her next film, *ZNMD*, proved a super hit. A buddy/road film set in stunning locales in Spain, it combined the aspirational drives of Bollywood cinema of the new millennium with a character-centred script, subtle dialogues and realistic acting. Akhtar added to this mix a comic lightness and sardonic edge that framed this exploration of the emotional vicissitudes of the over-privileged.

Akhtar then turned to a well-worn Bollywood terrain: the family drama with a brother–sister relationship at its core. *DDD* was another careful juggling act between aspirational aesthetics, carefully observed and well-written character studies and psychologically nuanced family dynamics. Though set on a cruise ship and featuring India's 1 per cent, the film showcases Akhtar's gift for subtly undoing Hindi popular cinema's habitual representation of *yaar* (friend), *pyar* (love) and *parivar* (family) while adhering closely to the glossy production values and star-studded extravaganzas associated with Bollywood cinema at this time. Once again, Akhtar's pungent satire of the lifestyles of the rich both stages and undermines the aspirational drives of millennial Bollywood from the inside and works to dislodge, rather than subvert, the formulas. She uses a number of stars, such as Anil Kapoor, Ranveer Singh, Priyanka Chopra and Anushka Sharma, but her strong commitment to ensemble acting also keeps the focus on performances. Like *ZNMD*, this is a rigorously scripted film co-written with long-time collaborator Reema Kagti.

Of particular note is Akhtar's method for keeping things real. Inspired to become a filmmaker after watching Mira Nair's *Salaam Bombay!* (1988), Akhtar has a documentary filmmaker's interest in anthropology. Her film scripts are built out of incidents and characters that she has directly witnessed and the upper-class milieus in which her films are set reflect, as it were, the world with which she is familiar. She describes her preference for mid- and wide shots and the near total avoidance of close-ups in *DDD* in these terms: 'I wanted to be on the outside looking in, I wanted the perspective of somebody who is watching these human beings and their weird behavior' (Mathew 2019). This tendency to look for material 'outside' that is then processed into a film subscribes to the logic of bourgeois aesthetics where film is one of diverse media that gives shape to reality.

CINEMA AND ITS OTHERS

These reformist motivations align Akhtar's work from *LBC* through *ZNMD* and *DDD* with a dominant rhetorical mode in Bollywood cinema in the new millennium that seemed fixated with gazing at its navel in order to historicise its own re-emergence as New Bollywood. Akhtar is also one of the chief architects of this new cinema as witnessed by *Gully Boy*, which marks a post-reflective phase in the evolution of Bollywood, signalled by a move away from the lifestyles of the 1 per cent to detailing a music scene emerging in the slums of Dharavi. When asked in a recent interview what she makes of the nation's obsession with Bollywood, Akhtar regrets that film culture in India is still all-pervasive and hopes that there will soon be diverse and thriving popular modes of entertainment including music. Other popular cultures, she notes, still remain subcultures in relation to the behemoth that is cinema and she hopes for more variety in this industrial environment (Pathak 2019). She links cinema's cultural domination to its capture of the infrastructures of exhibition and distribution and hopes that new media, including streaming platforms, will bring greater diversity of form, content and social identities to the entertainment sector. We might view her investigation of this film's subject matter, *gully* rap, as one such attempt to explore the popular beyond cinema. It is rare for Bollywood cinema to take as its subject a sovereign entertainment order, even if a subcultural one, with its own rituals, conventions and circuits of fandom and attempt to depict it with a modicum of sociological realism. This is particularly true of North Indian popular music, which seems entirely enmeshed with Bollywood. Consider, for instance, *Secret Superstar*, a recent film about a singer. Though the protagonist Insia (Zaira Wasim) first becomes a YouTube star, she needs Shakti Kumar (Aamir Khan), a Bollywood music producer, to realise her dreams. She in turn helps Kumar renew his repertoire with a fresh sound. The film illustrates how all new music is destined for the film industry. As such, it echoes a recent report in a trade publication that 'the local music industry is essentially synonymous with Bollywood, which releases over 1,000 movies annually, and soundtracks account for nearly 80% of the music industry's revenue' (Hu 2017).

In a similar vein, a collection of scholarly essays titled *More Than Bollywood: Studies in Indian Popular Music*, though focused on music beyond the film song, opens by conceding that 'India's commercial filmmakers often wielded the most financial interest in and control over India's popular song . . . and India's popular music [is] enmeshed in the needs and symbolic systems of the commercial cinema' (Booth and Shope 2013: 7). Further, the political economy of music remains closely annexed to film for 'the system of production, as it existed, wove authors, music companies, and film producers into a single industrial, symbiotic web' (7). So entangled is this production practice that though film songs are autonomous entities that generate value in multiple circuits, until the Bollywood amendment of 2012 to the Copyright Act, the authors of these songs (composers, lyricists, singers) had no rights over them except the fees they received for their services. All rights rested with the film producer and the music companies who bought this music. This made sense to some extent, since the commercial life of film songs was so closely tied to the commercial life of a film that it was hard to imagine popular music as a sovereign entertainment order.

Though musical idioms and performance cultures might emerge outside of cinema, the film industry typically tends to absorb these artists and styles into its own audiovisual register of film song. Historically, technological innovations and the emergence of new platforms like cassettes or cable television led to the burgeoning of popular music. Thus, with the advent of music television in the 1990s, we witnessed a minor explosion of pop singers such as Alisha

Chinai, Daler Mehndi and Adnan Sami, and while they moved the market for a while, by the end of the decade they had been incorporated by the industry. Rather than investing in talent development, Bollywood constantly raids the nascent popular music scene, as seen through ever-popular music-themed reality shows on television and more recently streaming platforms such as YouTube, for artists and content in order to refresh its styles. This industrial tendency has, in the recent past, taken to reincarnating pop hits from Punjabi and other regional languages as film songs (Gurbaxani 2018).

At the same time, now might be propitious for the future of non-film-based music in India. For one, the actual form and function of the film song has been one of the most dynamic areas of reform within Hindi cinema in the recent past, with new storytelling formats consigning music to the background (Gopal 2015; Gehlawat and Dudrah 2017). As film formats change and the song loses its formal and narrative centrality, Bollywood's ability to deliver musical hits is also diminishing. Moreover, with the song-and-dance sequence's place within filmic narrative being less stable and secure, banking on film music is increasingly a riskier enterprise. Industry professionals estimate that 'What we do for one Bollywood project is technically equivalent to what we do for four or five pop projects in terms of the investment' (Gurbaxani 2019). Not only is the outlay reasonable but the return on investment is quicker as well. At the All About Music conference 2019, Anurag Bedi, the business head of Bollywood-focused label Zee Music Company, said it takes an average of 'between three and seven years' to recover the investment on a Bollywood soundtrack. In contrast, Universal looks 'at a two to three-year horizon' for their non-film releases (Gurbaxani 2019).

Given these fiscal dynamics, the music industry is beginning to invest in web-based broadcast platforms that can foster a music culture independent of the film industry. The web might finally provide a low-cost model for distribution and an effective ballast against piracy. While models for monetising online musical content are still in flux, since views do not yet neatly translate into revenue and online artists need music companies and labels, there is great potential in this market. There are signs of a drift that may eventually challenge the commercial and industrial dominance of film songs. Major Indian labels such as T-Series (a music company that has 75 per cent market share) and international labels such as Sony and Universal are beginning to release what they term 'non-film music' and the transition to streaming platforms is feeding this movement. These trends can be seen in the following 2019 metrics: four of T-Series's highest-played videos are Punjabi or Hindi non-film songs: 'High Rated *Gabru*' (2017) and 'Lahore' (2017) by Guru Randhawa, '*Vaaste*' (2019) by Dhvani Bhanushali and Nikhil D'Souza, and '*Nikle Currant*' (2018) by Jassi Gill and Neha Kakkar. On the video-streaming platform's weekly India music charts, two out of the three tracks to hit number one in September were non-film songs (Gurbaxani 2018). 'It's the non-film music that's breaking boundaries. Non-film music in India has been at a constant rise in the last two years. It has definitely eaten into the massive pie that Bollywood once had', summarises Roochay Shukla, marketing manager at music industry services company Outdustry (Gurbaxani 2018).

And here lies the true significance of hip-hop, especially *gully* rap. Hip-hop as a genre in India has always had a somewhat tangential relationship to the film industry. Since 2016, though Bollywood movies have tried to incorporate hip-hop tracks, the scene itself circulates outside of Bollywood in terms of technology (hip-hop artists use new media and streaming platforms extensively) and ideology (as I will elaborate below, hip-hop's aesthetic and address is counter-Bollywood). As Shridhar Subramaniam, president of Sony Music India and chairman of the organisation Indian Music Industry, notes, '[We've been] waiting 30–40 years for the non-Bollywood scene to emerge, and it will only emerge if you have a bunch of artists who want to say something' (Gurbaxani 2018). This idea draws the connection between autonomy, expressivity and authenticity that has always been central to the definition of an 'artist' in the popular music industry and antithetical to the collaborative mode of production of film music where the composer, lyricist, singer, music director and film director all work in consort.

Since 2016, the rise of non-film or 'indie' music in India seems increasingly (and unsurprisingly) anchored in hip-hop. Here 'indie' signifies independent from the film industry rather than independent from major music labels since, especially lately, labels such as Sony have been very aggressive in courting hip-hop artists.[2] The political economy of popular music is so film-centric that, as one analyst puts it, those who sign on to music labels (no matter how mainstream) rather than go the film route are 'the plucky underdogs' of the music scene (UMG 2019). One of the first Indian rap albums, Baba Sehgal's *Thanda Thanda Pani* (1992) was an instant hit on arrival and went on to sell 5 million copies. Over the next two decades, hip-hop in India had a dual trajectory: commercial and underground/street.[3] The former centred in the North, particularly in the Punjab region, is represented by artists such as Yo Yo Honey Singh, Badshah and Raftaar, whose careers began to take off in 2011. Referred to as 'desi-rap', these artists approach hip-hop and rapping as a trend or, in the words of Badshah, 'In India we are creating mainstream hip hop music, rather than what real rap music is. The lyrics aren't that personal, since most of the music is catering to Bollywood. It is just trivial. It is a fashion here' (Goyal 2016). Raftaar, for example, suggests that he entered the scene by combining Bollywood music with hip-hop and it was only after gaining some success and familiarising listeners with the sound that he began to cultivate an individual style. This, he goes on to say, is critical for commercial success that proved more elusive for other artists who were purists (Allahbadia 2020).

Along a similar line, Naezy comments, 'The popular rappers in Bollywood just talk about girls and booze and parties, they are only talking about glamour and trying to sell a fake dream. I wanted to make music that spoke about fighting, and the murders and the violence that was a part of my life growing up – and is the same for millions of others living in ghettoes across India' (Lang 2019).[4]

Raftaar (and Badshah's) break with Yo Yo Honey Singh and his embrace of a different genealogy of hip-hop is enshrined in his diss track '*Fukra Flow*', where he calls Yo Yo an auto-tune 'bot'. Bohemia, another pioneer of hip-hop in India, renowned for his purist approach, calls out Raftaar, in turn, for being too mainstream (Noorani 2017). The phenomenon of the diss track, itself a durable element of US hip-hop culture, helps us see how these two dualities of hip-hop, mainstream/commercial and underground/political, are a predictable feature of its global reception in diverse geopolitical contexts. In the Indian context, *gully* rap, which roughly translates into 'street' rap, increasingly serves as the shorthand for referring to this underground scene, with overtly political lyrics that detail violence, poverty and the brutality of slum life. It is also characterised by its distance from Bollywood. Thus, Naved Shaikh, aka Naezy, growing up in a drug- and gang-infested neighbourhood and himself involved in petty crime, had to go to Tupac and the Notorious B.I.G to find the musical idiom that would enable him to detail all that was wrong with his world. In his view, 'this story of real life in India – of corruption and poverty and crime – is never told in popular Indian music' (Ellis-Petersen 2016). Vivian Fernandes, who raps as MC Divine, also grew up in a slum and had a hard life, and discovered rap in 2013 via a CD gifted to him by a friend. Soon after he began to rap first in English but, finding that that did not quite work, switched to Hindi. 'I have always written my own rap but it never felt convincing till I switched to Hindi. It was only when I started writing in Hindi that I was able to translate my thoughts into words effortlessly' (Roy Chowdhury 2019). Divine's Hindi, in turn, is deeply local and peppered with argot. He found fame on the internet as his music videos shot on a mobile phone went viral. Divine, too, is cautious about Bollywood and its predatory tendencies.

Though Divine and Naezy are the best-known *gully* rappers in India, there is a burgeoning scene that includes hip-hop collectives SlumGods and Swadesi that use rap to bring attention to social and ecological crises including rape, caste violence, lynching and environmental exploitation. These interventions are often deeply rooted in the localities and spoken in a slew of slang-heavy regional languages and dialects. Though the term *gully* rap has Mumbai roots concentrated in the slums of Dharavi, it has been more broadly applied to rap scenes in other parts of India that have the same attachment to a location, lingo, social critique and political orientation. For instance, in New Delhi we witness a rap scene growing in East Delhi, and while some of the rappers such as Raga and Prabh Deep may be from the *gullies*, the socio-economic profile of the rappers is more solidly middle class (Dua 2019).

Gully rap's focus on social oppression, deepening income inequality and exploitation by government receives a unique and powerful inflection in what is known as 'Dalit' or 'Ambedkarite' rap.[5] Though Dalit struggles have historically been expressed through music anchored in folk traditions, the turn to the globalised idioms of hip-hop is more recent. Rapper Sumeet Samos says that rap lends itself well to documenting *savarna*[6] atrocities and his songs indict both the right and the elite left (Dhingra 2017). Influenced by Divine, Dule Rocker (Duleshwar Tandi) raps in the Kalhandia dialect of Odia and hails from a region that is known as a Maoist stronghold.[7] His subjects are urgent and topical, ranging from corporate brutalism and farmer suicides to the plight of migrants during the Coronavirus lockdown and the Hathras rape where four upper-caste men assaulted and killed a Dalit teenager. He raps from his room and provides his own beats using FL Studio and then rapping over them. Like almost all of his comrades, Dule Rocker shoots his material on smartphones and releases it on social media, pre-eminently YouTube (Gurbaxani 2020).

Indeed, *gully* rap and its variants are rapidly emerging as instances of the subaltern popular. It is a pan-Indian phenomenon and includes in some instances guest artists from the Indian diaspora in Singapore, Malaysia, Sri Lanka and beyond. Anchored in specific communities and scenes, expressed in India's many languages and dialects, infused with slang, its mode of production is often collective, collaborative and lo-fi. The radical potential inheres not only in the social location of its subjects and the subjects they rap about, but also its promiscuous distribution on YouTube and other social media platforms. This use of new media by the hip-hop scene in India has been a characteristic from its inception and the now-defunct social media platform Orkut, popular in India, was the stage for many rap battles. South Indian rapper Brodha V, for instance, got his start on the Orkut forum Insignia Rap Battles started by Delhi-based rapper D'Brassic. This growth of hip-hop has since come to rely on YouTube, which serves as India's most popular platform for consuming music (and India, in fact, is YouTube's biggest music market). Despite aggressive promotion of music videos on YouTube by labels including paid views, YouTube is free and remains the platform of choice for DIY hip-hop acts hoping to grow an audience (Sood 2019).

Though underground scenes comprised of rappers, beatboxers, breakdancers, graffiti artists, producers, mentors, acolytes and fans might be strongly anchored in particular 'hoods', the distribution of this music through streaming services and social media jeopardises this very rooted authenticity as music companies and corporate producers swoop in to sign the next hitmakers. These big labels in turn marginalise the indie labels that first brought these musicians to the public's attention. In this dynamic ecology, popularity is both a threat and a reward, for it extracts the individual rapper out of the 'scene' and turns him into a commercial property. This is a dominant theme in the global itineraries of hip-hop, and the scene in India is also characterised by these struggles over authenticity. As Dharavi-based rapper Rapture (Sameer Inamdar) puts it, 'Rap comes from rebellion. It comes from a place of oppression, rage, emotions and struggles. Some people have started doing it because it's trendy to rap about your struggles. If you want to become a voice, then don't pretend. But this happens to a lot of movements – they get picked up and the essence fades away' (Sood 2019).

WORLDING A SUBCULTURE

Gully rap, then, might be considered as a musical genre of the subaltern popular. Its putative social origins in the slums; its populist address; its critique of poverty, inequality and of the structural barriers to mobility; its hardscrabble optimism and sense of locality; its indigenising and hybridising of the global popular in its aesthetics, as well as the multicultural world that it imagines into being, makes *gully* rap a contemporary avatar of the kind of public culture that Hindi cinema might once have aspired to be, but no longer is. Ashis Nandy once famously characterised Indian popular cinema – following Ratnakar Tripathy – as analogous to the urban slum, and its social efficacy was attributed to its ability to project a slum's-eye view of politics (1998). According to Nandy, the slum is a valid metaphor of Hindi cinema, for both entail an

> impassioned negotiation with everyday survival, combined with the same intense effort to forget that negotiation, the same mix of the comic and the tragic, spiced with elements borrowed indiscriminately from the classical and the folk, the East and the West. However, there is at least one other sense in which the metaphor of the slum seems apt: the popular cinema is the slum's point of view of Indian politics and society and, for that matter, the world. There is in both of them the same stress on lower-middle-class sensibilities and on the informal, not-terribly-tacit theories of politics and society the class uses and the same ability to shock the *haute bourgeoisie* with the directness, vigour and crudity of these theories. (2)

Akhtar, as we have seen above, took an active role in transforming Hindi cinema into the culture of, if not the *haute bourgeoisie*, certainly the aspirational classes which now look *at* the slums and the *gully* rap that emanates from there as 'other', being political and popular exactly in the sense that Hindi cinema once was. The *gully* boy Murad's ancestors are easily found in the archives of Hindi cinema in figures such as *Pyaasa*'s (Guru Dutt 1957) Vijay (Guru Dutt) or the Vijay (Amitabh Bachchan) of *Deewar* (Yash Chopra 1975), yet the film is not retro at all. Rather it is a fictionalised account of the *gully* rap scene in the world-famous slums of Dharavi, and its claims to authenticity derive not from the credentials of the director or stars who do not belong to this world nor the mode of production but rather from the verisimilitude of a uniquely cinematic nature: how authentically Akhtar and her team have captured the *gully* rap scene and its milieu. Bollywood stops looking at itself and connects with a world little known to its audience. When Akhtar speaks about what motivated her to make this film it is hard to miss the documentary impetus commingled with a human-interest story. She came to her material through an encounter with a rap by Naezy that went viral online, recalling, 'It was this guy with an insane vocal flow and he was just rapping and it was shot on a phone and it was all over the slums. He was rapping about his family, his mother, the state, the way society treats him, the fact that he is Muslim' (Ramnath 2019). Akhtar recognised right away that this was not the derivative, commercial version of hip-hop popularised in India through rappers like Yo Yo Honey Singh who sang of women, alcohol, cars and bling, but was rather authentic and engaging with the everyday reality of India's underclasses. Akhtar continues:

> I just wanted to meet him because I felt there is a story here because this voice, you know, the 20-year-olds, they are completely disenfranchised and they do not have any representation in the mainstream. The beauty about the internet is that they have access to and all their inspiration is American rappers. So they are suddenly educating themselves and they have taken it and made it their own and they are spitting their truth.

It is thus through the hip-hop scene's connection with the 'real' hopes, dreams and frustrations of India's underclasses, in other words, its street cred as a music scene, that Bollywood cinema re-engages social material (Ramnath 2019b). It is worth noting here that Akhtar approaches *gully* rap as a documentary filmmaker might: as social phenomenon worth bringing to the attention of Bollywood cinema's public. Verisimilitude is critical when trying to evoke a deeply rooted musical scene. Since *gully* rap rises from, reflects on and builds its critique out of an environment, the assembling of that world is really critical in order for the film to function as the sociology of a musical movement in addition to being about its protagonist's trajectory from college student to rap artist. Akhtar has always paid meticulous attention to production design and here she works again with the same designer, Suzanne Caplan Merwanji, who is known for the distinctive look she gifts Akhtar's films. Merwanji notes how these looks have diverse inspirations including photos, paintings and world cinema but never Bollywood. Perhaps the 'fresh' look that Akhtar's films achieve comes from this turn away from Bollywood's design repertoire.

In *Gully Boy*, Merwanji notes that they were not going for a 'style' but rather attempting to make it look 'real' (Ramnath 2019b). Initially, they had imagined shooting on location in the slums that skirt Mumbai (one of which, Kurla, had been Naezy's home) but eventually they decided that it had to be the more centrally located Dharavi, one of Asia's largest slums remarkable for its ethnic and religious diversity and a thriving informal economy. While it might have been made globally recognisable as the setting for Danny Boyle's *Slumdog Millionaire* (2008), Dharavi is the locus classicus for multiple Indian films (whether shot on location or re-created in a studio set) ranging from *Deewar, Parinda* (Vidhu Vinod Chopra 1989) to Ram Gopal Varma's *Indian Gangster Trilogy* (1998–2005), as well as 'art' films such as *Salaam Bombay*, *Black Friday* (Anurag Kashyap 2004) and *Aamir* (Raj Kumar Gupta 2008). Perhaps two of the most iconic films centred in Dharavi are in the Tamil language, Mani Ratnam's classic *Nayakan* (1987) and Pa Ranjith's *Kaala* (2018). The most celebrated items in this celluloid archive of Dharavi focus on the gangster as community hero and emphasise this neighbourhood's informal legal and extra-legal economies and resilience. Moreover, Dharavi's architecture, including its overcrowded low-rise buildings, jam-packed store fronts, narrow winding lanes and ubiquitous squalor, supply a densely textured mise-en-scène that makes it uniquely cinematic.

While this celluloid genealogy doubtless lends resonance to Akhtar and Merwanji's choice of Dharavi, they were also motivated by Dharavi's centrality in the emergence of their subject matter. Two of the earliest documentaries bringing attention to subaltern hip-hop in India are centred in Dharavi: *The SlumGods of Bombay – Hope, Hip Hop and the Dharavi Way* (a documentary commissioned by *The Guardian* newspaper in 2014) and *Dharavi Hustle* (Bajaoo 2016). The former, focused on the rapper Akku (Akash Dhangar) and his work with b-boys and breakdancing, draws attention to how hip-hop enables Dharavi to connect with the world as Dharavi youth, inspired by a movement that has its roots in the Bronx and South-Central LA, invent their own hip-hop culture firmly located in their environment and in the words of Akku create tracks that challenge the 'perception that tourists and foreigners have of our home. They think there is only poverty in Dharavi, but when they come here, they realize there is so much more to the place. People are industrious and hardworking; you will not find beggary here' (Ramnath 2019a). If Akku of the band SlumGods emphasises Dharavi as a space of hope and creativity, the artists featured in *Dharavi Hustle* turn to hip-hop as a lifestyle comprised of multiple elements including rapping, b-boying, graffiti and beatboxing that taken together help them to make sense of reality. The film documents the experiences of the everyday as well as analysing and critiquing the social forces and materialist structures that reproduce this reality. They claim there are twenty rappers in Dharavi and seven or eight crews, including pioneers such as 7 Bantai'Z, Bombay Mafia, Dog Z and Dopeadelicz, and all are deeply committed to the hip-hop creed of keeping it real to the struggle and hustle that is life in Dharavi.

Therefore, in spite of the immense technical challenges presented by shooting in such a densely populated area, Akhtar and Merwanji decided it had to be Dharavi. As Merwanji puts it, 'Most importantly, geographically it is in the heart of Mumbai. Dharavi is also surrounded by everything that the average slum-dweller aspires to, for themselves & their children, so this makes it all the more relevant & poignant as the main location for Murad's world and telling his story. It is a character in itself' (Shetye 2019).

As the rappers cited above underline, the connection between place and hip-hop is a crucial one that refers not only to Dharavi but all that surrounds it. Dharavi's physical proximity to affluent neighbourhoods like the Bandra Kurla Complex brings into sharp focus the figurative distance between growing income inequality and constraints to upward mobility that characterises the underclasses in a globalising India and is the subject of so much *gully* rap. This is brought out in the number '*Doori*' whose opening lines are '*Dekho to hum pas hai lekin, socho kitni doori hai, kaise yeh majboori hai*' ('See we are close and yet so far, so conscripted'). The song comes to Murad when he realises that despite occupying the intimate space of an automobile, the distance between him, the driver and his employer's daughter may not be traversed. Though she is clearly distressed, he is not her social equal so he may not comfort her. The song, the first one Murad records, then spirals out of this context to describe in greater detail other unbridgeable geographies that are particularly noticeable from the vantage of Dharavi. Despite being hardworking, enterprising and educated, what a young person from Dharavi (in particular a Muslim man such as Murad) can aspire to is tightly circumscribed in contemporary India, where cultural nationalism on the one hand and predatory capital on the other intensifies existing structures of domination that, as the film highlights, work concentrically from the family outwards. If the epistemic rupture of *gully* rap is the look from the slum and the ontology of the hip-hop artist is shaped by the slum, then a film about this musical genre must indeed pay attention to the material infrastructure that sustains this way of being and knowing.[8] The naturalism that motivates the film's production design then is inspired by *gully* rap's naturalist reading of subject and environment, artist and milieu: its slum's-eye view. In Akhtar's words, 'You had to be on the streets for this kind of a film – you could not be anywhere else. The locations dictated the camera movements, the lensing, the use of space, how the characters and their worlds were shot' (Mazumdar 2019). Akhtar and Merwanji decided to shoot on location in Dharavi but in order to have more control over sound, traffic and movement, they also built a set comprising of dwellings, shops and streets in an empty parking lot. This set served as a kind of mise-en-abyme – a slum within a slum – and was made to blend in with the surroundings. In addition, Merwanji and her team also 'dressed' several real locations to make them cohere with the constructed set. This production design's detailed and careful evocation of the world of Dharavi is artfully complemented by intimate cinematography, for as DP Jay Oza notes, he knew that 'if it looks fake or made up at any given second, then it'll fall flat on its face. I had to mould the actors into the world' (Mohanty 2019). The camerawork, mobile and restless, follows characters in their dense, claustrophobic lives and keeps the frames tight, only occasionally breaking away for a wide or high-angle shot. The visual code for representing slums, as Ranjani Mazumdar notes, has typically privileged aerial views (Ghosh 2019), but *Gully Boy* gives its audience an eye-level view, taking us inside while reminding us that we are nevertheless outsiders like the American tourists who are shown touring Dharavi, selfie-sticks in hand, paying extra to be let inside Murad's house.

Stylistically, the production design conjured three worlds. The first is Murad's world: his home and its environs, including his friend Moeen's (Vijay Varma) garage and places he hung out with his girlfriend Safeena (Alia Bhatt) and his friends. The second is the elite world beyond the railway tracks that Murad glimpses first as a driver and then through his producer Sky (Kalki Koechlin). But then there is a third world in the film: the spaces where *gully* rap happens within Dharavi and the city, the rooms, improvised recording studios, makeshift clubs, abandoned construction sites, restaurants and bars where artists meet, practise, perform, record, stage rap battles and cyphers.

The social critique that animates hip-hop as well as the speculative futures that artists imagine in their songs bring the first two worlds into a dynamic relationship roiled by desire and antagonism. If the number '*Mere Gully Mein*'

Figure 2.1 One of the worlds that *Gully Boy* depicts is the space where *gully* rap happens.

('In My Street'), first recorded in 2015 by Divine, feat. Naezy and then remade for the film and rapped by Ranveer Singh and Divine, introduced us to the riotous, joyful slum world of *gully* rap, the film's anthemic climactic number '*Apna Time Aayega*' ('My Time will Come') announces the right of the disenfranchised to dream a new world into being that undoes the spatial distribution of the haves and have-nots and rhymes into existence a future beyond the *gully*. Written for the film by Divine and Ankur Trivedi with music by Divine and Dub Sharma, the phrase '*Apna Time Aayega*', as Amaal Akhtar and Pragyan Mohanty note, echoes the words of another Muslim boy from the ghetto, Salim (Pawan Malhotra), who assures his friend Abdul (Ashutosh Gowariker) at a low point in his life, '*Tu dekhna, aapna bhi time aayenga*' ('You will see, even my time will come') in Saeed Mirza's *Salim Langde pe Mat ro* (1989) (Fernandes 2019; Shankar 2019). In contrast to Salim's dead-end life, Murad finds a way to channel his rage into art by discovering other worlds, first on the internet via US hip-hop and then, more locally, as MC Sher introduces him to the world of *gully* rap and Murad's recordings go viral. To the familiar triad of sustenance, '*roti, kapda aur makaan*' (food, clothing, shelter), Murad adds a fourth demand, internet, for indeed, hip-hop's ability to document the real world of the *gully* and potentially transform it relies on an encounter with virtual worlds and their networked publics.

World-making is central to hip-hop and *gully* rap shares with the various iterations of global hip-hop this drive to make and unmake worlds. As Karsh Kale, one of the film's two music directors observed, 'these guys . . . have built skyscrapers out of nothing' (Ghosh 2019). Therefore, a film about this spatially oriented subculture must be very attentive to the worlds that give rise to it, the worlds it inhabits as well as the new worlds it wills into being. The film's production design is very attentive to assembling the worlds of this subculture, for *gully* rap's onto-epistemology (its ways of knowing and being) is intimately entangled with its environment and a film that cannot detail this world (as well as its relationship to other worlds) with intimacy, respect and attention fundamentally fails. *Gully Boy*'s conjuring of these worlds through production, design and cinematography is precisely what allows us to experience *gully* rap as a sovereign entertainment order.

Through its meticulous and carefully detailed evocation of an urban and local musical scene located in the slums of Dharavi, *Gully Boy* acknowledges the real presence of other entertainment orders and their specific social worlds that can now be the subject of a Bollywood film rather than a musical genre that the film industry annexes through incorporation into its own soundtracks. The Hindi film industry has done the latter for most of its history such that to this day, popular music in India has been largely co-extensive with film music. The very fact that a controversy ensued over the film's release where hip-hop artists criticised the film's softening of the countercultural edges of the hip-hop underground or indeed its failure at authenticity is itself a testament to *Gully Boy*'s generic limits as a film about an autonomous musical subculture and its lifeworld (Oshin 2019; Shankar 2019). As such, it might be the most significant film to date that reflects on Bollywood's provincialisation within contemporary India's media landscape and the concomitant loss of its monopoly over the entertainment order, its transformation, in other words, from public culture to one of contemporary India's culture industries that include other regional cinemas, televisions, streaming, music and, arguably, Indian Premier League cricket. The fact that such a relocation of Bollywood's place happens through a film on the phenomenon of *gully* rap is additionally significant for it accepts that politically engaged popular entertainment that speaks to the struggles of the underclasses, once the province of Hindi popular cinema, has moved elsewhere. Bollywood can now make films about the politically disenfranchised and insurgent subjects using the limited grammar of commercial cinema but it is no longer necessarily addressed to this public. It is now securely a bourgeois entertainment form.

NOTES

1. Debashree Mukherjee identifies this genre as one that focuses on the actress as a figure who embodies both the enticements and anxieties around cinema and modernity. See *Bombay Hustle: Making Movies in a Colonial City* (Columbia University Press, 2020).
2. Sony is not the only player in the market. Universal launched a label focused on hip-hop titled Mass Appeal India by signing on India's highest-profile hip-hop artist Divine, one of the original *gully* boys of Akhtar's film. Interestingly, Divine had been with Sony for a while and then decided to go out on his own with Gully Gang Records (announced after the release of *Gully Boy*) but Universal clearly lured him back to a proven label. See Dredge 2019.
3. As scholars of hip-hop in other global locations note, this commercial/underground binary is a familiar one. Sujatha Fernandes notes that unlike the circulation of black popular culture at earlier historical junctures, the globalisation of hip-hop has always had a significant commercial component since its global travels have been heavily promoted by music conglomerates – Sony and Universal. As Ian Condry observes, in the Japanese context, the commercialisation of hip-hop in the 1990s is accompanied by a burgeoning underground scene comprising artists and fans from a broader range of socio-economic backgrounds and regions. See Sujatha Fernandes, *Close to the Edge: In Search of the Global Hip Hop Generation* (Verso, 2011) and Ian Condry, *Hip Hop Japan: Rap and the Paths of Cultural Globalization* (Duke University Press, 2006).
4. Sam Lang, 'Gully Rap: India's New Rap Scene', 1 August 2019. Available at <https://blog.traktrain.com/gully-rap-indias-new-rap-scene/> The historiography of 'rap' as originating in African American neighbourhoods in the South Bronx and South-Central LA is a durable one in the Indian hip-hop scene. Artists here attached to a particular canon and a specific account of hip-hop as driven by graffiti, b-boys, beatboxing and diss tracks. There is less awareness of the global black roots and trajectories of hip-hop through Caribbean and African diasporas, for instance. *Gully Boy* too espouses this historiography.

See Antonio Tiongson, *Filipinos Represent: DJs, Authenticity and Hip Hop Nation* (Minnesota, 2013).
5. This phrase is used by Greeshma Rai and references Dalit leader B. R. Ambedkar (Dhingra 2017).
6. The term *savarna* refers to those who belong to any of the four castes: Brahmin, Kshatriya, Vaishya and Shudra.
7. Odia is the official language of Odisha.
8. I am inspired here by Priya Jaikumar's theorising on 'spatial historiography' in *Where Histories Reside: India as Filmed Space* (Duke University Press, 2019).

WORKS CITED

Akhtar, Amaal (2019), '*Gully Boy* and the legacy of *Salim Langde pe Mat ro*', *The Hindu*, 26 April 2019. Available at <https://www.thehindu.com/entertainment/movies/apna-time-aayega-gully-boy-and-the-legacy-of-salim-langde-pe-mat-ro/article26951915.ece>

Allahbadia, Ranveer (2020), 'Raftaar on career secrets, life goals and rap culture in India', *The Ranveer Show*, 1 May 2020. Video, 45:47. Available at <https://www.youtube.com/watch?v=Q_YAiVux8TY>

Athique, Adrian and Douglas Hill (2010), *The Multiplex in India: A Cultural Economy of Urban Leisure*, New York: Routledge.

Booth, Gregory and Bradley Shope (2013), *More than Bollywood: Studies in Indian Popular Music*, Oxford: Oxford University Press.

Dhingra, Sanya (2017), 'Dalit rap on the knuckles of casteism', *The Print*, 29 April 2017. Available at <https://theprint.in/theprint-profile/dalit-rap-on-the-knuckles-of-casteism/158/>

Dredge, Stuart (2019), 'UMG's new venture shows the power of independent Indian hip hop', *Music:)ally*, 21 August 2019. Available at <https://musically.com/2019/08/21/umgs-new-venture-shows-the-power-of-independent-indian-hip-hop/>

Dua, Mansi (2019), 'Beyond *Gully Boy*, Delhi's underground rappers are jamming their way to stardom', *Indian Express*, 14 February 2019. Available at <https://indianexpress.com/article/entertainment/music/beyond-gully-boy-delhi-underground-rappers-are-jamming-their-way-to-stardom-5582714/>

Dudrah, Rajinder and Ajay Gehlawat (2017), 'The evolution of song and dance in Hindi cinema', *South Asian Popular Culture*, 15: 2–3, pp. 103–8.

Ellis-Petersen, Hannah (2016), 'Poverty, corruption and crime: How gully rap tells the story of real life', *The Guardian*, 14 May 2016. Available at <https://www.theguardian.com/world/2016/may/16/poverty-corruption-and-how-indias-gully-rap-tells-story-of-real-life>

Ghosh, Devarsi (2019), '*Gully Boy*'s music', *Scroll*, 27 January 2019. Available at <https://scroll.in/reel/908804/gully-boy-music-four-years-18-songs-54-collaborators-and-an-absolutely-nuts-ranveer-singh>

Gopal, Sangita (2011), *Conjugations: Marriage and Form in New Bollywood Cinema*, Chicago: University of Chicago Press.

Goyal, Samarth (2016), 'There is not hip hop rivalry here, claims Badshah', *Hindustan Times*, 23 June 2016. Available at <https://www.hindustantimes.com/music/there-s-no-real-hip-hop-rivalry-here-claims-badshah/story-lZUge1xrWVsWbNfiHsdYzL.html>

Gurbaxani, Amit (2015), 'Audible past, or What remains of the song-sequence in New Bollywood Cinema', *New Literary History*, 46: 4, pp. 805–22.

— (2018), 'The rise of Indian hip hop', *Music Ally*, 16 September 2018. Available at <https://musically.com/2018/09/06/indian-hip-hop-huge-opportunity/>
— (2019), 'Is Bollywood losing its dominance of the Indian music industry?', *Music Ally*, 5 November 2019. Available at <https://musically.com/2019/11/05/bollywood-losing-dominance-indian-music-industry/>
— (2020), 'From Bollywood domination to most preferred language on Youtube charts', *Firstpost*, 18 October 2020. Available at <https://www.firstpost.com/entertainment/from-bollywoods-domination-to-the-most-preferred-languages-what-the-youtube-india-charts-reveal-about-the-listenership-in-the-country-7512661.html>
Hu, Cherie (2017), 'How India, the global music industry's sleeping giant, is finally waking up', *Forbes*, 23 September 2017. Available at <https://www.forbes.com/sites/cheriehu/2017/09/23/how-india-the-global-music-industrys-sleeping-giant-is-finally-waking-up/#1eda5a5c30bf>
Kumar, Akshaya (2019), 'Consolidating Bollywood: Spectacularity without stardom', in S. Heijin Lee, Monika Mehta, and Robert Ji-Song Ku (eds), *Pop Empires: Transnational and Diasporic Flows of India and Korea*, Honolulu: University of Hawai'i Press, pp. 138–54.
Lang, Sam (2019), 'Gully rap: India's new rap scene', *TrakTrain*, 1 August 2019. Available at <https://blog.traktrain.com/gully-rap-indias-new-rap-scene/>
Majumdar, Rochona (2016), 'Art cinema: The Indian career of a global category', *Critical Inquiry*, 42: 3, pp. 580–610.
Mazumdar, Ranjani (2019), 'The Mumbai slum: Aerial views and embodied memories', *Mediapolis*, 3: 4. Available at <https://www.mediapolisjournal.com/sections/threads/>
Mohanty, Pragyan (2019), 'Before Murad, Saeed Mirza's Salim Langda was the OG *Gully Boy* dreaming of "Apna time aayega"', *Qrius*, 3 February 2019. Available at <https://qrius.com/before-murad-saeed-mirzas-salim-langda-was-the-og-gully-boy-dreaming-of-apna-time-aayega/#:~:text=Apna%20time%20aayega%2C%20Gully%20Boy%2C%20Saeed%20Mirza%20Before,of%20circumstances%20that%20are%20both%20disadvantageous%20and%20dehumanising>
Nandy, Ashis (1998), 'Introduction: Indian popular cinema as a slum's eye view of politics', in Ashis Nandy (ed.), *The Secret Politics of Our Desires: Innocence, Culpability, and Indian Popular Cinema*, India: Bloomsbury Academic, pp. 1–18.
Noorani, Reza (2017), 'Diss tracks heat up Desi hip-hop', *Entertainment Times*, 22 July 2017. Available at <https://timesofindia.indiatimes.com/entertainment/hindi/music/news/diss-tracks-heat-up-desi-hip-hop/articleshow/59701132.cms>
Oshin, Fernandes (2019), '*Gully Boy* Azadi or Kanhaiya Kumar who hit the seditious note?, *Free Press Journal*, 17 February 2019. Available at <https://www.freepressjournal.in/analysis/gully-boy-azadi-or-kanhaiya-kumar-who-hit-the-seditious-note>
Pathak, Ankur, '*Gully Boy*: Zoya Akhtar on her politics, Alia's violence, and Ranveer's "Brown-face"', *Huffington Post*, 22 February 2019. Available at <https://www.huffpost.com/archive/in/entry/zoya-akhtar-gully-boy-interview_in_5c6e3a56e4b0e2f4d8a2a6d4>
Prasad, Madhava (2003), 'This thing called Bollywood', *Semina*, 525. Available at <https://www.india-seminar.com/2003/525/525%20madhava%20prasad.htm>
Rajadhyaksha, Ashish (2009), *Indian Cinema in the Time of Celluloid: From Bollywood to the Emergency*, Bloomington: Indiana University Press.
Ramnath, Nandini (2019), 'Zoya Akhtar on *Gully Boy*', *Scroll.in*, 17 February 2019. Available at <https://scroll.in/reel/913542/zoya-akhtar-on-gully-boy-i-wanted-murad-to-be-the-kind-of-man-i-want-to-see-in-the-world>
— (2019b), 'Designing *Gully Boy*', *Scroll.in*, 3 March 2019. Available at <https://scroll.in/reel/915126/designing-gully-boy-when-nobody-knows-whats-a-set-and-what-isnt-that-is-the-best-compliment>

Roy Chowdhury, Rishita (2019), 'DIVINE: One for the streets', *Sunday Guardian Live*, 23 March 2019. Available at <https://www.sundayguardianlive.com/culture/one-streets-divine>

Shankar, Karthik (2019), '*Gully Boy* and its mixed political messaging', *Firstpost*, 19 February 2019. Available at <https://www.firstpost.com/entertainment/gully-boy-and-its-mixed-political-messaging-zoya-akhars-film-is-praiseworthy-but-has-superficial-politics-6093591.html>

Shetye, Archit (2019), 'Through the lens of cinematographer Jay Oza', *Homegrown*, 15 April 2019. Available at <https://homegrown.co.in/article/803523/through-the-lens-of-cinematographer-jay-oza-gully-boy-made-in-heaven-ghoul-and-more>

Sood, Akhil (2019), 'Why India's gully rap scene is liberating the country's youth', *RedBull*, 26 July 2019. Available at <https://www.redbull.com/us-en/why-gully-rap-is-liberating-indian-youth>

Suresh, Mathew (2019), 'Zoya Akhtar on filming *Gully Boy*, Azadi, the Ranveer-Alia connect', *The Quint*, 13 February 2019. Available at <https://www.thequint.com/entertainment/bollywood/ranveer-and-alia-gully-boy-director-zoya-interview#read-more>

CHAPTER 3

New Forms, New Stories: Zoya Akhtar's Short Films

Amber Shields

There is something fitting about how Zoya Akhtar's entry into short films starts with her work in *Bombay Talkies* (Zoya Akhtar, Dibakar Banerjee, Karan Johar and Anurag Kashyap 2013). As a point of commemoration, the film was a curious creation that was tied to the industry but was not wholly part of it. Commissioned as an anthology production to celebrate a hundred years of Indian Cinema (marked by the release of the 'first' Indian film, *Raja Harishchandra* [Dadasaheb Phalke], in 1913) and named after the Indian production house Bombay Talkies, the film was anything but the typical cinema hall fanfare. Instead, it offered a mixed point of reflection from distinct perspectives that looked forward as much as it looked back. Its directors ranged from industrial kingpins like Karan Johar to those quickly establishing themselves as the next generation like Akhtar to the more popular 'indie' filmmakers Dibakar Banerjee and Anurag Kashyap. Its form, while representing some of the sensibilities of these directors' styles, overall leaned more towards the 'indie' than commercial and the film was notable for a lack of song-and-dance sequences;[1] though there was a tie back to Bollywood's present with a closing song containing many of the industry's biggest stars. The stories ranged in themes from the dreams that the cinema creates to the acceptance of the realities we live far from these dreams and even broached taboo topics not often seen in the blockbusters such as suppressed homosexuality and breaking societal gender roles. Thus, like Akhtar's other works, this film was hard to categorise. Instead, it represented something new being created as the industry was trying to re-envision itself for a new millennium.

As such, the film left questions of not only what type of commemoration it was, but if it was a true commemoration of the past it purported to be celebrating. In a special dossier reflecting on the meaning of this particular commemoration,

Meheli Sen perhaps best describes this '*hatke* (different)' film and the questions it raises:

> I would like to ask whether *Bombay Talkies*, as a film as well as a celebratory event, forces us to reckon with this new milieu of the Bombay industry – the new ecology, wherein the mobilization of a seamless mediascape seems to be of paramount interest as well as maximum profitability? Aided by the multiplex within the overarching impetus toward corporatization and streamlining, this is an era of strategic alliances and newly engendered promiscuities. Filmmakers associated with the 'indie' genre are keen to tap into the energies harnessed by Bollywood; the commercial industry, on its part, grows more capacious, cannibalizing other cinematic formations with impunity. Indeed the exchanges, transactions and cross-pollination between the two formations are so great that it is becoming virtually impossible to tell them apart. (2015: 78)

Bombay Talkies came out at a time of dramatic shifts locally and globally in terms of production. Though its raison d'être, the hundred-year anniversary of the industry, represented a time to look back, really what the shorts seemed to be grasping here was a chance to look forward. As Sen describes, *Bombay Talkies* embodies those questions of the present and was a confrontation point between two formations, the 'indie' and 'commercial', that were able to merge in this third- way form. In moving forward, the following two Netflix-produced omnibus films directed by the same group of directors, *Lust Stories* (2018) and *Ghost Stories* (2020), further complicates the romantic entanglement of entertainment production by adding a third partner to the production mix: online streaming services. Thus, even between anthologies there is a substantial shift in the market, with each work highlighting some of the changes of production shaping the industry.

The 'promiscuities' that Sen refers to are not only seen in production, however, but can also be seen in the stories through all three films. New modes of production have allowed for new stories, and all films exhibit an exploration of more serious and often controversial topics that only recently have begun to be seen sparingly in mainstream Hindi cinema. The types of stories and how they are told further cement this form as a vehicle for ushering in a divergence from past understandings of the commercial. This trend begins to shed light upon the possibility of the short film as a place of formal and content experimentation, allowing directors to pursue the paths that might not always garner the interest and funding needed to realise a feature.

Zoya Akhtar's short films provide two points of examination. First, they are a compelling example to examine in terms of how this format is growing and, consequently, how its appeal to both new and established directors is pushing the production and form of Indian film. Second, it is a greater glimpse into Akhtar as a filmmaker and how through the greater freedom of the short she pushes herself to experiment with different forms, characters and stories that differ from her feature films. Examining these works offers a nuanced glimpse at some of the other themes examined in this book: namely, Akhtar's relation to change in the industry and her representation of gender. Further, her shorts show a broader examination of the confluence of gender, sexuality and class not realised in her features. In her short films seen in *Bombay Talkies*, *Lust Stories* and *Ghost Stories*, similar to her Amazon Prime series *Made in Heaven* (Zoya Akhtar and Reema Kagti 2019), it is possible to see a more direct take by Akhtar on controversial social topics that adds to our understanding of her work beyond what is seen on the big screen.

THE BOOM OF THE SHORT FILM IN INDIA

On the one hand, *Bombay Talkies* might have still represented direct ties to the film industry due to its subject, its choices in directors and its overall length (combining all shorts into one larger film to make it the length of a feature film). On the other hand, it begins to not only, as Sen observes, take more from the 'indie' genre, but it also begins to solidify the groundwork of a surge in the short film form in India during that decade. From social message films such as *Aids Jaago* (Mira Nair, Santosh Sivan, Farhan Akhtar and Vishal Bhardwaj 2007) to festival specials like *Mumbai Cutting* (Jahnu Barua, Rahul Dholakia, Rituparno Ghosh, Shashanka Ghosh, Manish Jha, Anurag Kashyap, Sudhir Mishra, Ruchi Narain, Ayush Raina, Revathi and Kundan Shah 2008) to special theatrical releases like *Shorts* (Neeraj Ghaywan, Vasan Bala, Anubhuti Kashyap, Shlok Sharma and Gitanjali Rao 2013) and the thousands of individual shorts that cover all genres, this form has become an increasingly enticing way for filmmakers to reach audiences while also pushing themselves to explore new possibilities of their craft. Indian-American filmmaker Mira Nair, who has made shorts for anthology films such as the Indian-based *Aids Jaago* and the transnational production *11'09"01* (Youssef Chahine, Amos Gitai, Shôhei Imamura, Alejandro G. Iñárritu, Claude Lelouch, Ken Loach, Samira Makhmalbaf, Mira Nair, Idrissa Ouedraogo, Sean Penn and Danis Tanović 2002) as well as standalone shorts, indicates the appeal of the form through her comments about it: 'I am addicted to the SFF [short film format] . . . The medium insists that you be rigorous in how much you can speak in the story and in how short a time. It's a great way to practice your craft. I love how the short film tests the rigour of every medium of cinema' (Manjulaa 2017). The possibility for creativity, inspired as much by the form as by the greater production freedoms, attracts established directors as well as new directors hoping to gain attention, making the short film an intriguing mode of exploration.

While production has increased, significantly aided not only by intrigue with the form but by technological developments that make filmmaking more accessible, so have distribution opportunities. The development of existing outlets as well as the growth of new ones make this film format even more appealing as there is an ever-increasing ability to ensure that these films reach wider audiences.

One of the main locations where shorts have historically found a welcoming home is the film festival. Generally, festivals' focus on the 'art' over the 'commercial', select audiences, greater embrace of experimentation as well as impetus for finding the next great filmmaker make them a perfect place for short films to find enthusiastic viewers. Though in most major film festivals, shorts can still find themselves overshadowed by feature-length productions, there continues to be a robust exhibition of the format on these important stages. Most of the world's biggest and most prestigious international festivals such as the Cannes Film Festival, Berlinale, Sundance Film Festival, Toronto International Film Festival (TIFF) and International Film Festival Rotterdam (IFFR) have short film exhibitions and prizes. Some of the biggest film festivals in India, from the International Film Festival of India to the Jio MAMI Mumbai Film Festival to the Kolkata International Film Festival, also showcase short films. Short films have also found a home in the growing market of Indian film festivals held abroad that include the New York Indian Film Festival (NYIFF), Indian Film Festival of Los Angeles (IFFLA) and the Bagri Foundation London Indian Film Festival (LIFF). These festivals are increasingly catering not only to diasporic audiences, but are finding diverse audiences drawn in by their interest in a particular topic or director or general curiosity to learn more about a cinema that is sometimes still eclipsed in larger international festivals (Rosario 2018). Film festivals dedicated either solely or predominantly to short films have also become increasingly pervasive both worldwide and in India, with some of the latter including the International Documentary and Short Film Festival of Kerala (IDSFFK), the Jaipur International Short Film Festival, the Mumbai International Film Festival and the Bangalore International Short Film Festival. The film festival still provides an important venue for the short film not only to be seen, but to be rewarded in its own right, and the growth of film festivals specifically dedicated to the short film shows that in India there is an appetite to consume these films not just as extras or sides, but as the main fare.[2]

Though short films still have a strong relationship with festivals, this is no longer the only or even the primary method of viewing short films. Wider consumption of short films beyond festivals can be attributed to new forms of access to these works, specifically digital media. The growth of entertainment consumption through digital media, ranging from YouTube to OTT (over-the-top) services, has increased exponentially in India in the 2010s and has seen even more tremendous growth starting in 2020 in response to the lockdown and severe reduction of group activities like going to the cinema due to the COVID-19 pandemic. In 2019, digital streaming platforms overtook film entertainment to become the third-largest segment of the Indian media and entertainment industry and growth of this segment only grew faster during the pandemic, which saw a 31 per cent increase in paid subscriptions to OTT platforms in the first four months of lockdown (Amin 2021). Global giants like Netflix, Amazon Prime Video and Disney+ have invested heavily in the market and can be seen as key drivers in this increase. However, local media companies like Jio TV and Jio Cinema and Eros Now have also turned their focus on increasing viewership. With this quickly growing market, all media producers are trying to find new ways to entice their audiences and grow viewership for their content both at home and abroad.

One way that Netflix and Amazon Prime Video have sought to increase their appeal is through the production of their own content. While companies like Eros Now already have a large catalogue of Indian content, Netflix and Amazon Prime Video are quickly trying to make up for this gap. Netflix Indian original films went from thirty in 2018 to ninety in 2020 and Amazon Prime Video jumped from ninety to 110 (Amin 2021). There is a range in the types of originals, which include series and feature-length films as well as short films. Netflix has produced both the second and third anthology films featuring Akhtar, Johar, Banerjee and Kashyap (*Lust Stories* and *Ghost Stories*) and most recently released *Ajeeb Daastaans* (Neeraj Ghaywan, Kayoze Irani, Shashank Khaitan, Raj Mehta) in April 2021 and *Ray* (Srijit Mukherji, Abhishek Chaubey and Vasan Bala) in June 2021. Further, as they look to expand their regional language content to meet the demand of consumers who are seeking non-Hindi language content at almost the same rate as Hindi language content on streaming services, they have again used the short in this pursuit. In 2020, Netflix released *Paava Kadhaigal,* a Tamil-language omnibus film featuring four shorts by acclaimed directors Sudha Kongara, Gautham Vasudev Menon, Vignesh Shivan and Vetrimaaran. Centred around the theme of honour killings and the caste, religious and LGBTQI+ discrimination that can lead to them, the film features prominent Tamil film industry actors such as Simran, Anjali and Gautham Menon as well as 'indie' darlings like Kalki Koechlin, again demonstrating a blurring of borders between industries and forms. It has since gone on to release the Telugu original omnibus film *Pitta Kathalu* (Nag Ashwin, B. V. Nandini Reddy, Tharun Bhascker and Sankalp Reddy 2021) and the Tamil-language anthology series *Navarasa* (Priyadarshan, Karthik Subbaraj, Vasanth, Arvind Swami, Bejoy Nambia, Karthick Naren, Gautham Vasudev Menon, Srajun KM and Rathindran R. Prasad 2021) created by Mani Ratnam.

Netflix's growth in the market has been supported by its substantial investment and its ability to draw industry names. Srishti Behl Arya, Netflix's director of international original films, India, cites the latter as due to 'some of the country's biggest actors, directors and producers . . .enjoying the opportunity to develop content that wouldn't pass muster in risk-averse mainstream Bollywood films' (Shackleton 2020). Netflix not only offers the appeal of an increasing Indian and global audience, but also a greater freedom to explore new ideas and content that makes it an exciting place for production, experimentation and innovation.

The short film form has proven advantageous not only to this sense of exploration, but more practically to the difficulties of producing content under constrained circumstances, such as the COVID-19 pandemic. Amazon Prime Video released both Tamil- and Hindi-language anthologies: *Putham Pudhu Kaali* (Sudha Kongara, Gautham Menon, Suhasini Maniratnam, Rajiv Menon and Karthik Subbaraj 2020) and *Unpaused* (Raj & DK, Nikkhil Advani, Tannishtha Chatterjee, Avinash Arun and Nitya Mehra 2020). Both films were written, shot and produced during the pandemic and tell stories set during or inspired by the COVID-19 lockdown. Here the short form shows an ability for producing a quick response to current topics as well as the ability to film under more difficult circumstances.

The mixing of industries, and how this has been enhanced by the streaming platform, can be clearly seen in the cases of growing short film streaming platforms such as HumaraMovie, Pocket Films and Royal Stag Barrel Large Short Films. HumaraMovie is a premium site for independent cinema and carries a large range of short films made by festival winning directors as well as famous popular directors. Not only a distributor through their streaming platform, they have also become a major producer of shorts and encourage people to submit both finished films and scripts. In terms of production, in 2014 they started a mentored film programme called 'Shuruaat' that paired experienced and new filmmakers. The first anthology released was *Shuruaat Ka Interval* (Aarti S. Bagdi, Amrit Raj Gupta, Krishan Hooda, Shishir Jah, Atanu Mukherjee, Rukshana Tabassum, Ankit Tripathi and Palash Vaswani 2014) and in 2016 they released another shorts anthology, *Shor Se Shuruaat* (Amira Bhargava, Rahul V. Chittella, Satish Raj Kasireddi, Pratik Kothari, Arunima Sharma, Supriya Sharma and Annie Zaidi), which had segments mentored by directors like Mira Nair and Zoya Akhtar. The third anthology, *Shuruaat Ka Twist* (Heena Dsouza, Avalokita Dutt, Praveen Fernandes, Hanish Kalia, Sanjiv Kishinchandani and Gaurav Mehra), was released in 2019. These films have been shown at festivals and have had theatre premieres that are attended by some Bollywood stars (usually the mentoring directors or star actors). While centring their platform, which allows them to maintain a sustained audience of subscribers, HumaraMovie represents the multifaceted growth of the media industry where companies see mixing in formats (HumaraMovie now also produces feature-length films), styles and industry positions. Further, through their mentoring, they show the possibility of the short as a way for new filmmakers to develop their voice and perhaps find a spot in an industry heavily shaped by family connections.

Pocket Films is one of the largest distributors of Indian short films and has a YouTube channel of over 2 million subscribers (Mehrotra 2019). They were created in 2009 with the desire to help promote and monetise short films. Their distribution has grown beyond their YouTube channel and they now have a weekly TV show on NDTV Prime called *Prime Talkies with Pocket Films* that features their shorts and interviews with directors; they have also organised theatrical screenings of shorts (see https://pocketfilms.in/about_us). They are currently growing in their work with film festivals as they not only curate viewings of their shorts at international festivals but have started to expand their work as a festival hub where they will grow their festival hosting and submission services and create a database to help connect filmmakers with industry professionals.

One last short film distributor worth mentioning here is Royal Stag Barrel Large Short Films. The site hosts an open contest in which anyone can submit a film to be considered for the Large Short Film's Short of the Week. These films are distributed on their Facebook page with over a million followers (Mehrotra 2019). While a place to discover new filmmakers and stars, one of the things that makes Large Short Films stand out is their ability to attract star power. Leading filmmakers like Sujoy Ghosh, Anurag Kashyap and Imtiaz Ali have made Large Short Films and scrolling through their catalogue, one sees some of the most recognised faces of Bollywood and Hindi independent cinema appear. By bringing popular names to work within this format, Large Short Films thus perhaps represents one of the best examples of the confluence of industry with the more independent short film market.

These and the many other sites and channels providing regular access to short films, ranging from ShortsTV's 24/7 HD TV short films channel to Mumbai-based film club Aabobo focused on screening and creating a community of filmmakers, offer the chance to individuals to create, to experiment and, for newcomers, perhaps to be found. However, the proliferation of such sites and content does not necessarily mean the short has become a road to fame. Further, as the popularity of the short film has grown, attracting major independent and Bollywood directors and stars, the competition to get views has grown. Individual films made by major directors or featuring popular actors featured on Royal Stag Barrel Large Short Films, for example, can garner more than a million views, with some reaching 5, 10, 15 million. In 2021, the short film *Chutney* (Jyoti Kapur Das 2016) starring actress Tisca Chopra had garnered more than 132 million views. The popularity that some of the more star-studded Royal Stag Barrel Large Short Films garner shows that even shorts can be influenced by the star-driven industry and that not all filmmakers have equal access to creating a name for themselves in this film format.

However, popularity and the chance of discovery are not the only ambition of the short film form. In an interview about the expansion of the short film into the Indian market, Carter Pilcher, founder of the company Shorts International, emphasises that because the format allows more films to be produced more quickly, the growth of the short film 'is about the success of the category and not just one short film' (Pratap 2018). Thus, turning to look at Akhtar's short films, it is important to remember that while they are at once individual films that provide a platform for Akhtar as a director to experiment and show a different side of herself as a filmmaker, they are also part of a larger movement that relies on the success of the format as a whole to allow for the short to continue to thrive as a space of experimentation. The growth in production and distribution methods for the short film is one demonstration that this form as a whole has continued to be a success and, as such, is growing as a space for even established filmmakers like Akhtar to experiment with new forms and new stories and thus shows a new side of her as a filmmaker.

AKHTAR'S EXPLORATION OF NEW PATHS THROUGH THE SHORT FILM

Zoya Akhtar's work in *Bombay Talkies* is a launching point for her short film work which, with each successive film, continues to grow into its own. *Bombay Talkies* is an appealing entry point as it is, of all three anthologies, the film that most closely walks the line between industry and independent, new forms. In that intermingling, the film offers a point of reflection as to the short film's possibilities which, in turn, impact Akhtar's work as they allow her to pursue a different kind of production.

One of the main shifts allowed by the short is the ability to address a different kind of audience. The question of who is being addressed was a particularly salient point of discussion in critical analysis of *Bombay Talkies* as the film is at once a celebration of the industry yet also a move away from the past industry, and its perceived audiences, in many regards. In terms of viewers, Sen argues that the film is 'made for more worldly audiences who frequent urban multiplexes', as evidenced especially by the characters who 'are perhaps somewhat familiar, but whose obsessive attachment with the popular film is not shared by the target spectator of the film as a whole. The passionate film fan – the "masses", in Bollywood's parlance – is carefully held at an arm's length from the mature consumer-spectator of this tribute text' (2015: 79). In her introduction to a dossier on *Bombay Talkies*, Anupama Kapse elaborates, 'in a nation that is known for being crazy about films, the infantile film fan of *Bombay Talkies* is not *apna* [of/for the people], as the extravagant medley that it concludes with claims. Three of the film's four shorts feature children, but their cinephilia sits uneasily with the discerning, mature audience the film addresses itself to' (2015: 63). Understanding who the audience are is paramount to understanding what the film is and does, and both Sen and Kapse agree that the audience here is not the same as the subject of the film.

Rachel Dwyer underscores the importance of understanding the audience in relation to following the development of a new Indian 'middlebrow' cinema starting in the 1990s.[3] Dwyer cites *Bombay Talkies* as one place to do so as it exemplifies a shift towards a 'middle ground of Hindi cinema' that has developed over the years in relation to the country's changing middle class (2016: 51). In these circumstances, Dwyer sees the middlebrow as

> occupying the middle ground between the highbrow, the arts that elicit intellectual responses as they may be challenging and uncomfortable, and the lowbrow, or cultural texts that elicit emotional, basic or bodily responses. The middlebrow is also the area of culture that reflects middle-class self-improvement and auto-didacticism, associated with institutions like book clubs, reading groups, literary festivals and ticking off lists such as '10 best films', '100 best books' and 'films to see before you die'. (2016: 52)

The important thing to underscore in the process of finding a middle ground is that while this form of cinema catering to middle-class audiences enjoys taking from both the highbrow (connected with independent) and lowbrow (connected with the mainstream industry) to create a new style and broach new themes, it does so in a way that is 'challenging without being disturbing' (2016: 64). Social issues and themes abound in these films, but they are still audience friendly, giving their middle-class viewers something to think about but not necessarily confront. This is an important distinction in Akhtar's short works, which walk that middle ground; unlike some short films that deliver a more direct call for social change such as the 2020's *Devi* (Priyanka Banerjee), Akhtar experiments with bringing up issues that merit serious conversations, though still in a way that is accessible and audience-pleasing. Unlike in her features, which also embed serious themes in audience-pleasing fare, here the message and theme are more central as it is the main crux of the film and is not surrounded by competing storylines, location shots, song-and-dance numbers and other features that support (and possibly overwhelm) the story and themes in her feature-length films. Thus we see in her shorts her industry sensibilities that guide her to make a film for a certain audience coupled with her experimentations in subject and form as she encounters a new type of audience that is looking for some message though still not direct confrontation.

Having this different audience allows Akhtar's segment '*Sheila ki jawani*', as well as the other three shorts in *Bombay Talkies*, to be a '*hatke*' film (Sen 2015).

'Sheila ki jawani' tells the story of young boy Vicky (Naman Jain) who dreams of being a dancer and who finds his inspiration from Bollywood superstar Katrina Kaif. At once a whimsical tale that shows a bright-eyed young child lovingly adoring his favourite star through film sequences, such as the item song 'Sheila ki jawani' from which the film gets its title,[4] to his imagined encounter with Kaif who appears to him as a fairy godmother late one night, the story of the film is prompted by a more serious threat of toxic masculinity, unbending gender expectations and the possibilities of future homophobia and/or transphobia. The film focuses on the conflict between Vicky and his father (Ranvir Shorey), who dreams of his son participating in what he deems appropriate gender practices. The opening scene of the film shows a miserable young Vicky on the soccer pitch, reluctantly joining the game and running in circles without purpose, clearly not wanting to be there. When he tries to ask his father to let him quit this sport that he loathes, his father complains about the extra money he is spending on coaching and refuses to listen to the boy's desires. This conversation happens as Vicky's sister requests money from her father to attend a school field trip that she is very excited about, only to be turned down because her father does not have the money and regards this opportunity as having little importance. The father has clear expectations for his children and discriminately apportions resources to fulfil his vision.

The conflict between father and son turns violent when not only does Vicky not want to participate in the activities selected by his father, but when his father sees him breaking what he deems to be gender norms. When he catches his son in a dress, high heels and lipstick, passionately performing a song in his living room to his sister, the father cannot control his anger and hits his son, threatening to 'break every bone in his body' if he ever catches him dressed up again. Gender stereotype nonconformity incites violence and the child must learn to hide his true passions from his father. However, as the boy learns this reality, he also learns to find furtive ways to live out his identity. The story thus climaxes not with the beating of the boy, but rather with his idea to practise the art form that he loves while helping his sister raise money to go on her school trip. When their parents go out for the day, Vicky decorates an abandoned warehouse and sells tickets to the neighbourhood to watch him perform 'Sheila ki jawani'. Though the neighbours enter the scenario with scepticism, and the young neighbourhood boys even start to taunt Vicky when he comes on stage all decked out in drag, once the performance begins everyone is won over. The film ends on a happy note, with Vicky living his dream and the neighbourhood (though not his father) accepting of this dream.[5]

Though the film does present, as Dwyer describes of middlebrow cinema, some challenging themes, it does so in a way that is made less disturbing as in the end we see the young child conquer these challenges through his ingenuity. This film clearly represents a middle ground as the challenging themes of the story that could be found in highbrow cinema are still shrouded in spectacle as Bollywood offers an escapist solution to the real issue at hand, showing that the film has not quite escaped industry nor become completely highbrow.

While *Bombay Talkies* might have garnered attention for what it was, *Lust Stories*, the second omnibus film by the group, gained notice for what it was saying. The film stood out as all four segments centred on women and their desire and was viewed by many to be an if not perfect, at least refreshing reflection on a topic and from a point of view rarely shown in Bollywood features. The reviews praised the film for being one of a few recent films that not only 'delightfully pushes boundaries to tell real stories about real women' (Ghosh 2018) but that 'spearhead[s] the sexual revolution of Bollywood's women' (Upadhyay 2018) and represents 'a step forward in Bollywood's sexual awakening' (Roy 2018).[6] In displaying female sexual desire in such a direct manner, a portrayal that is sorely underdeveloped and can still be shocking in most world cinemas, *Lust Stories* is perhaps the most fun and most challenging of the three anthologies as it celebrates and confronts a topic that should be marked with joy but is too often shrouded in taboo.

Zoya Akhtar's segment opens with Sudha (Bhumi Pednekar) and Ajit (Neil Bhoopalam) loudly having sex. Sudha here is clearly enjoying herself and is actively playing a part in the act that satisfies her as well as Ajit. Introduced in a position of pleasure and power, the next scene offers a slight surprise as we see Sudha pragmatically clean up and resume her role not as a wife, girlfriend or lover, but rather as Ajit's maid. As Sudha goes about preparing breakfast and cleaning up after Ajit, he ignores her, not maliciously but also pragmatically, easily slipping into his role as the 'master' of the house who has no relationship with the lower class/caste domestic help. Following her introduction, Sudha is notably quiet as she is shown scene after scene silently fulfilling her role within the enclosed space of the apartment in a peaceful rhythm. Sudha exudes a sense of security and confidence in her role that leads to her graceful command of the space as she moves through it with an air of certainty and purpose.

This rhythm and command are disturbed, however, when Ajit's parents come to visit and arrange his marriage. The small confines of the apartment become increasingly claustrophobic as Sudha must move between these now crowded spaces silently serving the arrangement that threatens her interests. The kitchen is invaded by Ajit's mother, who comes in giving directions on how to serve the guests. The voices of the visitors pierce the silence of the tiny space and Sudha is able to hear with clarity the reverberating conversations that pass through the walls and down the halls. Again she sees her spaces invaded as Ajit takes his bride-to-be (Nikita Dutta) into the space where Sudha reigns: the bedroom. Sudha silently observes them in conversation, an act we have not seen between her and Ajit, as she waits to serve them tea.

Figure 3.1 Sudha hears the whispers invading her confined space.

Throughout the film, we do not know what is going on in Sudha's mind. We can feel the walls of the space she has created close in on her, but it is unclear whether she wants to marry Ajit or keep their relationship as it is, or even if she loves him. When the engagement is announced, it feels like the end of something for Sudha, but it is unclear what is ending or what consequences this change will bring. Sudha takes the sweet offered to her to celebrate the betrothal and leaves the flat (for the first time in the film we see her outside of this space). To the outsider it might appear that it was just a normal day, and this is confirmed as the maid from the neighbouring flat happily starts chatting with her as they wait for the lift. However, Sudha's smile at the end as she bites into the sweet again puts her in the position of power over her pleasure: her relationship with Ajit might have ended, but that does not mean her ability to satisfy her lust and desires has and she will go on without him.

This work stands out among the rest in the anthology for though it tells a story about lust, it also broaches other societal topics such as class divide. There are obvious power dynamics in this relationship, as Sudha is a lower-class employee who is treated by those around her as a silent fixture of the house rather than a real person. Though marked by exploitative elements, this is a story of a relationship where Sudha actually shows that she has more control than that which might be attributed to her at first glance. She enjoys the relationship (or at least the sexual elements of it) and addresses its end on her own terms. While Akhtar's films are usually filled with words, from voiceovers to dialogue to poetry, this film stands out for its silences and all that is conveyed through the power of the portrayal of space and Sudha's navigation of it that tells of lust, power and the games played to conquer them.

The uniting factor of the third omnibus film is not only a theme but a genre. *Ghost Stories* is each director's attempt to make a horror film, and for that reason is perhaps the biggest stretch as this is a genre that none of the directors are known for and that has relatively little presence in the Indian film market. While *Lust Stories* was warmly received, *Ghost Stories* got middling reviews that noted that most, aside from Dibakar Banerjee's segment, were a 'miss' (Thakur 2020) and were unable to get the genre quite right. Ankur Pathak summarises: 'if you're looking for some old-school spooks, *Ghost Stories* doesn't cut it. But if you manage your expectations just a little bit and sacrifice instant amusement for delayed gratification, you may not be too disappointed' (2020). As each director grapples with this shift to varying success, this film best underscores the importance of the short film as a place to experiment and grow, an act which doesn't always result in someone getting it right the first time.

Like in *Lust Stories*, Akhtar's segment in *Ghost Stories* also uses a claustrophobic space to convey themes of class, gender and horror. In this story, a young woman, Sameera (Janhvi Kapoor), in lust and in love, waits for her married boyfriend to rendezvous with her at her latest work assignment: caring for an elderly, bedridden woman (Surekha Sikri) in her home. As the young, vivacious Sameera waits for love and the hope of escape it carries in this suffocating house of death, the tension builds as the sounds of doorbells ringing and something dragging, heightened by the old woman's declarations of someone coming, create an alarming sense that these two women are not alone. The creepy feeling of the house is confirmed by Sameera's lover (Vijay Varma), who once he arrives quickly leaves again, abandoning his jilted lover to her fate. The culmination of the story is when the girl, curious about the sounds, follows them and finds the dead body of the old woman she thought she had been caring for who, it is revealed, has been dead for several days.

Though the film manages to inspire mild anxiety and does well creating a menacing sense of space, the horror is not really in the ghost story but rather in the social situations that have created this scenario. Caretaking has been transformed from a family duty to a profession that reinforces class hierarchies. Sameera has taken this job out of necessity and has little interest in her work, which is presented as unenjoyable and dirty. She is shown working alone to care for a woman she does not know: she bathes her, empties her bedpans, makes her food and must listen to her strange stories and requests that make little sense to her. Through her conversations we learn that she has been orphaned and must take what work she can get as she tries to build a life for herself.

This small passage about her being orphaned leads to another of the horrors of the film: shifting family structures. The old woman has a son that she waits for expectantly, but her care service is primarily hired out. When the death of the old woman is revealed, it is blamed on the son who was supposed to have come to care for her for a few days but didn't show up, leaving his mother to starve to death. Ghosts may be scary, but in this day and age the possibility of family abandonment and the fear of dying alone are much more real horrors that one must confront and that the film highlights.

With all her short films, Akhtar tries out different forms to tell stories that have a pointedly more direct social message. From silence to genre, she experiments with new types of filmmaking that might not otherwise appear in her work. She also brings up new themes, from gender stereotyping and violence to women's lust to class power relationships. These films are not filled with stars nor do they contain the heavy dialogue or ensemble casts that her have stood out in her features. They focus on one story developed through one character and thus can leave a sense of a more direct message. Though these films sit within the realm of what Dwyer describes as the Indian middlebrow, and as such are 'challenging without being disturbing' (2016: 64), they represent some of Akhtar's most experimental and political works.

CONCLUSION

While short anthology films like *Bombay Talkies* might represent 'strategic alliances and newly engendered promiscuities' (Sen 2015: 78) between the industry and independent cinema, in the short time between the much-publicised release of this film and the release of the third anthology by these directors in 2020, the short film has shown that it has taken on its own identity. There are increasingly more opportunities for filmmakers, and in turn, this form, to grow as new modes of production and distribution ensure that the short film is seen by more audiences both in India and the world. As the form becomes more popular, it attracts more established filmmakers who, even though they have the name and recognition to make features, can turn to this form for something that even they might not be able to get in a more cautious industry: the freedom to experiment. Thus, though this further intertwining of industry and independent might represent to some, as Sen suggests, Bollywood's 'cannibalizing other cinematic formations with impunity' (2015: 78), which it has done with other media forms such as music (see Gopal, this volume), it has turned out to be not a direct cannibalisation as the short film form has proven able to maintain some of its own integrity.

Akhtar is an example of this as, despite her industry connections, she enters each short with a fresh take that demonstrates another side of her as a filmmaker. In this form she breaks away from some of her more known trademarks – large ensemble casts, narrative voiceovers, extravagant and complicated settings, rich dialogue and popular actors – and instead finds a new way to tell a story. As she branches further into new formats, like the streaming series, and new stories, as represented by her 2019 feature *Gully Boy*, the short perhaps remains as a point of inspiration that continues to offer the freedom and space for her to grow as a filmmaker in different directions.

NOTES

1. Karan Johar's and Zoya Akhtar's shorts did contain tributes to the song-and-dance sequence within their films.
2. For more on the history and growth of film festivals, see, for example, the *Film Festival Yearbook* series (general editor Dina Iordanova) as well as *Film Festivals: History, Theory, Method, Practice* (Valck et al. 2016).
3. Dwyer notes that this term is not often used in relation to Indian Cinema or Bollywood in particular, though she does highlight it as having potential to shed light on what is happening in the country's cinema due to the rise of the middle class. It should also be noted that her work on middlebrow Indian cinema appears in a book exploring the middlebrow globally and therefore part of the decision to use this particular term is related to its context.

    Further, while Dwyer mainly focuses on a middlebrow cinema she sees starting to develop in the 1990s, she does acknowledge prior 'middlebrow' cinemas, such as India's 'parallel cinema' from the 1970s and 1980s, which she describes as a 'new wave of art cinema that also overlapped with the middlebrow' (2016: 52).
4. The item song '*Sheila ki jawani*' picturised on Katrina Kaif appears in *Tees Maar Khan* (Farah Khan 2010).
5. This story can be compared to one of the storylines that emerges in the recent film *Dolly Kitty Aur Woh Chamakte Sitare* (Alankrita Shrivastava 2019) in which Dolly (Konkona Sen Sharma) is confronted with how to address her son identifying as a girl. Both children confront frustrated and violent reactions from their parents; however, in Shrivastava's story there is a final acceptance by Dolly and perhaps a greater hope of reconciliation between generations.
6. *Veere Di Wedding* (Shashanka Ghosh 2018) is another popular example of a film that also pushed these boundaries.

WORKS CITED

Amin, Ruhail (2021), 'Bells jingled all the way for OTT', *Business World (India)*, 1 January 2021.

Business World India (2017), 'Royal Stag Barrel Select continues sponsorship of 19th Jio Mami', *Business World (India)*, 31 August 2017.

D'Mello, Wayne (2016), 'The fresh filmmaking voices of Shor Se Shuruaat', *Film Companion*, 15 December 2016. Available at <https://www.filmcompanion.in/features/bollywood-features/fresh-filmmaking-voices-shor-se-shuruaat/>

Dwyer, Rachel (2016), 'Mumbai middlebrow: Ways of thinking about the middle ground in Hindi cinema', in Sally Faulkner (ed.), *Middlebrow Cinema*, London: Routledge, pp. 51–67.

Edidin, Peter (2007), 'AIDS awareness films for India', *The New York Times*, 30 November 2007.

Ghosh, Suktara (2018), 'Review: Netflix's *Lust Stories* pushes boundaries to offer a real ride', *The Quint*, 18 June 2018. Available at <https://www.thequint.com/entertainment/movie-reviews/lust-stories-review-netflix#gs.x0e2CEvR>

Kapse, Anupama (2015), 'Afterthoughts on the Indian cinema centenary', *South Asian Popular Culture*, 13: 1, pp. 61–4.

Manjulaa (2017), 'Why short films have begun to make it big', *The Hoot*, 27 July 2017. Available at <http://asu.thehoot.org/research/special-reports/why-short-films-have-begun-to-make-it-big-10217>

Mehrotra, Suchin (2019), 'Have you made a short film? Here are 13 platforms to help you find an audience', *Film Companion*, 21 May 2019. Available at <https://www.filmcompanion.in/features/short-film-features/have-you-made-a-short-film-here-are-14-platforms-to-help-you-find-an-audience/>

Pathak, Ankur (2020), '*Ghost Stories* Review: Netflix's horror anthology has 3 Misses and a win', 2 January 2020. Available at <https://www.huffpost.com/archive/in/entry/ghost-stories-netflix-movie-review-horror-dibakar-banerjee-karan-johar-zoya-akhtar_in_5e0dd1d6c5b6b5a713b6300b?guccounter=1&guce_referrer=aHR0cHM6Ly93d3cuZ29vZ2xlLmNvbS8&guce_referrer_sig=AQAAAC1I8Q8hSArIFIOEpNE0OKnPA9CeeGuUy6qcPOX9iv4FbuzuLAQJnm7yjVksCX-RvSwWYKnYdvxbptOOkJ4FMPE9u0xs0PID3lXiPaYUMPmwuf8-5sTlz6OSmKiuv9Mcw6jaLle9nnoI8ounu5RUZmDdnFXPlKoq4dSepJjsuvXg>

Pratap, Rashmi (2018), 'We can take Indian short films to 70 million homes', *The Hindu: BusinessLine*, 29 November 2018. Available at <https://www.thehindubusinessline.com/news/we-can-take-indian-short-films-to-70-million-homes/article25625422.ece>

Rosario, Kennith (2018), 'As Indian film festivals mushroom across the globe, desi cinema is drawing new audiences', *The Hindu*, 5 May 2018. Available at <https://www.thehindu.com/entertainment/movies/as-indian-film-festivals-mushroom-across-the-globe-desi-cinema-is-drawing-new-audiences/article23773557.ece.>

Roy, Priyanka (2018), 'Lust and lost love: *Lust Stories* is a step forward in Bollywood's sexual awakening', *The Telegraph*, 18 June 2018. Available at <https://www.telegraphindia.com/entertainment/lust-amp-lost-love/cid/1431440>

Sen, Meheli (2015), 'Bombay Talkies and the Indian cinema centenary', *South Asian Popular Culture*, 13: 1, pp. 77–80.

Shackleton, Liz (2020), 'Srishti Behl Arya on Netflix India's original films strategy', *Screen International*, 31 January 2020.

Thakur, Tanul (2020), 'Movie review: Three misses, one hit in Netflix's *Ghost Stories*', *The Wire India*, 3 January 2020. Available at <https://thewire.in/film/ghost-stories-netflix-movie-review>

Upadhyay, Karishma (2018), 'How *Veere Di Wedding* and *Lust Stories* spearhead the sexual revolution of Bollywood's women', *First Post*, 19 June 2018. Available at <https://www.firstpost.com/entertainment/how-veere-di-wedding-and-lust-stories-spearhead-the-sexual-revolution-of-bollywoods-women-4540411.html>

Valck, Marijke de, Brendan Kredell and Skadi Loist (2016), *Film Festivals: History, Theory, Method, Practice*, London: Routledge.

CHAPTER 4

Zoya Akhtar as a Screenwriter: Making Niche the New Mainstream

Vyoma Jha

This chapter explores Zoya Akhtar's career as a screenwriter and defines her signature style of filmmaking. On the face of it, the four feature films written and directed by Akhtar, *Luck by Chance* (2009), *Zindagi Na Milegi Dobara* (2011), *Dil Dhadakne Do* (2015) and *Gully Boy* (2019), may not appear to have much in common, either in terms of the story or setting. However, a central thread running through her films is the high quality of their ensemble performances. A deeper analysis of the creative influences in her life and her writing style reveals that Akhtar is motivated to make films for the mainstream audience even if her choice of subjects appears rather niche. Akhtar's scripts invariably inhabit an urban Indian milieu (even when abroad, the characters bring this urban mentality with them) and tend to stem from her own social environment and personal experiences. Further, the very particular settings of each film, from the Hindi film industry to luxury European holidays to the *gully* rap scene of Mumbai, make her work seem as if she must be targeting a specific audience, as the worlds her characters inhabit are ones with which most audiences have little in common. In spite of these specificities, she is skilful in ensuring the widespread appeal of these stories by weaving them around universal themes such as self-esteem, freedom, family or class. These themes are explored throughout her films not just through one character, but through the multiple, well-crafted and intriguing lead and supporting characters who each bring a distinct story and personality to the film and reinforce the universality of the films' themes as they spill beyond one character and, inevitably, from the specific to the popular.

Akhtar's signature style of filmmaking is writing a strong ensemble that takes a niche story to a mainstream audience. Her writing process can be broken down into two key elements: a love for observation and a collaborative spirit.

While her keen understanding of human behaviour spills over into the wide range of characters she writes, her collaborative style allows her to benefit from others' life experiences and develop authenticity in each character's graph. Ultimately, it is a combination of an inherited love for film and a voracious appetite for studying people that makes Akhtar the eclectic scriptwriter that she is, with her ability to develop rich storylines with even richer characters.

GROWING UP WITH WRITERS

'Stories were a part of my system' (Akhtar 2015)

Born and bred in Mumbai, Akhtar has been steeped in the inner workings of the Hindi film industry owing to her parents' connection with and love of film. Her father, Javed Akhtar, was one half of India's most celebrated writing duo in Hindi films: Salim-Javed (Salim Khan and Javed Akhtar). Her mother, Honey Irani, has also had a long association with the Hindi film industry; she began her career as a child artist and later turned into a screenwriter and filmmaker. Growing up surrounded by literature and films, Akhtar recalls how watching films would be followed by long discussions at home about the scenes, characters, cinematography, lighting etc. (Akhtar 2015). It was also normal to see actors, directors, musicians or poets around the house at all times. As a result, she believes her mind was trained to look at the finer details of films from a young age.

When she was around ten years old, Akhtar's mother studied at the Film and Television Institute (FTII) in Pune, which resulted in her brother Farhan Akhtar and her growing up in an environment of films and filmmaking. She credits her mother for her early education in films, from watching movies on a home projector to critiquing the story, screenplay and dialogues. They were immersed in films and her mother would frequently procure prints from theatre owners and exhibitors (Akhtar 2011a). Although she was exposed to all kinds of films, from Hindi cinema to foreign films to American musicals, she didn't aspire to become a filmmaker as she didn't relate to the 'terrible' Hindi cinema of the 1980s (Akhtar 2009, Akhtar 2011a, Akhtar 2015).

Akhtar's early interest was in writing and not filmmaking. But watching Mira Nair's *Salaam Bombay!* (1988) changed her outlook towards filmmaking. The movie had a huge influence on her desire to make movies and she credits it for shaping her filmmaking sensibilities, saying 'it was about my city and told in a way that it opened my eyes to a whole new world of storytelling' (Akhtar 2009, Akhtar 2016). Early on in her career, Akhtar chose to work with independent Indian and Indian-origin filmmakers, such as Mira Nair, Dev Benegal, Mahesh Mathai and Kaizad Gustad, and began exploring the space 'out of the mainstream' (Akhtar 2009). Ultimately, her first experience of working on a mainstream film in the Hindi film industry came in 2001 for her brother Farhan Akhtar's directorial debut, *Dil Chahta Hai* (DCH).

She and Farhan had written their first scripts around the same time, but *DCH* got cast first (Akhtar 2016) and was promptly made while Zoya had to wait almost seven years until her film *LBC* could go into production. It was a surprising wait considering she is an 'industry kid'. However, she strongly believes that while having insider status can afford an advantage in terms of access, no one will agree to do a film simply because of that fact (Akhtar 2019c). She recounts how it was impossible to cast her first film, with no mainstream actor willing to play the leading role. After meeting six actors who did not want to act in the film, but did not tell her to change the script either, she decided to wait and focused her attention on other projects. According to her, 'the audience was completely different at that point' (Akhtar et al. 2009), and she thinks people didn't 'get' the script (Akhtar 2009). Despite the 'ridiculous' situation of not having any lead actors (Akhtar 2009), she didn't have any insecurities about the script and stuck to her guns until the film finally went into production. Akhtar's difficulty in making her first film despite having a complete script signals the changing landscape of Hindi cinema in the twenty-first century, where major movie stars were still reluctant to sign onto films that did not showcase them as the quintessential Hindi film 'hero'. Ultimately, it was her brother, Farhan, who took on the lead role in *LBC* as he was a relatively new actor unburdened by a pre-existing image in the audiences' minds.

THE WRITING PROCESS: STORY, CHARACTERS, DIALOGUES

'When you're a writer, you're a scavenger' (Akhtar 2018)

The writing process and the role of the script has changed dramatically in Bollywood over the decades. According to filmmaker Shyam Benegal, Bollywood functioned like Hollywood in the 1940s and 1950s, with directors using bound scripts that adhered to a storyline. By the mid-1960s, stars began to triumph over the story and screenwriters did not get much credit (Bose 2007: 32). This trend changed in the early 1970s, when the prolific writing duo Salim-Javed began fighting for credit and better pay while also moving away from writing stories to suit the star (Chaudhuri 2015: 10). This again shifted by the late 1980s and through most of the 1990s, when screenwriting in Hindi films was entirely ad hoc, relying on oral narrations of stories, scripts and dialogues written on film sets while the shooting was occurring (Shah and Kapur 2018: 16–17). By this time the star-centric nature of green-lighting film projects had taken over and aspiring writers, producers or directors just needed to persuade a male star about their story idea or script for the film to be viable (Ganti 2013: 339). The corporatisation of the film industry in the early 2000s, however, brought with it a new discipline of full scripts being written prior to shooting (Ganti 2013; Zankar 2013: 279). Once again, stories were considered essential to a film's success, and reputed production houses started working with bound scripts and improved the pay for screenwriters (Shah and Kapur 2018: 16–17). The 2000s also marked the advent of multiplex cinemas in the country and the introduction of a unique, low-budget, non-formulaic genre called the 'multiplex film', often referred to as *hatke* (eccentric or offbeat) cinema (Gopal 2011: 125).

Akhtar's work represents this new wave of 'multiplex films' in the Hindi film industry, in terms of making non-formulaic feature films as well as her propensity to work with bound scripts. Sangita Gopal identifies a new category of multiplex films, the multiplot film, which features several couples loosely connected by a place or circumstance. She argues that this kind of representation of conjugality becomes 'a powerful strategic tool for rethinking the notion of couplehood and its relations to the social in modern India' (Gopal 2011: 126). In this regard, Akhtar's films can be described as 'multiplot' since they tackle different relationships in the same script. However, unlike the films in Gopal's analysis, Akhtar's scripts do not rest solely on depicting new-age romance and conjugal relationships. The 'love story' between a 'hero' and a 'heroine' is not central to Akhtar's narratives.

Since her first film, a running theme across Akhtar's movie scripts is a strong core message and the high quality of their ensemble performances. In writing ensembles, Akhtar appears to be paying homage to the multi-starrers of the 1970s, even as she goes a step further to break from the stereotypical characters in a Hindi film: the hero, the heroine, the villain, the best friend, the comic relief, the mother, etc. Instead, Akhtar weaves her stories around multiple characters, not always the hero and the heroine, who could all be considered protagonists that drive the story forward. *ZNMD* and *DDD* are particularly illustrative of this quality as it is impossible to diminish the importance of all three of the friends or all four family members in the respective films. Akhtar has also left us with memorable supporting characters that have their own arc during the film, even if they're not the main protagonists. For instance, the producer Romy Rolly (Rishi Kapoor) who is trying to keep up with a changing Hindi film industry in *LBC*; both Murad's mentor MC Sher (Siddhant Chaturvedi) and Murad's childhood friend Moeen (Vijay Varma) who left an indelible mark on the narrative in *Gully Boy*; and the young lovers Noorie Sood (Ridhima Sud) and Rana Khanna (Vikrant Massey) in *DDD* who strike up a holiday romance as the backdrop to an old family rivalry. Akhtar possesses a unique ability to write unforgettable cameos in her films as well, from Shah Rukh Khan playing himself in *LBC* to the fleeting role of *apni* (our) Albina (Srishti Shrivastava) in *Gully Boy*, and even skilfully turning the high-end Hermès Kelly bag into the independent character '*Bagwati*' in *ZNMD*.

Before proceeding to discuss the underlying themes in Akhtar's scripts, it is important to understand her process of writing. How does she flesh out the character graphs and individual plotlines while retaining the film's overarching narrative? Akhtar believes good screenwriting happens only when you have clarity of thought about the film's central idea: what is the single point the film is trying to make? Each film rests on a central thematic frame: self-esteem in *LBC*, freedom in *ZNMD*, family in *DDD* and class in *Gully Boy*. Her process for discovering the story idea depends on what is happening in her life and the headspace she finds herself in at the time (Akhtar 2019d). Akhtar has revealed that *LBC* came from an extremely personal space of living in the film industry and grappling with its nebulous concept of success and failure; *ZNMD* was inspired by her own travels, especially road trips, and her wanting to tell a story about the meaning of life; and *DDD* is a commentary on the long-standing issue of men and women being treated unequally in Indian families, which was inspired by the lives and travails of people in her wider network of friends (Akhtar 2015). Meanwhile, the idea for *Gully Boy* emerged from a chance viewing of a video by rapper Naezy and the strong desire to uncover the growing *gully* rap scene in Mumbai (Akhtar 2019).

An analysis of a screenwriter's work is incomplete without a deconstruction of three essentials: storylines, characters and dialogues. With regard to each of these script essentials, Akhtar has created a unique individual style of writing while also being an active collaborator. She has co-written three of her four feature films and a streaming series with long-time collaborator Reema Kagti. Although they wrote the story and screenplay of their first films independently,[1] they started co-writing with their second directorial ventures, *ZNMD* for Akhtar and *Talaash* (2012) for Kagti, and have continued ever since, forging one of the only female-writer duos in the Hindi film industry to date and following in the steps of her father's famous writing duo, Salim-Javed. In recent times, Raju Hirani and Abhijat Joshi have also been a successful writing pair, but only one among them is a director (Hirani). Akhtar and Kagti are a unique writing pair since they are both accomplished directors and they work on each other's film scripts and have co-written a streaming series as well.

Akhtar describes their approach to writing as being very organic, where they let the story lead the way (Akhtar and Kagti 2012). The process begins with some serious brainstorming, during which time they spend days talking through and developing ideas until they crack the film's core. In Akhtar's words, 'We don't write for a while, we just talk. We just talk, talk, talk, we just like really literally marinate in it' (Akhtar 2019d). At this point, they create the blueprint for the film by writing down all the scenes in a line each. Once this blueprint is locked, Kagti writes the screenplay for the film, following which

Akhtar develops the dialogues and characterisation. The writing goes back and forth between the two, with each improving the other's writing. Ultimately, the final word on the script rests either with Akhtar or Kagti, depending on who will be directing the film (Sahani 2015).

She describes Kagti as a 'sibling' and admits that she feels they have to work on each other's films. Between the two, Kagti is the more disciplined writer and Akhtar admits that she'd never meet deadlines if she worked on her own (Bhatia 2012). Kagti prefers to write at a desk, while Akhtar tends to lie down on a couch with her laptop (Bhatia 2012). The mantra for successful co-writing with Kagti is that they don't agree on everything since they bring their own personalities and experiences to the table, which in turn prevents the script from becoming unidimensional. They do, however, share the same value system and have a similar gaze towards the overall story that allows for a strong partnership on the final script (Akhtar 2019d).

In terms of developing characters, Akhtar derives inspiration from a mix of real-life observation and fiction. In her own words, 'you take a prototype or something that exists around you, and then you fictionalize it' (Akhtar 2019c). Akhtar is a self-confessed people-watcher and admits that she 'loves observing human behaviour and is obsessed with how people interact' (Akhtar 2019c). Kagti too acknowledges that Akhtar is 'very observant about people and very good with layering [characters]' (Akhtar and Kagti 2015), and recounts how during a friend's wedding in Delhi, Akhtar was furiously taking notes on her phone and a lot of these anecdotes made it to their streaming series, *Made in Heaven*. Ultimately, the characters are a product of their combined vision, with Akhtar taking the lead on nuancing the character graphs. In doing so, you can see how her early education in sociology and literature at St Xavier's College (Mumbai) comes into play. Her writing rests heavily on ethnographic research and she spends time immersing herself in the surroundings and subcultures in which she plans to set her movie. This is particularly evident in the case of scripts that are outside her comfort zone. For *Gully Boy*, for instance, there were extensive interviews with the real-life *gully* rappers, and Akhtar and Kagti spent a lot of time hanging out with them in their daily surroundings, including their homes, streets and musical gigs. This period of observation went on for a long time, following which the two began ideating the film's characters, their conflicts and the central theme. The final story flows from these early conversations based on in-depth observations (Akhtar 2019b). In the case of *Talaash*, both Akhtar and Kagti spent countless hours at police stations, making contacts and visiting them at their homes or their social hangout spots like the Bombay Gymkhana (Akhtar and Kagti 2012).[2]

Akhtar is well known for writing everything down; she's said that 'the blueprints for my films are solid, with dialogue and everything' (Ramnath 2019). However, some of the best moments in her films are a result of on-set improvisation by the actors. For instance, in *Gully Boy* the playful gibberish rap by Moeen in the Benetton showroom, '*whatte whatte wow wow vada pav*', was developed during a workshop with the actors and retained for the film. The touching moment when Murad folds the hand towel and places it back exactly where it was in Sky's bathroom was an improvisation by Ranveer Singh. In *DDD*, the iconic *hain?* (huh?) by Neelam Mehra during the family fight was entirely to actor Shefali Shah's credit. Akhtar notes that 'great actors co-create the characters and bring a lot to the table' (Akhtar and Khurana 2019). But it is a testament to her preparedness with strong, well-bound scripts that actors are able to go a step further to bring characters to life.

All her scripts, including those co-written with Kagti, are written in English. While English has always played a prominent role as a 'necessary lingua franca' in the Hindi film industry, it has increasingly become the 'language of production, creativity and decision making since the mid-2000s' (Ganti 2017: 122). Moreover, the trend of having 'bound scripts' (complete typed script with dialogues) in advance has led to an increase in the use of English-only screenwriting software such as Final Draft (Ganti 2017: 125). Akhtar follows this generational trend of writing scripts in English, in great part owing also to her English education at St Xavier's College (Mumbai) and later while pursuing a diploma in film production at New York University.

Once the final script is ready, she works with a dialogue writer to turn the script into Hindi and sets off the process of bringing the story and characters to life through dialogues. This marks the second round of collaboration in Akhtar's scriptwriting process. With each movie she has brought in the expertise of a dialogue writer who understands the milieu in which the film is set. She relies on these associations to define the language of the film, which in turn provides a greater degree of authenticity to the story and its characters. She has worked with her father and brother, Javed Akhtar and Farhan Akhtar, as well as others such as Vijay Maurya and Anurag Kashyap.

In her first film, Akhtar relied on her father's insider knowledge of film industry people to add nuance to the script. The film ended up with inside jokes, banter and conversations that drew from Javed Akhtar's personal experiences in the industry. In her next two movies, *ZNMD* and *DDD*, the dialogues were penned by her brother, Farhan Akhtar. Talking about her brother, she relates how they share a similar aesthetic and sense of humour, leading her to regularly consult him regarding questions about scripts, screenplays and editing. Since his involvement in the writing process is from the script stage, he gets the essence of the film 'effortlessly' and is able to translate the script into dialogues (Sahani 2015). According to her, in both instances of working with her father and brother, it was their astute observations of these worlds that brought the characters to life (Akhtar and Akhtar 2011).

Nandana Bose, however, argues that Akhtar's reputation of being an unconventional filmmaker is 'overstated' (Bose 2017: 224) and that her collaborative nature of filmmaking and familial dependence limits her own creative vision and artistic range (Bose 2017: 218). She states that Akhtar 'works within the stylistic conventions and limitations of Bollywood by adhering to a formulaic framework of industrial production that mandates the inclusion of elaborate song and dance spectacles, multi-stars and melodrama, with the corporate gloss and sheen of new money that funds the Bollywood new wave' (Bose 2017: 223). Baradwaj Rangan, a noted film critic, has also pointed out that Akhtar's tendency to script Hindi dialogues by literally translating them from English can sound jarring and absurd (Rangan 2011). But Akhtar's latest film, *Gully Boy*, dispels these kinds of criticism as it demonstrates precisely how an external collaboration with writers and artists can enliven the characters in the script. In this case, they relied on National Award-winning writer Vijay Maurya to bring in an authentic *Bambaiya*[3] language for the central characters in Murad's life: his girlfriend, Safeena (Alia Bhatt), his best friend, Moeen, and his family (Vijay Raaz, Amruta Subhash and Jyoti Subhash). The next step was bringing local rappers such as MC Altaf, Kaam Bhaari, Rahul Piske and Emiway Bantai on board, which added another level of authenticity and accuracy to the language the rappers speak. This was especially apparent in the character of MC Sher and the various rap battles that move the story forward. The real-life rappers became consultants on the script and would tell Akhtar whether or not a scene in its final form was working. Akhtar adds that 'our main focus was on getting the Bombay that Murad engages, the Bombay that engages him, where is he welcomed, where is he allowed, where is he not, etc. So, the approach was very particular – through him, through Murad's eyes' (Bhattacharya 2019).

In fact, Akhtar has consistently defied expectations and people's attempts to define her work. After the poor box office performance of *LBC*, she seems to have realised the importance of a film being profitable. Despite the critical acclaim and love that *LBC* received from industry insiders, it failed to bring audiences to the theatres. Each of her subsequent films, starting with *ZNMD*, has been a conscious effort to paint a narrative that is attractive on the big screen, even if it emerges from the familiar social strata that she inhabits in real life. Although some have labelled her the 'princess of posh pain' who only makes films about 'rich people' (Akhtar 2017), Akhtar has managed to tell stories that appeal to a mainstream audience because of their universal messaging.

DIFFERENT THEMES, SIGNATURE STYLE

'Your stamp will be created only if you're true to yourself' (Akhtar 2015)

Akhtar has developed a signature style of storytelling in Hindi films: taking well-defined characters in a niche backdrop to weave a critique on broader social issues and relations. For instance, *LBC* champions the self through the prism of the Hindi film industry. *ZNMD* focuses on a group of affluent friends taking a road trip through Spain, but at its heart the film's message is a more universal theme about finding contentment in life. *DDD*, although about a wealthy South Delhi family vacationing with their friends on a luxury cruise in the Mediterranean, is essentially a commentary on the modern-day dysfunctional Indian family, with parents' high expectations, children's double lives and 'sticky' social and cultural norms. *Gully Boy* uses the nascent hip-hop scene in Mumbai to critique the growing class divide in Indian society. In each of these films Akhtar begins by defining the overall vision for the film and uses different vehicles to explore the central theme: the Hindi film industry (*LBC*), a group of friends (*ZNMD*), a family (*DDD*) and the burgeoning rap scene in Mumbai (*Gully Boy*). As a result, each film is unique in terms of its context and landscape, and yet the unifying thread is the way the script is designed.

Akhtar's first script was about the film industry, as it was a deeply personal space and she grew up with a keen understanding of the different facets of showbiz. However, the underlying theme was universal: the question of who defines success and failure. This is developed through the journey of the two protagonists, struggling actors Sona (Konkona Sen Sharma) and Vikram (Farhan Akhtar), whose different ideas of self-worth and self-esteem radically alter their careers and life (Akhtar 2011b). Through their paths we see Akhtar's emphasis on the importance of self-esteem and how one's idea of self-worth can shape their destiny. Even though the script is not primarily about the Hindi film industry, Akhtar provides an insider's view of its working. She says, 'the movie is about people, it could be set in any industry, but is set in the [Hindi] film industry because that's what I know' (Akhtar et al. 2009). However, in order to avoid the pitfalls of being an industry kid, she was very aware during the writing process not to include insider jokes that would alienate audiences.

She also describes how the writing of *LBC* stemmed from her personal struggles of being an industry kid and yet feeling like a 'fish out of water' (Akhtar 2011a). She has said how the idea of success and failure in the film industry is defined by others around you, and not necessarily measured by personal contentment. Does self-esteem have any bearing on your future and destiny? Having worked with independent filmmakers and acquiring a different sensibility than mainstream Hindi cinema, she has said that 'for the film space I'm a bit arty, and for my artist friends I'm filmy. So [I'm] always somewhere stuck in the middle' (Akhtar 2011a). Therefore, *LBC* came from the need to talk about finding balance in your life away from the trappings of how others define success.

In the film there are several scenes where she highlights how one's self-esteem can determine their destiny. Vikram is extremely self-assured and confident and never loses the opportunity to put himself out there. He approaches Nina (Dimple Kapadia), a famed actress of the past, during a party and introduces himself with a small anecdote that she's likely to remember and which comes back to play a crucial role in him being signed on for a film. In another scene with Sona, he dismisses the action of saving an eyelash to make a wish, saying he 'doesn't need luck'. During his final audition, Vikram throws off his competition by making him believe that the producers have all but decided to work with him. These scenes illustrate how Vikram's strong sense of self makes him believe that success and failure are choices. While he chooses success in his career, the same level of self-assuredness (or self-absorption) fails him in his relationships and makes him confront his own unhappiness.

Sona, on the other hand, begins the movie with low self-esteem and is hopeful of a turnaround in her career only with the help of a small-time producer who she perceives as a well-wisher. The scene where she wins the fridge marks a turning point in her character's self-belief, after which she decides to make her own opportunities and grab success. She chooses to rid herself of others' definitions of success and find happiness in the one thing that she wanted to do all along: act.

The story of *ZNMD* was inspired by Akhtar's own travel experiences of taking road trips with friends. She was clear about wanting to make a film with three friends who take a journey together that ends up being a cathartic experience for all of them. The common thread in each protagonist's arc is about finding contentment: for Arjun (Hrithik Roshan) it is about slowing down in his professional life to make room for life's experiences, for Imraan (Farhan Akhtar) it is getting answers from his estranged biological father, and Kabir (Abhay Deol) needs to discover whether his personal life is headed where he really wants it to go. Set against the backdrop of a bachelor trip and adventure sports, Akhtar creates a narrative that's not just high on adrenaline but has great depth. Akhtar has said that the stunts came into the script at a later stage, when she and Kagti realised that the friends were just moving from place to place without a trigger for their self-realisations. Ultimately, they decided to weave in the three adventure sports as a plot device to move each of the three individual arcs. As Akhtar notes, 'it wasn't just adrenaline, but also poetic' (Akhtar 2016). The script skilfully explores the friends' interpersonal equations, as well as each character's individual arc, without losing the entertainment quotient. It also appears that following the dismal box office performance of *LBC*, the choice to cast three leading male stars and to set the movie in a foreign landscape was an attempt to meet the unsaid demands of the Hindi film audience for an escapist, visually appealing spectacle with 'heroes' who are a big draw at the box office. With *ZNMD*, Akhtar also storyboarded certain sequences in a movie for the first time. She relied on storyboards for the technical scenes that required action or VFX directors. Adding that you 'can't be random with such stuff' (Akhtar 2018), she worked on storyboarding the underwater, skydiving and bull chase sequences.

Coming off the success of *ZNMD*, Akhtar's next outing was a multi-starrer entertainer. Initially *DDD*'s plot about a wealthy Delhi-based family taking their friends on a Mediterranean cruise holiday to celebrate their thirtieth wedding anniversary faced some criticism for being a story only about 'rich people'. However, Akhtar was quick to clap back at critics, saying that 'Indian audiences don't like to watch poor people on screen' (Akhtar and Kagti 2015). At the heart of the film, however, is a story about family, especially Indian families. The film revolves around the Indian phenomenon of parents interfering in their children's lives, even when the kids have become adults. The universality of the theme, according to Akhtar and Kagti, would hold true even if money was taken out of the equation. The story reveals the subtle (and not too subtle) ways in which patriarchy is entrenched in Indian families despite their economic status and that it does not exist only in the lower strata of Indian society. Although the cruise holiday and Mediterranean locales were not essential to the story, Akhtar and Kagti decided to use the ship as a metaphor. Just as in the middle of the ocean one cannot leave the ship, in life, too, you can't leave your family and are stuck with each other (Sahani 2015). The confined nature of the ship ultimately closes the walls in on the family and their brewing problems, forcing them to confront each other and their feelings about how broken their relationship is (see Chapter 5 in this book).

Not one to be weighed down by audiences' expectations, Akhtar said: 'I only make what I want to make and not what people expect from me' (Akhtar and Khurana 2019). Her most recent feature film, *Gully Boy*, has taken a complete U-turn from her films situated around the lives of the upper middle class and wealthy in India. Following the protagonist Murad on his journey to pursue his dreams to become a rap artist, it is a classic underdog story based on the *gully* rap scene emerging in Mumbai's slums. It uses this backdrop to showcase how art cuts across class, economic divide, caste and religious borders in what becomes overall a commentary on the growing class divide in India.

Figure 4.1 The Mehras board the ship in this tale of the modern Indian family.

Another tool in Akhtar's arsenal has been the use of motifs to illustrate the film's central message. She maintains that 'the elements are quite subliminal and not in-your-face' and come up in production design or on set rather than the writing process (Film Companion 2018). These motifs play a critical role in her films and come at a pivotal time in the characters' lives. In *LBC*, Akhtar uses birds throughout the movie to imply the different stages of ambition. First, early in the movie, we see framed pictures and figurines of birds all around Sona's house, and in the same scene Vikram is wearing a printed T-shirt with a single bird, perhaps suggesting his first flight to the city of dreams in search of a successful career in the Hindi film industry. Second, Sona's friend starts a gossip column titled 'A little bird told me', a nod towards how ambition will soon tear the lives of the two protagonists apart. Third, we see birds in flight on Vikram's T-shirt when he runs into Shah Rukh Khan, the scene highlighting that success can be a heady feeling and blind you to reality. Lastly, we see the flight of birds across Vikram's film billboard as Sona walks past it, a signal of choosing happiness over ambition.

In *ZNMD*, Akhtar uses natural landscapes, interspersed with Imraan's poems, to signify a pivotal moment of self-realisation in the characters' arcs. The close-up shots of Arjun after the deep-water dive, the wide shots of the roads when the three friends drive out of Buñol and Imraan's melancholic walk against the sunset after his meeting with his biological father are also moments of melding nature with self-realisation. Each of these scenes moves the narrative forward against the backdrop of nature, almost as if the characters' worries are insignificant in the grand scheme of things.

The most impactful scenes in *DDD* happen in front of a mirror: Kamal Mehra (Anil Kapoor) checking himself out and completely ignoring his wife before stepping out for their anniversary dinner, Neelam filling an emotional void by binge-eating chocolate cake after being embarrassed by her husband's philandering ways, and Ayesha (Priyanka Chopra) quietly asking Manav (Rahul Bose) for a divorce while he talks over her. In essence, the mirror is reflecting the true picture behind these relationships and captures more than just emotions: it displays the breakdown of relationships.

In *Gully Boy*, Akhtar uses bridges to illustrate the levels of class divide in society. First, the secret meetings between Murad and Safeena on the bridge between their neighbourhoods underlines the class divide between the two and complicates their love story even though they belong to the same religion. During the end credits, their meeting at the railway station appears to mark a new phase of their relationship: Murad standing on top of the overbridge reflects his changing economic status and efforts to secure a future for their relationship. Second, the use of the flyover in the song '*Doori*' (Distance) brings out the deep cleavages between the haves and the have-nots, whereby the distance between them cannot be reduced even if they're put in close proximity. Third, after Murad moves his mother and brother out of their father's home, the moving trains on the railway bridge imply his move up the economic ladder marked by his early success as a rap artist.

MADE IN ONE OF THE MANY INDIAS

'Can't I have both awards and critical acclaim, as well as box office?' (Akhtar 2011c)

The underlying belief in Akhtar's writing process has always been that 'if a film is good, people will watch it' (Akhtar and Akhtar 2011). In keeping with that, she has written scripts that have consistently pushed the boundaries of filmmaking in the Hindi film industry by blurring the years-long divide between 'art' and 'mainstream' cinema. Her annoyance with the distinction between the two is evident when she says, 'everyone who makes a film wants people to watch it and wants to make money back . . . it is not a home video' (Akhtar and Kagti 2012). She says, 'as a storyteller, I want to make movies for the audience. I want them to watch it and like it, and also have it make money' (Akhtar 2017).

Akhtar's scripts until now have stemmed from a very personal space, either through things that she has witnessed in her immediate surroundings or that inspire her in the moment. While it could be said that she is playing safe, I argue that Akhtar writes about different kinds of India (albeit in an urban setting, until now) and masterfully brings these niche stories into the fold of mainstream. Her self-confessed passion for people-watching finds its way into her films through a wide array of characters. The ensemble casts navigate the complexities of modern relationships between lovers, friends, families, communities and societies. It is this voracious appetite for studying people that makes Akhtar the eclectic scriptwriter she is, delivering rich storylines with even richer characters.

Akhtar's writing has also matured over the years, with her two most recent films (*DDD* and *Gully Boy*) providing a social commentary under the garb of mainstream entertainment, that is, A-list movie stars, big budget productions and the quintessential song-and-dance in Hindi cinema. Her recent streaming series, *Made in Heaven*, also tackles issues like economic inequality, gender and religious politics and morality through the lens of big fat Indian weddings. In the closing lines of *LBC*, Sona says that no one in Mumbai asks one their caste and that you only prove yourself through your hard work. This dialogue was a blink-and-you-miss-it reference to the existing caste divide in Indian society. In *Gully Boy*, ten years after her first film, Akhtar's nuanced take on the class divide shows the growth in her writing and a new confidence to convey her ideological beliefs. Until then, she had written films that were well within her comfort zone both in terms of the setting and the characters. *Gully Boy*, however, was a marked departure from all of the expected notions of a Zoya Akhtar film. It was mounted in a landscape very unlike her previous films and took on the very unlikely (and risky) task of merging hip-hop with mainstream Hindi cinema. In doing so, the city of Mumbai became a character in her film and she engaged the city as it would be engaged by Murad. *Salaam Bombay!* was seminal in shaping her aesthetics as a filmmaker, and with *Gully Boy* you can see how Akhtar has come full circle to make a movie that truly blurs the lines between mainstream and independent cinema in the Hindi film industry.

With the launch of her production house, Tiger Baby Films, Akhtar wants to 'take untold stories and marry them into the mainstream' (Akhtar 2019b). So far, her scripts tell simple stories with an ensemble cast in niche settings, breaking away from formulaic Hindi film plots. However, she continues to ensure their mainstream appeal by creating compelling narratives around a single unifying theme, as well as in the final treatment and production value. A welcome by-product of her films being produced by her brother's production company, Excel Entertainment, is that she has been able to mount these stories on a large scale with big stars and bigger budgets. Akhtar has creatively leveraged her unique position within the industry to carve out her own signature style of filmmaking: making niche the new mainstream. From redefining how Indians travel around the world to introducing *desi* (local, or Indian) hip-hop, it will be interesting to see what unexplored phenomenon Zoya Akhtar captures in her next script.

NOTES

1. Kagti hilariously describes Akhtar's first film script as 'a 1000-page thesis' (Bhatia 2012).
2. Bombay Gymkhana is a premiere *gymkhana*, or sports arena, in Mumbai. It is an elite, members-only club located in the posh locality of South Mumbai.
3. *Bambaiya*, or Bombay Hindi, is a Hindustani-based pidgin spoken in Mumbai. While the vocabulary is largely from Hindustani, the predominant substratum influence on *Bambaiya* is Marathi, which reflects Mumbai's location in the wider Marathi-speaking state of Maharashtra.

WORKS CITED

Akhtar, Zoya (2019), '*Gully Boy* interview', interview by Anupama Chopra, *Film Companion*, 6 February 2019. Video, 22:53. Available at <https://www.youtube.com/watch?v=Zs_58AocYi4&t=68s>

— and Ayushman Khurana (2019a), 'Tape cast with Ayushman Khurana', *Film Companion*, 18 February 2019. Video, 19:24. Available at <https://www.youtube.com/watch?v=QPmThPur9ls&t=74s>

— (2019b), '*Gully Boy* postmortem', interview by Anupama Chopra, *Film Companion*, 15 February 2019. Video, 29:49. Available at <https://www.youtube.com/watch?v=o8V7Z4n5hko&t=832s>

— (2019c), 'ScoopWhoop Townhall ft. Zoya Akhtar', interview by Sattvik Mishra, *ScoopWhoop Unscripted*, 17 February 2017. Video, 31:40. Available at <https://www.youtube.com/watch?v=nQbP1ximAo4&t=13s>

— (2019d), 'Zoya Akhtar tells us about her filmmaking process', *The Quint*, 21 February 2019. Video, 4:36. Available at <https://www.youtube.com/watch?v=813gY4lCplg>

— (2018), 'My first film', interview by Anupama Chopra, *Film Companion*, 29 October 2018. Video, 27:54. Available at <https://www.youtube.com/watch?v=_B2wChETV5g>

— (2017), 'The *Firstpost* Show: Zoya Akhtar', interview by Renil Abraham, *Firstpost*, 2 April 2017. Video, 12:15. Available at <https://www.youtube.com/watch?v=mvWYcnARJU0>

— (2016), interview by Lakshmi Pratury, *INKTalks*, 28 June 2016. Video, 13:48. Available at <https://www.youtube.com/watch?v=CJQXl_zuTrQ>

— and Reema Kagti (2015), '*Dil Dhadakne Do* postmortem', interview by Anupama Chopra, *Film Companion*, 15 June 2015. Video, 19:59. Available at <https://www.youtube.com/watch?v=V4DGmAXNPt4>

— (2015), 'Guftagoo with Zoya Akhtar', interview by Irfan, *Rajya Sabha TV*, 27 October 2015. Video, 26:12. Available at <https://www.youtube.com/watch?v=4crcniaQw38>

— and Reema Kagti (2012), 'Zoya & Reema on *Talaash*', interview by Faridoon Shahryar, *Bollywood Hungama*, 26 November 2012. Video, 12:02. Available at <https://www.youtube.com/watch?v=MAm9-AdSnVU>

— and Farhan Akhtar (2011), 'Farhan & Zoya on *Zindagi Na Milegi Dobara*', interview by Faridoon Shahryar, *Bollywood Hungama*, 12 July 2011. Video, 18:07. Available at <https://www.youtube.com/watch?v=CUVdScuPOS4>

— (2011a), 'Cinema and me: Zoya Akhtar', interview by Pragya Tiwari, *Tehelka*, 27 June 2011. Video, 21:09. Available at <https://www.youtube.com/watch?v=IbcABY5c6vw>

— (2011b), interview by Anuradha Sengupta, *Beautiful People*, CNBC, 15 July 2011. Video, 16:47. Available at <https://www.youtube.com/watch?v=gjlWrz7KEEc&t=16s>

— (2011c), 'Characterization in *Zindagi Na Milegi Dobara*', interview by Taran Adarsh, *Talking Cinema*, 12 September 2011. Video, 10:32. Available at <https://www.youtube.com/watch?v=gwsx3q5XQAk>

—, Farhan Akhtar and Javed Akhtar (2009), interview by Anupama Chopra, *Picture This*, NDTV, 17 January 2009. Video, 4:26. Available at <https://www.youtube.com/watch?v=B9pROJbdQvo>

— (2009), interview by Koel Purie Rinchet (Parts 1–9), *On the Couch with Koel*, Headlines Today, 28 February 2009. Video, 21:52. Available at <https://www.youtube.com/watch?v=d8IxU-TKJ2Q>

Bhatia, Vivek (2012), 'We can never co-direct a film – Zoya and Reema', *Filmfare*, 5 December 2017. Available at <https://www.filmfare.com/interviews/we-can-never-codirect-a-film-zoya-and-reema-1844.html>

Bhattacharya, Suryasarathi (2019), '*Gully Boy*: Inside Zoya Akhtar's ode to Mumbai's "asli" hip hop sub-culture', *Firstport*, 15 February 2019. Available at <https://www.firstpost.com/long-reads/gully-boy-the-making-of-zoya-akhtars-ode-to-mumbais-asli-hip-hop-subculture-6088871.html>

Bose, Mihir (2007), *Bollywood: A History*, New Delhi: Roli Books.

Bose, Nandana (2017), 'Globalization, reflexivity and genre in Zoya Akhtar's films', in Ayesha Mohan Iqbal Viswamohan and Vimal Mohan (eds), *Behind the Scenes: Contemporary Bollywood Directors and Their Cinema*, New Delhi: Sage, pp. 215–26.

Chaudhuri, Diptakirti (2015), *Written by Salim-Javed: The Story of Hindi Cinema's Greatest Screenwriters*, Gurgaon: Penguin Books.

Farzeen, Sana (2019), 'Reema Kagti: *Made in Heaven* has all the ingredients for a delicious drama', *The Indian Express*, 7 March 2019. Available at <https://indianexpress.com/article/entertainment/web-series/made-in-heaven-reema-kagti-5615130/>

Film Companion (2018), 'Zoya Akhtar on the use of motifs in her films', *Film Companion*, 24 May 2018. Available at <https://www.filmcompanion.in/zoya-akhtar-motifs-dil-dhadakne-do-luck-by-chance/>

Ganti, Tejaswini (2016), '"No one thinks in Hindi here": Language hierarchies in Bollywood', in Michael Curtin and Kevin Sanson (eds), *Precarious Creativity: Global Media, Local Labor*, Oakland: University of California Press.

— (2013), 'Corporatization and the Hindi film industry', in K. Moti Gokulsing and Wimal Dissanayake (eds), *Routledge Handbook of Indian Cinemas*, London: Routledge, pp. 337–50.

Gopal, Sangita (2011), *Conjugations: Marriage and Form in New Bollywood Cinema*, Chicago: The University of Chicago Press.

Majumdar, Anushree (2019), 'Family construct is what makes us and breaks us: Reema Kagti', *The Indian Express*, 13 March 2019. Available at <https://indianexpress.com/article/entertainment/web-series/reema-kagti-film-director-interview-5623379/>

Ramnath, Nandini (2019), 'Zoya Akhtar on *Gully Boy*: "I wanted Murad to be the kind of man I want to see in the world"', *Scroll*, 17 February 2019. Available at <https://scroll.in/reel/913542/zoya-akhtar-on-gully-boy-i-wanted-murad-to-be-the-kind-of-man-i-want-to-see-in-the-world>

Rangan, Baradwaj (2011), 'Bullet-point report: *Zindagi Na Milegi Dobara*',16 July 2011. Available at <https://baradwajrangan.wordpress.com/2011/07/16/bullet-point-report-zindagi-na-milegi-dobara-396492/>

Sahani, Alaka (2015), 'I don't think any family is normal, says *Dil Dhadakne Do* director Zoya Akhtar', *The Indian Express*, 7 June 2015. Available at <https://indianexpress.com/article/entertainment/bollywood/i-dont-think-any-family-is-normal-says-dil-dhadakne-do-director-zoya-akhtar/>

Shah, Gayatri Rangachari and Mallika Kapur (2018), *Changemakers: Twenty Women Transforming Bollywood Behind the Scenes*, Gurgaon: Penguin Books.

Zankar, Anil (2013), 'Scriptwriting: In and out of the box', in K. Moti Gokulsing and Wimal Dissanayake (eds), *Routledge Handbook of Indian Cinemas*, London: Routledge, pp. 273–86.

PART II

Reworking Bollywood Themes

CHAPTER 5

The Heterotopia of Family Relation-Ship in *Dil Dhadakne Do*

Debnita Chakravarti

This chapter is a Foucauldian reading of Zoya Akhtar's 2015 film *Dil Dhadakne Do*. As Bollywood has continued to etch its presence indelibly on the global cultural platform, 'attracting all kinds of new audiences for various reasons in its continuous quest to monopolise global cinema' (Kaur and Sinha 2005: 29), Akhtar has been one of a cadre of young directors contributing to this growing prominence. While Akhtar has been part of this wave narrating the stories of a new India, her films still hold some of the stylistic and narrative techniques that appeal to the majority of the audience who seek their ticket's worth of entertainment from their weekly sojourn to the mall multiplex. In all her works she has endeavoured to remain true to 'real' problems, even as her characters indulge in the box office-stipulated quota of songs and dances. In *DDD*, Akhtar delves into issues of marital discord and family fracas crystallised along the lines of class and gender.[1]

The family in crisis has been an underlying theme that has taken on several forms in many of the most popular Bollywood films. Since the emergence of Bollywood as a culture industry and film form in the post-liberalisation 1990s, popular Hindi cinema has often resolved its anxieties about the tussle between traditional family values, Indian culture and westernised modernity by reaffirming the importance of the normative Indian family. Even as the family undergoes crisis in films such as Aditya Chopra's *Dilwale Dulhania Le Jayenge* (1995), Sooraj Barjatya's *Hum Aapke Hain Koun. . .!* (1994) or Karan Johar's *Kuch Kuch Hota Hai* (1998) and *Kabhi Khushi Kabhi Gham* (2001), this is resolved by firmly adhering to family ties and values in order to achieve a wholesome conclusion that restores the status quo of a normative Indian family. Breaking from this 'family knows best' tradition, more recently the family in crisis has become a subject of more critical scrutiny. A diverse range of films has depicted themes ranging from the frustration of misunderstanding or consuming obligations between generations, *Dear Zindagi* (Gauri Shinde 2016) and *Piku* (Shoojit Sircar 2015), to the exposure of family abuse, *Highway* (Imtiaz Ali 2014), to the breakdown of marriages and the facade of the 'perfect' family in films like *Oye Lucky! Lucky Oye!* (Dibakar Banerjee 2008), *Titli* (Kanu Behl 2014) or *Kapoor and Sons* (Shakun Batra 2016), the latter of which also addresses the continued widespread prejudice against homosexuality.

Akhtar's film *DDD* also broaches the subject of the family in crisis. Set on a Mediterranean luxury cruise liner where Kamal (Anil Kapoor) and Neelam Mehra (Shefali Shah) are celebrating their thirtieth wedding anniversary accompanied by their son Kabir (Ranveer Singh), daughter Ayesha (Priyanka Chopra) and dog Pluto, along with relatives and a whole range of friends and family, this film at first offers to tell a modern-day family success story. These are 'the well-known Mehras of Delhi high society' – a prominent business family that has risen from humble beginnings to amass their wealth and achieve their social standing. Their son is being groomed to take over the family business and their daughter is well married and has even become a successful businesswoman in her own right. They are wealthy, well-dressed and can celebrate in style by inviting friends and family to join their anniversary on a luxury cruise. Though everything is beautiful on the surface, the film is really one of crisis: once confined to the space of the cruise ship, this veneer begins to chip away to reveal that all is not right with the Mehra family.

Analysing the film closely, I argue that looking at it through the concept of heterotopia will allow us not only a deeper understanding of its particular themes but will also enable us more generally to use this approach as a mode of reading film as a social text. In this film, Akhtar uses the milieu of the rich in order to delve into the heterotopia of the family structure. Every family is unique, but the shared concerns of safeguarding social appearance and reputation even at the cost of individual unhappiness make the family an intriguing case study using the Foucauldian power apparatus of heterotopia.

Both the setting of the cruise ship, which Michel Foucault designates as an ideal heterotopic setting,[2] and the crisis that unfolds inside lend the film to be read through the lens of heterotopia. In his seminal essay, 'Des Espace Autres' (1967, translated as 'Of Other Spaces' in 1984), Foucault expounds most fully on this concept. In designating our era to be engaged with space as opposed to the nineteenth century's obsession with time, he expresses his interest about those spaces 'which are endowed with the curious property of being in relation with all the others, but in such a way as to suspend, neutralise, or invert the set of relationships designed, reflected, or mirrored by themselves' (332). He recognises these spaces as being connected to others even as they contradict them and divides them into two categories: utopias and heterotopias. Calling the former fundamentally unreal, he shifts his attention to the second kind of spaces which are, by contrast, real and effective. These spaces Foucault calls 'heterotopias', which he defines as actual spaces of difference or otherness within the dominant social order, as counter sites to imaginary utopias, in that heterotopias form part of the reality they reflect even as they contest and invert the same. They exist within society but are in effect separate from it, for in them the modes of social functioning are 'represented, challenged and overturned' (332). It is this idea that comes to play out in *DDD*, as the family as a unit not only finds itself as being represented but being challenged and overturned.

The chapter reads *DDD* through this concept of heterotopia. It identifies the many ways in which the film negotiates with this concept in its varied aspects and complex nuances, where it often blends not only different but directly contradictory features in itself. The chapter is structured along the three qualities that Foucault mentions of heterotopia: representing social norms, challenging the same and overturning these modes by replacing them with new ones. As Akhtar presents and works through these qualities, she not only represents a reworking of the Mehra family who through this process are challenged to change, but also a reworking of the family film. *DDD* is a film that rejects the false utopias of films like the 1990s family romance dramas and instead highlights the importance of other spaces to work through the crises that can stay hidden in the normal day-to-day, or even the less than normal utopias. Just as films like *Highway*, *Piku* or Akhtar's own *Zindagi Na Milegi Dobara* (2011) rely on the space of the open road to bring to light certain secrets and realities buried deep, so too does *DDD* rely on the cruise to begin the process of not just recovering but repairing the family unit. As the Mehra family use this other space to rework their family, Akhtar uses *DDD* to rework the family film to become a space to confront the crises and changes the family is facing. While the film continues to function within a narrative arc where the family unit is repaired and restored at the end, its subversion lies in the fact that the crises it explores are those that are foundational in creating a normative family.

REPRESENTING NORMS AND CREATING ILLUSION

Keeping up appearances is just a part of everyday life for the Mehras and their guests, and this routine of preening and posturing follows them onto the ship as they enter this new space still enacting their old habits. This paradox, which will become the source of conflict in the film, is represented in Foucault's discussion of the mirror. Foucault starts his discussion with this curious item as it is both a utopia for the illusion of its reflected image and a heterotopia because it does exist as an object. It is unreal in its essence though it functions to contextualise the subject vis-à-vis its surrounding space. One might view the cruise ship in *DDD* as functioning as a heterotopian mirror, one which 'represents' modes of social functioning. It is a temporary, artificially constituted social space which does not have permanent existence – temporary 'societies' gather into it and disperse after a set time span – but it posits a true representation of the real world from which it sets sail.

Further, Foucault specifically mentions ships as heterotopias of illusion and compensation. Heterotopias construct alternative areas for the emergence of subjectivity and the dynamics of intersubjective negotiations which in doing so reveal the countercurrents of human existence. These sites are then necessarily in constant engagement with the norms and expectations imposed on them by the societal apparatus. The group on the ship constitutes a microcosm of the super-rich Delhi and Mumbai milieu, complete with its cut-throat rivalries of social one-upmanship and corporate competitiveness, not to mention the snobbery, affectations and superficialities of the Indian upper class. This is their norm and illusion, and the film starts by drawing us into that image and underscoring the importance it plays as something so vital that the characters will sacrifice almost anything to uphold it.

Akhtar posits the Indian family setup as being governed by many of the same rules as the Foucauldian heterotopias. Most of them have certain regulations regarding being let in and out of these spaces, and the right to inhabit them at all. The cruise ship is one such controlled and contained space. 'I wanted a place where they can come together but can't leave easily,' Akhtar has said (Dundoo 2015). Guests enter by invitation, and it is difficult to leave at will, as Kabir and subsequently his family discover at the end of the film. Entry and exit into the family are similarly strictly regulated by concerns of societal appearance, making the illusion of this appearance so important to hold.

The cruise has been organised to celebrate Kamal and Neelam's thirtieth wedding anniversary. Having married at a young age when their biggest concern was romance rather than business or social expectations, they have gained social success and plan to celebrate in style by inviting friends and business colleagues on a cruise of Greece and Turkey. The celebrations are everything befitting of this couple: sumptuous gift baskets, glamorous banquets, open bars, Turkish baths, hot-air balloon rides and tours through exotic locales. Each day is like a fashion show, with every member of the family and guest party dressed in the latest styles. There are speeches about love, friendly chatter and Kamal and Neelam are the perfect hosts for it all.

As 'god's gift', Kamal and Neelam's only son, Kabir, also plays the expected part. He is the picture-perfect son, following in his father's footsteps as he is groomed to take over the family business AyKa. He is young, handsome and charming, slipping in and out of conversations with guests and leaving them with a smile or laugh from his flattery. Kabir is a supportive shoulder to cry on and a people pleaser as he looks to support his mother, sister and the family friend Noori (Ridhima Sud) in searching for their happiness.

Ayesha is the dutiful daughter who has arranged the whole cruise but, as she no longer officially belongs to the family, gets no credit. She is married to Manav Sanga (Rahul Bose), who belongs to another business family socially on par with the Mehras. The cruise liner guest list includes Manav and his hypochondriac mother (Zarina Wahab). Ayesha's marriage has been arranged by her parents to be fully befitting of social standards and both of the families expect her to portray their ideal of the content domestic wife. Even when she is confronted with her former boyfriend, Sunny (Farhan Akhtar), Ayesha must play the role of wedded bliss. When he enquires after her, she replies that things are 'perfect' and that she has been very 'lucky' when it comes to her husband. Even when during a casual group chat at a bar Manav pompously advertises his 'progressive' outlook in 'allowing' his wife to work and Sunny challenges him about what authorises him to give her permission, Ayesha goes back and confronts Sunny about his audacity in demeaning her husband before others. This is the relationship that Ayesha ended up with and that she must continue to defend even when the cracks are so visible.

This illusory masquerade of happiness which must be maintained for social purposes is one of the main themes that the film addresses. Behind every closed cabin door each family has their own set of problems, but when they emerge into the common lobby or deck, they are perfectly poised pictures of contentment. This is emphasised in the scene where every member of the cruise comes together for a group photograph, manufacturing a smile with difficulty, often managing only a grimace, in order to fit into the image of what is expected of them. The fragility of this veneer is exposed time and again when the film underscores how 'friends' gossip continuously and caustically, how the reality fails to be effectively concealed by the elaborate charades and how 'civilised' society keeps up a fiction of wellness at the cost of the individual.

The fancy facades conceal ugly underbellies of defunct marriages and toxic relationships, crumbling fortunes and desiccated dreams, which are gradually exposed as the plot unfolds. The Mehras go in viewing the reflected image of what they see as their utopia, though only by coming to examine it closely can they begin to acknowledge that it is an imagined space and, with that, come to manifest the second quality that Foucault mentions by challenging the norms of the society it represents.

A CRISIS OF NORMS

While the Mehras enter the ship carrying with them this illusory image that even they know is a false reflection, the ship proves to be a difficult space to keep up appearances. The ship in this film answers to the description that Foucault gives about heterotopias having the ability to juxtapose varied locations, often incompatible with each other, in the same space. He gives the examples of the garden, the theatre stage and the film hall, which superimpose aspects of different locales onto themselves. The cruise ship is a conglomeration of a wide variety of people on board, in terms of both guests and staff, which moves from port to port, country to country, during the journey.

Along with this coming together of separate places in the same space, heterotopias often further reveal the characteristic of dovetailing multiple time frames. Past and future moments impinge upon the present in what Foucault designates as the heterochronic character of certain heterotopias. The ship, moving along its route in the cinematic present, also moves simultaneously backward and forward in time. Incidents in the present are traced back to past happenings which have progressed into creating the circumstances on board the ship. As spaces and time frames cross paths in this heterotopic space, the Mehras lose their loosely held control on their narrative and find themselves confronting the various crises in their lives that they have fought so hard to deny. The ship thus becomes a place of crisis where it is the family structure itself that is in question.

To begin with, there is the Mehras' fraught relationship. The celebration of their anniversary, as well as social success over the past thirty years, is underscored by the fact that their veneer as a happy couple is quickly cracking as time and success has cost them their intimacy. They can hardly have a civilised conversation with each other in the present under the weight of growing resentments that have piled up over the years. Kamal has been unfaithful in their marriage, going on trips with other women, including his secretary, under the pretence of business trips. At the very beginning he states with a flourish to his golfing mates that he has to leave for lunch with his wife because 'I never keep a lady waiting', only for us to discover that it is just an empty excuse. His only interaction with his wife has been reduced to reminding her that she squanders the hard-earned money of her self-made husband on her fashion labels and taunting her for her failed diet plans. He even derides her in her interactions with her son by mocking her with the appellation 'Mother India', the hallowed ideal of Indian motherhood from the landmark 1957 film of the same name.

Her marriage problems have caused Neelam to lose her self-esteem, leading her to binge-eat and diet in manic cycles. In her husband's eyes, she has become the image of the perpetually nagging socialite wife who searches vainly for fulfilment in her kitty parties[3] and her attempts to preserve her fast-fading youth through the latest expensive fashion trends. As such, the character of Neelam runs the danger of being portrayed as a stereotype who serves as a backdrop to frame her husband or the family's crisis but who is not given space to experience her own crisis. This is not uncommon in mainstream cinema where, 'as wife . . . the woman has been victim of every imaginable kind of suppression, oppression, subordination and humiliation. Her role has almost always been clearly framed without shades of grey or scope for fluidity, interpretation, question' (Chatterji 1998: 62). In the hands of Akhtar, however, Neelam acquires complex nuances.

As they have grown in prosperity, Kamal and Neelam have grown apart as a couple until they have a wall of bitter remonstrances and recriminations dividing them. Her role as her husband's partner in the days of their struggle has been exchanged for that of a necessary social appurtenance. While she maintains this role and carries out these duties, she does so with her own strength of character. She continues to go to the kitty parties that are expected of her and that are a source of societal information, even though she knows her friends are gossiping about her with equal maliciousness the minute she turns her back. She also does not meekly accept her position in the marriage, countering her husband's verbal and emotional abuse by similar abrasive language. This crisis is not self-contained, however, and Neelam's insecurities seep into the general negativity that afflicts the family, affecting all their decisions and becoming an instrument to subjugate her daughter into continuing in a dysfunctional marriage. The dynamic that she shares with Ayesha liberates the character from becoming a unidimensional victim.

Apart from their personal problems, the Mehras are also facing a financial crisis. While Kamal and Neelam show little interest in fixing the personal problems in their relationship, they are united in guarding the financial well-being of their family. The couple hopes that the cruise will help their floundering business by providing the opportunity to set up a relationship between their son Kabir and the daughter of their family friend and successful businessman Lalit Sood (Parmeet Sethi), Noorie. The Mehra couple embark on the trip with the strategy that this marriage of convenience will lift their failing fortunes once they enlist the considerable clout of Sood as a business partner through the alliance of their children. This crisis involving their failing business is assigned the space of the cruise ship to sort itself out by making sure that Kabir and Noorie enter into an alliance. Thus, while their relationship is failing, Kamal and Neelam hope to save at least the financial aspect of it through setting up another relationship.

However, if the ship becomes a heterotopia of personal and professional crisis for Kamal and Neelam, it is simultaneously one of deviance for their children Kabir and Ayesha. Kabir finds himself not only pulled into this scheme by his parents, but also in their plans for him to become the head of the family business despite the fact that he has no interest in doing so. As a son, Kabir also finds himself in crisis as he is expected to follow his parents' wishes and live out their dreams for him even though they do not correspond with his dreams. Though Kabir is shown attending the meetings and making the presentations his father requires of him while he trains to be the next company leader, his sad and distant demeanour convey he is not happy in this role. When he tries to bring up these concerns at home, he is rebuffed by his mother who tells him he is exactly where he needs to be. Kabir is expected to continue fulfilling these family expectations even on the ship as he becomes a pawn in his parents' plot to arrange the marriages of family and business through the relationship of Kabir and Noorie.

For Kabir, however, the ship and the ports it docks in represent the realm of possibility. When the ship docks in Istanbul, its 'romantic' name is emphasised and it is described as a land of possibilities where anything might happen, a statement which becomes the prescient preamble to the unlikely romance between Farah (Anushka Sharma) and Kabir. Farah is a dancer on the ship who is part of the ecosystem of the ship rather than a transient guest. Her and Kabir's mutual attraction is evident in their first meeting and after Kabir's dogged pursuit they become lovers on the cruise. This is a deviant relationship not only as it breaks the ship's rules about relationships between workers and guests, thus threatening Farah's livelihood, but it is also a relationship that will not be acceptable to Kabir's family. Farah is not considered suitable by his parents to be admitted into their privileged social circle as she comes from a more modest background, belongs to a different religion, works for a living and is a cabaret dancer, a profession looked down upon severely by the 'respectable' audience of the same performances.

In order to secure the relationship, and the life he wants, Kabir must expose the system in crisis. He needs to manipulate his parents as well as the Soods in order to extricate himself from the arranged marriage and leave Noorie to marry the man she loves, Rana Khanna (Vikrant Massey). Time frames are bridged as thought bubbles emanate from Kabir's head to show us his elaborate 'future' ruse by which he might get away with keeping the aeroplane he desires without having to actually marry the girl he does not. He also must convince his parents and Farah that he is serious about their relationship. The situation of the family in crisis actually proves useful to Kabir, and also his sister Ayesha, in that by looking at the flaws in the system they are able to make an argument to deviate from the system.

Just like her mother, Ayesha carries the extra burden of being in a system that has stricter rules and expectations for women. Everything she feels or desires is seen to be a challenge to the system. Like her mother, Ayesha is expected to remain silent about her unhappiness in her marriage. Her husband is oblivious to her as an individual with her independent aspirations. He expects her to follow dutifully in his mother's footsteps in upholding the traditions of their family where wives, far from working, would barely have the nerve to talk to their male relatives. He insists on their need to have a baby as soon as possible, which is reiterated by his mother and his parents-in-law repeatedly. Ayesha, however, is on birth control, a fact that she cannot share with either her husband or her parents. She shares her secrets with her brother, who in turn confesses to her his deepest desire to keep the family plane for himself.

Another reason for her dissatisfaction is the fact that as the married daughter of the family, she is not considered to be a 'Mehra' anymore. When the film opens to zoom in on an invitation card for the anniversary cruise aboard the *Pullmantur Sovereign*, we find that the invites have gone out in the name of Kabir Mehra only, even though Ayesha has been the one organising every detail of the trip. When questioned about this discrepancy, her father's answer is that the inclusion of Ayesha's name, who now is part of her husband's family, would have confused their guests into thinking that their son-in-law had also paid for the cruise, which would have reflected badly on Kamal.

This distancing by her parents saddens Ayesha, as does their insistence that Kabir rather than she must inherit their business. The fact that Kabir neither has the inclination nor the acumen for it fails to be a factor in her parents' decision. They do not consider her at all for the role, even though she has proved her business proficiency in making her online travel agency start-up portal *Musafir* the second-largest in its bracket in a short time. For her parents the only marker of her success as their daughter is to remain in her marriage and produce children as her contribution to both her families, despite her unwillingness to do either.

Ayesha is continually held to different standards than her brother. Even though the Mehras' company is called AyKa after both their children, Ayesha and Kabir, Ayesha is not even considered in the plan of company succession as by virtue of gender only the son can inherit it. Sons are considered the 'gift of god' as the family name continues through them. They might meet young women and be considered eligible men of the world; if their daughters venture out with the same intention of mingling with the opposite gender, they are severely frowned upon and their character called into question. Their only options are secrecy or open rebellion. A son might have had multiple marriages but will remain a son forever; a daughter is her parents' child only until she marries, whereupon she is 'transferred' into her new family for good.

Ayesha was 'parcelled off' at the age of twenty-one to Mumbai after marriage. Her father refuses to let her return to the Mehra residence if she chooses to leave her husband's home. Ayesha's attempts to convince her extended family meet a wall of uncomprehending resistance. Her husband is indignant at her complaints, her mother-in-law fails to understand what the fuss is about, her mother feels she is unappreciative of what is essentially a viable marriage and her father is too enraged at the threat of having his social prestige undermined by his daughter's divorce to actually listen to a word she says. When Ayesha rushes out from the closed cabin where she must confront and explain her desires to the whole family, she seeks refuge at the far end of the deck, along the edge of the ship. The move is a metaphor for her abandoning the suffocating space for the fresh air outside, but the fact that her move is limited within the ambit of the ship is symbolic of her restricted freedom against which she struggles in vain. The vessel is her heterotopia both of crisis and deviance, representative of her claustrophobic marriage which she revolts against without success, where she cannot thrive but which she cannot leave.

The many different shortcomings, oddities, aberrations and machinations of the people on board the ship are observed by an unlikely interpreter. The family's moments of crisis are framed by the narration of the only non-human in this group, Pluto Mehra, the gravely sagacious pet bull mastiff voiced impeccably by Aamir Khan with monologues written by Javed Akhtar who has the humour-laced detachment of the world-weary philosopher. The choice of the narrative voice is inspired as it allows the entire group of people on board to be put under scrutiny with no exclusions. The dog continues a sustained commentary, right from the first sentence which posits man as one of the animals on this planet that differs from its fellow creatures. He emphasises that they are the only species which celebrate special dates, thus broaching the idea of the wedding anniversary, the celebration of which is the raison d'être of the cruise. Pluto muses at length on the oddities, frailties and weird ways of his bunch of two-legged mammals, calling his family 'our madhouse'. The dog introduces each member of his human family in turn, and they are defined by their greatest vulnerability, their bugbear or their dominant fear. He expresses amazement that the only animals capable of using a sophisticated language system fail so spectacularly at conveying their thoughts, feelings and emotions even to their closest relatives. He further ponders on the unspoken awkwardness of first love, and the general human inability to let the object of their desire know about their amorous inclinations. In this respect, his family becomes a microcosm of this world, for which he can see no hope of achieving effective communication. He notes how humans decry hypocrisy in others while practising the same duplicity themselves under the guise of worldly-wise ways; he calls them chameleons who can change their colours at will. Noting that the only danger to the dominant human species is from others of their own kind, Pluto compares their risk radar to a dog's. Pluto emphasises how other animals leave their offspring alone once they grow up, whereas Indian parents never stop interfering in their children's lives, not allowing them to make their own choices. He alerts us to the fact that not only do parents refuse to relinquish control over their children's affairs, they also have a very different set of rules based along gender lines.

These general observations on the condition of being human would not have been possible had one of the cruise guests functioned as our point of entry into the world of the cruise ship. An omniscient narrative, too, would have missed the privileged point of view that Pluto possesses. His position is key as part of the family but not quite privy to their most intimate concerns and private acts without being implicated in them directly. 'I needed someone who would observe the dysfunctional family from afar, and it couldn't be just a director's voice' (Dundoo 2015), Akhtar says, and in employing this unconventional narrative voice the film gains the same kind of under-the-stairs perspective that a *Gosford Park* (Robert Altman 2001) provides, but at a further remove, which works in its favour.

DEVIATION AND RENEWAL

It is fascinating to note that among the examples of heterotopias that Foucault mentioned was the *hammam*, a site of purgation and renewal, belonging to the subset of heterotopias of crisis. The film features a scene in a Turkish *hammam*, though this space in and of itself fails to fulfil its function of sublimating the crisis and providing a solution for the same. It does, however, become another space of challenging norms that, along with the many spaces on the ship, begin to culminate in the larger moment of purgation and renewal in which the family must deviate from the expected norms to save themselves.

In the Turkish *hammam*, where the women are sprawled out relaxing at one of their ports of call, Ayesha tries to talk to her mother about the issue of divorce, questioning her as to why she chooses to stay with her father even after being fully aware of his sexual shenanigans. Neelam brusquely cuts her short with the adage that every marriage runs into problems which must be solved, and that running away from them is too easy. She advises her daughter not to let her professional success get the better of her, and to concentrate her energies on the home front, stressing that Manav is a perfectly suitable husband who will always provide for her. The conversation ends there, with the space of the *hammam* unable to lead to a solution. It does, however, begin to plant the seeds of deviation for both women, which only come to fruit later when they are back in the heterotopic space of the ship.

For Ayesha, this happens when she is finally able to admit to her husband and family that she wants a divorce. The importance of such utopian illusions in the context of maintaining social prestige is apparent in the vehement responses to her proposal of divorce from not only her husband and mother-in-law but also her own parents, who insist that she should stay in the marriage 'for her own good'. Ayesha's decision to divorce her husband on grounds of incompatibility meets with complete incomprehension and outright resistance from not only her mother-in-law but also her own parents. A daughter's exit from her own family and her entry into that of her in-laws by virtue of her marriage is treated as an irrevocable and irreversible process even by parents who are so- called 'modern', 'progressive' and 'educated', by all measurable standards.

Ayesha's divorce is even more deviant as, though it is not said, there is the underlying understanding that the person she is compatible with is her former boyfriend Sunny. Her youthful dalliance with Sunny, the son of the manager Amrish Gill (Ikhlaque Khan) in the Mehra firm, had been firmly nipped in the bud before it could come in the way of her arranged marriage; Kamal had sponsored Sunny's study abroad to get him away from his daughter, a ploy that, the cruise reveals, has not succeeded in erasing Sunny from Ayesha's heart. While he is admitted and even welcomed onto the ship by virtue of his being an established award-winning journalist that has given this humble son of the Mehras' manager a certain standing in society, he is still not part of the same social circle. Both he and Ayesha have been rudely made aware of their different stations in life and the fact that their proximity makes her parents nervous. The inequality of their social status is made apparent by Amrish Gill's confession to Ayesha that he *had* to come for the cruise as Kamal had invited him himself, which amounted to more of an order to be present than just a polite invitation. Though not the intention of Kamal, Sunny's presence not only rekindles Ayesha's young love, but he also reminds Ayesha that she is a powerful woman who deserves to be recognised as an individual and supported in her own right.

While Sunny and Kabir support Ayesha in her decision, in order to get acceptance for this deviation by her parents, they too must undergo their own deviation of societal norms. The ship's clinic becomes a place to finally address the family crisis and affect a therapeutic purge. Kamal's sudden illness lands him in the hospital setting, where his worried family gathers around him. Here the exacerbated family tensions, provoked by the crisis of what they felt was Kamal's near death but was actually a case of bad gas, boil over and the family must confront the illusion. While Neelam lashes out at Kamal, venting her frustration that he never thinks about her, it is Kabir who really exposes the several cracks in the family. He points out his parent's hypocritical family standards, telling Ayesha and Kabir what to do when they themselves are miserable in their marriage because Kamal is openly cheating on his wife and Neelam does not have the courage to leave Kamal. Kabir stands behind Ayesha, thus giving space to the divorce discussion, and finally admits to his family that he is in love with somebody who does not meet their standards: she is a dancer and she is a *musalman* (Muslim), he tells them. With everything finally out in the open, it becomes up to the family in the following scenes to embrace their deviance of the strict norms and start working towards renewal.

The process begins on board the ship itself. Back in their quarters, Neelam and Kamal finally discuss their unhappy marriage and thus begin the process of rekindling their love. The parents also come to approve of the wishes of their daughter, renewing their familial bond and commitment to love and protect Ayesha. Neelam reaches out for her daughter's hand when she faces her husband and mother-in-law and Kamal confronts his son-in-law in defending his daughter from the latter's aggressive patriarchal sense of entitlement over her and her decisions.

The different personal crises of the four members of the Mehra family along with several of their friends and associates come to a head with Kabir realising that Farah has been fired from her job as a dancer on board the ship because of her relationship with him and has disembarked at the previous port. The ship has set sail when he discovers her gone and he tries to convince the staff to let him get off. When they tell him that is impossible at the moment and he can only go ashore at the next port, he embarks on a plan that is unexpected and desperate in equal measure: he jumps off the cruise ship and starts swimming towards land. But before he takes the plunge, a literal correlative of his commitment to his lover, he asks his father, 'Papa, can I depend on you?' When a perplexed Kamal nods in the affirmative, he says, 'Good, because you are my lifeboat.' It takes Kamal a moment after his son is overboard to realise that Kabir was giving him a hint about how to rescue him from the guards who intend to arrest him for his rash action. With the help of his guests who rally around him in this emergency, Kamal evades the security personnel on board and gets on a lifeboat to save his son. He is joined by his wife and daughter and the loyal Pluto, and they speed off towards the lone figure of Kabir out on the open sea pursued by the furious ship guards. They must rescue Kabir and reach the shore before the ship security gets to him, and this completely sudden, enormous and unimaginable crisis does what no amount of discussions and negotiations could achieve: it brings the family together. Their physical proximity on the tiny inflatable raft signifies the final closeness that they manage to achieve in the face of grave danger. Away from the ship, the space of the lifeboat affords the Mehras a topos of reclamation and regeneration, becoming the most effective heterotopia of crisis that achieves the final resolution of the film.

Figure 5.1 The Mehras find a space of regeneration on the lifeboat.

On the lifeboat, Kabir's complaint that his family never really talked, that everyone spoke but on the surface without addressing the 'real issues' that needed to be tackled, fades away in the bright sunlight as the four finally embrace each other without their rancour and reservations. They face an uncertain immediate future from the time they will land to the resolution of their personal and professional problems, but for the moment the family experiences a rare happiness as they are tossed on the blue waves. Pluto can finally feel that his family, and people in general, can change with love and freedom, and we are left with the sense that the Mehras can now face their troubles bolstered with the security of their togetherness, before we are engulfed into the colourful song that accompanies the final credits.

CONCLUSION

Foucault ends his discussion of heterotopias with the ship, which he calls the 'heterotopia par excellence'. He calls it 'a floating part of space, a placeless place, that lives by itself, closed in on itself and at the same time poised in the infinite ocean' (336). This chapter has argued that the ship, even as it contains the elements of the larger social world from which it has sailed away, repositions and reconfigures them within itself. The many issues that had been swept away without articulation, or after aborted attempts at discussion, resurface in this unfamiliar setting. The social sanctions governing every decision, be it professional or personal, lose their sway in the tossing of the vessel enough for voices of protest to be raised. Well-laid plans veer away from charted courses to allow individuals to helm their own futures, however uncertain or unconventional, until the final resolution leaps out unexpectedly into the open waters of vicissitude, to be collected pell-mell into the tenuous but optimistic freedom of a sailboat. The smaller vessel posits an overturning of and a compensation for the normative modes of social functions. These multiple catharses are contained in the topos which functions as one of the most eloquent examples of this Foucauldian concept in a recent cultural text.

The Mehra family had boarded the Mediterranean cruiser with all their baggage, and the gradual unravelling of family tensions and trials make the film a compelling sociological study. *DDD* may be seen to present a study of the Mehra family that represents a growing pattern of portraying the family unit in crisis. While popular Hindi cinema has traditionally crystallised its mores and values around the idea of the ideal family, *DDD* challenges this ideal, laying it bare as a reflection rather than the reality of the family. At the same time, rather than acting as a prescriptive or condemning commentary on the family, *DDD*'s uniqueness is its ability to straddle the convention and the contrary, the predictable and the astonishing, the old and the new, becoming a film which is as commercially successful as it is artistically satisfying. The family comes away as that which faces challenges at all levels but also offers the hope of change and rejuvenation that, even though it might only come about in a certain space, can then be carried into the future.

NOTES

1. How gender stereotypes determine social norms has been explored in detail by critics like Deepa Gahlot and Rajeswari Sunder Rajan.
2. The cruise ship as an ideal heterotopic setting is used in other films as well, such as most recently *Let Them All Talk* (Steven Soderbergh 2020), in which a famous author embarks on a cruise of reconnection with her best friends and family and herself, and *Like Father* (Lauren Miller 2018), in which a jilted bride reconnects with her estranged father (and herself) on her honeymoon cruise.
3. A kitty party is an informal gathering of women that is usually held on a monthly basis. In addition to being a space for socialising, an important aspect of the group is the 'kitty', which refers to the money that is collected every month through contribution. This is given to one member using a lottery system. Kitty parties are popular in South Asia among certain sections of society.

WORKS CITED

Dudrah, Rajinder Kumar (2006), *Bollywood: Sociology Goes to the Movies*, New Delhi: Sage.
Dundoo, Sangeetha Devi (2015), 'A voice from afar', *The Hindu*, 9 June 2015. Available at <https://www.thehindu.com/features/metroplus/why-aamir-khan-was-chosen-for-the-voice-of-pluto-in-dil-dhadakne-do/article7298285.ece>
Foucault, Michel (1997), 'Of other spaces: Utopias and heterotopias', in Neil Leach (ed.), *Rethinking Architecture: A Reader in Cultural Theory*, New York: Routledge, pp. 330–6.
Kaur, Raminder and Ajay J. Sinha (2005), 'Introduction', in Raminder Kaur and Ajay J. Sinha (eds), *Bollywood: Popular Indian Cinema through a Transnational Lens*, New Delhi: Sage, pp. 1–32.
Sunder Rajan, Rajeswari (1996), 'The prostitution question(s): (Female) agency, sexuality and work', in Ratna Kapur (ed.), *Feminist Terrains in Legal Domains: Interdisciplinary Essays on Women and Law in India*, Delhi: Kali for Women.

CHAPTER 6

Sabka Time Aayega: Language and the City in *Gully Boy*

Kamayani Sharma

This chapter looks at Zoya Akhtar's *Gully Boy* (2019) to examine the relationship between Mumbai and its working-class communities and language, particularly poetry. The city plays a central role in the film as that which inspires, intrigues, gives and denies its people in a complicated relationship that demands to be examined. By using *gully* (street) rap to capture all these sides of Mumbai and reflect on the social and economic realities of its residents, *Gully Boy* represents the conflict between the city and its citizens.

This reflection is inspired by Murad (Ranveer Singh), the film's subaltern Muslim protagonist, who because of his position has a compelling outsider-insider relationship to this consuming space. Murad traverses the city from slums to skyrises, encountering and living through the tension that Mumbai, at once a city of dreams and a city of deprivation and exclusion, holds. In *Gully Boy*, this tension is explored by drawing on two enduring Hindi film character types to fashion Murad as a *shayar* (poet) who also carries the baggage of the *tapori* (urban vagabond). In the form of rap lyrics and dialogue, language becomes a way for Murad to chronicle, occupy and claim various parts of the cinematic metropolis that at once claims and rejects him as this vagabond figure, becoming the poetic voice of the city's tensions.

I present this argument in four sections: in the first, I examine how the rise of Mumbai as the 'global city' and its relationship with its proletarian citizens play out through Murad's engagement with Mumbai. In the next section, I show how Murad navigates this urbanscape using *gully* rap, making him a descendant of the *shayar* figure. The third section draws a contrast between Murad and two previous incarnations of the urban *shayar* – *Pyaasa*'s (Guru Dutt 1957) Vijay (Guru Dutt) and *Namak Haraam*'s (Hrishikesh Mukherjee 1973) Alam (Raza Murad) – to discuss how *Gully Boy* departs from the politics of those films by adhering to a neoliberal order. In the final section, I interpret the *shayar/tapori* characterisation of Murad by examining his language and class location in the context of a need to emphasise the 'local', showing how language becomes a mode of subversion. By tracing the relationship between representations of Mumbai and its languages in Hindi cinema embodied by Murad's liminal status as both *shayar* and *tapori*, I show how the film captures the dynamic between Mumbai and its marginalised citizens.

BETWEEN TWO WORLDS

The rise of Mumbai as the 'global city' and its relationship with its proletarian citizens plays out through Murad's engagement with the city. While Mumbai might represent a 'global city' of dreams to some, Murad is shown to be in conflict with his immediate physical and social environment. As a talented young rap artist from Dharavi, Mumbai, one of Asia's and the world's largest slums, Murad must fight against his socio-economic circumstances and class expectations to emerge as a national rap sensation. At times this puts him at odds with his family and even his childhood friends and sweetheart, as well as at odds with the new world he is trying to enter. This incompatibility between *haqeeqat* (reality) and *khwaab* (dreams) is explicitly articulated towards the climax of the film, though it is also present throughout in the form of the urban landscape which Murad navigates. The two poles of Murad's movement are the slum of his birth and the aspirational glitz of success elsewhere in the city, and it is his desire and eventual ability to move between these worlds that form the narrative arc of *Gully Boy*.

Gully Boy is a quintessential Mumbai film, a subset of Hindi movies that span genres as different as the social melodrama, the crime thriller, the urban romance and the coming-of-age drama. *Awaara* (Raj Kapoor 1951), *Deewar* (Yash Chopra 1975), *Don* (Chandra Barot 1978), Basu Chatterjee's films from the 1970s, Saeed Mirza's films from the 1980s, *Satya* (Ram Gopal Varma 1998) and *Wake Up Sid* (Ayan Mukherjee 2009) are some classic examples from across the decades. This subgenre, in which the city is a prominent character, has existed since the early years of Indian cinema because of the city's modernity and infrastructural significance as the locus of the Hindi film industry. From the 1990s to the 2010s, globalisation exacerbated the class divide in Mumbai, creating a situation where an ever-widening gap in wealth is becoming apparent in civic infrastructure, ghettoisation and gentrification occurring side by side. Mumbai's marginalised communities must develop vernacular forms of expression such as *gully* rap that can both record and resist the sociopolitical disenfranchisement that the city symbolises, while also celebrating its emancipatory facet. Throughout the film, the tension between the city and its disenfranchised citizenry plays out in the form of Murad's ascent from slums to skyrises. Caught between the Mumbai of the poor and that of the wealthy, Murad's multifaceted experience of the city is ultimately directed towards an interpretation of its neoliberal globality, marked by interiors and architecture, as aspirational.

Zoya Akhtar's filmography complicates her approach to filming the geography of the proletariat. A filmmaker whose two preceding feature films, *Zindagi Na Milegi Dobara* (2011) and *Dil Dhadakne Do* (2015), were heavily invested in the world of the affluent, she states that she was conscious of the need for an immersion in Murad's world to prevent the 'Bandstand gaze' from taking over, an allusion to an affluent Mumbai area that could well be the home of the characters in some of her other films (Akhtar 2019a). Often criticised for making films only about the rich, Akhtar widens her horizons beyond 'a certain narrow strata of Indian society whose lives have been transformed by the embrace of a neoliberal, capitalist economy in post-1990s India' to also include Mumbai's poor (Bose 2017: 220–1). This reversal is apparent in a sequence early on in the film in which, in one smooth take, a local guide leads a party of foreign tourists through the sunny streets of Dharavi into Murad's home. The shots of the tourists entering the house are composed from Murad's perspective, the scene ending with him surprising one with a rendition of Nas' 'N.Y. State of Mind'. It is a somewhat backhanded commentary on the transactional workings of the global tourism industry that reduces poverty and subalternity to a cynical spectacle, but delivered almost as a riposte to the 'cine-tourism' of *ZNMD* and *DDD* (Bose 2017: 221).

Murad's character is partly constituted by Dharavi, the central Mumbai slum that is a fabric of his existence even as it hems him in. Akhtar had her production designer, Susan Caplan Merwanji, build a set within Dharavi, deciding to shoot on location for greater authenticity. 'You have to be there . . . you can't do it from the outside,' Akhtar has said (Akhtar 2019a), elaborating on the importance of filming *Gully Boy* where it is taking place and affirming its status as one of those films that Geoffrey Nowell-Smith states 'would have been impossible without the ontological link between nominal setting and actual location' (2004: 103). The inside/outside binary is key to understanding Murad's trajectory and changing relationship to the space of the city as a site of consumption. Merwanji noted the need to convey 'how circumscribed Murad is by his environment', while also discussing the need to create a geometry of horizontal and vertical arrangements that propelled the protagonist higher and higher as the film progressed, transporting him from his father's skyless hovel to his own tiny rented flat with a window (Ramnath 2019). As with *haqeeqat* and *khwaab*, when depicting a slum on screen there are 'many possible relations between filmic and profilmic spaces' to do with the ethical stakes of the dominant modes of cinematic representation that is documentary and realism

(Krstic 2017: 7–8). Akhtar has cited *Salaam Bombay!* (Mira Nair 1988) as an inspiration (Bose 2017: 221), though *Gully Boy* departs from that film's neo-realist mode by sticking more closely to the diktats of mainstream Bollywood and its popular conventions. This is true to Akhtar's practice, which, while deliberately naturalistic, lies 'within the stylistic conventions and limitations of Bollywood by adhering to the formulaic framework of industrial production' such as elaborate set design, song-and-dance sequences and a romantic subplot (Bose 2017: 223).

Gully Boy's narrative is spatialised in terms of Murad's movement out of the slum and into the Mumbai of the wealthy through his use of language. It is his ability to navigate both parts of the city that allows him to relate to Mumbai as simultaneously insider and outsider to portray its contradictions. Long shots of Dharavi's rooftops and clustered houses dwarf Murad against his world, but his verbal artistry opens doors for him that lead to another, more affluent one. Acknowledging the simultaneity of these starkly different versions of the same city, Ranjani Mazumdar makes a point about how Mumbai's extreme poverty is always in conflict with its global ambitions, necessitating other strategies of coping: '. . . the transformation of the interior provides the fleeting imaginary possibility of transcending the physical geography of the cityscape' (2007: 115).

For Murad, caught between inside and outside, Sky (Kalki Koechlin), a music production student studying at the Berklee College of Music in the US who offers to produce the song *'Mere Gully Mein'*, embodies an entry into these interiors so removed from his own. The hip cafe where she first meets Murad and MC Sher (Siddhant Chaturvedi), her huge apartment whose bathroom Murad tries to measure in steps and the professional studio she makes available for their use – these are interiors that were denied to Murad until he became accepted and recognised for his poetry. Similarly, it is at the apparel showroom a friend works at, outside of the slums, where Murad learns of the rap battle he goes on to win, thus getting the chance to open for the American rapper Nas at his India concert. At the same time, by way of the jam sessions, rap battles and cross-class sociality of artists and their supporters occurring in different parts of Mumbai, *Gully Boy* 'chooses to impress upon us that spaces of emancipation need to be explored within the interstices or the in-between spaces that "dual-city" (belonging to both the rags and the riches) provides' (Mohanty 2019).

Throughout the film, Murad's in-betweenness is emphasised through the inside/outside motif elaborated via the use of language. In one scene, the camera tracks Murad's father and his newlywed second wife as they walk through Dharavi towards Murad, the *shehnai* of wedding music playing. As Murad plugs in his earphones, standing outside their house, to listen to the American rapper A$AP Rocky's 'Everyday', the soundtrack switches to his aural perspective. His father yanks out the earphones and we hear the *shehnai* again, only for Murad to reinsert them and switch back to A$AP Rocky as he enters the house, using his music as a personal opposition to his father's second marriage and a defiance of his orders. Through the use of diegetic sound and an inside/outside motif, language is once again a form of rebellion, this time against a patriarchal order.

Murad's liminal status as both insider and outsider is again underscored in the sequence, set to a dreamy song with a retro quality, in which he accompanies Sky and her wealthy friends in a car across Mumbai. The rapid-edit montage sequence comprises a combination of overhead shots, long shots and tracking shots to reveal the city at different scales, skyscrapers looming in the background, rows of shops, the BEST (Brihanmumbai Electric Supply and Transport) city bus stops, construction sites and long roads illuminated by street lights. The group spends the night graffitiing metal sheets cordoning off construction sites, storefront windows, neon advertisements, politician's flyers and walls of seemingly distinguished buildings. This montage suggests a neoliberal-bourgeois vision of the contemporary Indian city and equates success with the material regime of finance capital, a globalised economy and, thus, the powerful elite in the company of whom Murad is exploring his city.

For Murad, language becomes at once a marker of origin and vehicle for successfully traversing the geography of Mumbai from its seething margins to its glamorous centre. A personification of Mumbai's megacity dualities, Murad negotiates between the material and symbolic polarities of the city using language, the foremost incarnation being his rap lyrics. If one considers the rap sequence, '*Mere Gully Mein*' ('In my Hood'),[1] the bright, vivid tones and dynamic cinematography put Murad and his collaborator MC Sher in charge of showing off Murad's neighbourhood (similar to Sher's own) as they tell its story. Native informants, they are the focus of the camera, on the screen and off it, performing their space, their bit of Mumbai, for consumption not just by their 'homies' (as their shout-out to Bombay 17 during recording indicates) but by a much greater audience that may not be conversant with this particular area or society but to whom it is nonetheless alluring. Indeed, this is the song that proves to be a breakthrough for Murad in terms of his popularity and diegetic propulsion. Mazumdar describes the sequence:

> The choreography is spatialized to provide a sense of synergy between what is viewed as embodied knowledge of Dharavi and the content of the lyrics. With drones, tracks and handheld camerawork, the sequence consciously maps the location with its rooftops, narrow alleys, and more. (2019)

The music-video-within-the-film sequence of '*Mere Gully Mein*' celebrates the place where the *gully* rappers on whom the film is based grew up. Just as the streets and city of Mumbai hold such an important part in the rise of these rappers, so too do they play a key role in *Gully Boy*.

Through its representation in the film, the city becomes a map of the complex relationship between its multilingualism and its class-caste and religious divisions. This sort of articulation of Mumbai's social landscape in terms of its languages is not new in Hindi cinema, itself a product of migrations and the import of northern Indian habitus into a global city: 'Mumbai's relationship to language has always been fascinating particularly in the context of a powerful film industry that emerged in a non-Hindi speaking state [Maharashtra]' (Mazumdar 2001: 4873). *Gully Boy*'s urbanscape acknowledges the many linguistic communities that constitute Mumbai and Hindi cinema and the newer forms of cultural practice that this multilingualism and polyglossia generate.

Murad's poetry in the form of *gully* rap addresses the concerns and draws on the imaginary of his neighbourhood, understood and appreciated by those with whom he shares a linguistic heritage, inflected by both region and class. At the same time, his public performances encapsulate for a global consumer base Mumbai's socio-economic asymmetries and the complicated bond its marginalised residents have with it. Murad's engagement with Mumbai is a playing out of the vexatious relationship between subaltern citizens and the metropolis they belong to (and which belongs to them) – frustrating and freeing at the same time. Through the polyglossal mode of poetry and everyday speech, he straddles the borders of two worlds, the definition of 'inside' and 'outside' constantly shifting as he deploys language to move between both.

POET IN THE CITY

In Hindi cinema's history, the impoverished *shayar* has often represented melancholic masculinity that is harnessed to critique the socio-economic status quo, his words describing and condemning the realities around him, serving as both record and judgement. The *shayar* has been the voice of the oppressed, inhabiting or operating on the periphery of a society that he deems unjust and corrupt, and from which he has been excluded.[2] The *shayar* figure in Hindi cinema can be understood as a somewhat gentrified nod to the subcontinent's legacy of protest poetry and political balladeering within the archive of popular Hindi cinema.[3] The examples I am referring to are *Pyaasa*'s Vijay and *Namak Haraam*'s Alam: for the *shayar* figure in these films, language becomes a way to affirm their subjectivity in a world that they are in conflict with. Murad navigates this urbanscape using *gully* rap, making him a descendant of the *shayar*.

From the 1950s, the *shayar* has been a rebellious, contrarian figure who confronts and counters the prevailing order, casting a more direct message in poetic terms. Murad is a subaltern hero whose poetry propels him out of his marginalised context and into a global arena. The film presents the device of poetry as emancipatory and communitarian, a polyglossal bulwark against the hostility of the city and society. While he shares with his predecessors the use of language as a form of resistance to the prevailing order and his poetry carries the social themes of his predecessors, Murad nonetheless departs from them politically and is celebrated by neoliberal, capitalist consumer society, as I will discuss in the next section. By giving Murad a feel-good happy ending, *Gully Boy* refashions the *shayar* from tragic figure to successful hero, his songs of protest now palatable spectacles.

Similar to his navigation of class that is spatialised in the form of Mumbai's geography, Murad embodies a continuum between the old, elite codes of Urdu poetry and new ones based in *Bambaiya* patois. While Urdu does not have a monopoly on poetry, in Hindi cinema it has historically been the language of poets – *Pyaasa*'s Vijay, *Palki*'s (Mahesh Kaul, S. U. Sunny 1967) Naseem (Rajendra Kumar), *Namak Haraam*'s Alam or *Saajan*'s (Lawrence D'Souza 1991) Aman (Sanjay Dutt). In *Gully Boy*, Murad's poetry/*gully* rap incorporates both the Urdu of *shayari* (poetry) and the flow of his predominantly lower-class Muslim neighbourhood's street talk. As Murad's friend and fellow rapper MC Sher notes, *gully* rap is rhythm plus poetry, and Murad already has the legacy of the latter bequeathed to him by his Bollywood forebears.

Mumbai's legacy is its multilingual poetic traditions, for it 'is a lived city as well as an imagined one, imagined and retold through its various lives in different languages, spaces, representations and vocations' (Nerlekar and Zecchini 2020: 2). *Gully* rap is one such contemporary subaltern poetic tradition of Mumbai, its fame (and name) and appeal based on its rootedness in the Mumbai *gully*. A fictionalised version of the real stories of *gully* rap pioneers Naezy and Divine (Kappal 2019), *Gully Boy*'s backdrop captures the vibrant rap scene that has taken off in Mumbai within the past decade. Divine started to rise in popularity through the release of his song '*Yeh Mera Bombay*' ('This is My Bombay' 2013) and both he and Naezy became international sensations with their collaboration on '*Mere Gully Mein*' (2015). While recording the film's version of Divine and Naezy's career-making hit, Murad proudly identifies himself with '*Bombay satra*' ('Bombay 17'), the postcode for Dharavi. In doing so at the moment in the film when he asserts his artistry as a multilingual rapper, he establishes the link between his practice and the specific geography of Mumbai that he belongs to and that endows him with that polyglossal facility.

Like the older *shayar*s but more explicitly than them, Murad deploys language as a type of protest against an unjust socio-economic system, giving voice to those oppressed by it. In the track '*Mere Gully Mein*', Murad and MC Sher rap in a mixture of *Bambaiya* Hindi (*bantai, bacchi, bamai*), English (We gettin' money-money) and Urdu (*daulat, shauhrat, mohabbat*) to tell the story of a neighbourhood in a way that is unique to it. *Bambaiya* Hindi or Mumbai

Hindi is a pidgin native to Mumbai, a mix of Hindi-Urdu (Hindustani) and Marathi, used mostly by the working-class communities of the city. Popularised in Hindi cinema as the language of lower-income characters (*taporis*, petty criminals, domestic workers, etc.) or those with similar origins (gangsters), the use of *Bambaiya* marks a character as being from Mumbai's underclass. Language becomes a form of political agency, not only because they are wordsmiths but also because of the polyglossia of their *gully* that affords them a rich lexicon and free range.

Akhtar emphasises that the Mumbai we see in *Gully Boy* has been determined largely by Murad's engagement with it: 'we just saw the city through him' (Akhtar 2019a). As Murad moves through the city and encounters people from its various parts, his language shifts too, a conscious effort on Akhtar's part (Akhtar 2019b). In college he attends English lectures, at home he speaks Urdu, with his neighbourhood friends he speaks *Bambaiya* and with his fellow rappers he tweaks all of these languages to imbue everyday speech with rhythm and flow. The spatial and the lingual frequently are co-constitutive – the homes of his friends in various pockets of Mumbai gesture towards the city's polyglossia. Examples include MC Sher's Marathi-speaking father in their *chawl* (tenement), Sky's plush apartment in which she switches between Hindi and English, and Safeena's middle-class home in which her mother (Sheeba Chaddha) chastises her for using the formal second person address of *aap*.

There is another, more literal thread that connects Murad to the Urdu *shayars* of the past: director Zoya Akhtar is the descendant of generations of well-known Urdu poets from the paternal side of her family. This includes her grandfather Jan Nisar Akhtar and father Javed Akhtar, who, apart from being an established screenwriter responsible for penning scripts that featured the subaltern Mumbai of the 1970s and were responsible for a hardening of Bollywood language (Masud 2005), has contributed poetry, lyrics and dialogues to her films, including this one. Javed Akhtar collaborated with Divine and Rishi Rich on the song '*Doori*' ('Distance'), which melded Hindustani, English and the cadence and perspective of Murad's life in Mumbai.

'*Doori*' appears in the film as a recited poem and in its musical form hews to the traditional Hindi film song more than any of the other rap songs on the film's soundtrack. Akhtar recounts another instance of collaboration that gestures towards a congruency between poetry of seemingly divergent types: initially Divine wrote the track '*Apna Time Aayega*' as '*Sabka Time Aayega*'. It was Javed Akhtar who suggested he change *sabka* (everyone's) to *apna* (mine) because '*apna* is what you own . . . it'll make you feel something' (Akhtar 2019a). In this way, Javed Akhtar's interventions, rooted as they are in a more classical register, prove to be reconcilable with *gully* rap, subtly endowing Murad's poetic voice in the film with the ancestral craft of multiple generations of *shayars*.

These aspects of the film, both the profilmic and extra-filmic, indicate that the political angst and anti-establishment content of Murad's songs connect him to the Hindi film character type of the *shayar*. As is the case with these older examples, his poetry is a record of the tension between the city and its citizens. However, unlike these earlier representations, Murad's attempt to navigate Mumbai through poetry – moving between the 'inside' and 'outside' as discussed in the previous section – is a rewarding journey. Murad is positioned as a new kind of *shayar* hero for the neoliberal era who, paradoxically, can rage against the machine and yet benefit from it.

A NEW KIND OF *SHAYAR*

Though belonging to a line of *shayars* in Hindi cinema, Murad represents a new version of the old mould; unlike the traditional poet who is often a tragic figure who remains at the margins of the city, *Gully Boy*'s poet protagonist is on his way to achieving success and rising to national (and perhaps international) fame. This is most apparent in the way he moves through the city, from the periphery of his subaltern neighbourhood to the centre, the glitzy upscale venue where he gives his closing performance and finally 'arrives' onto a global arena. Drawing a contrast between Murad and two previous incarnations of the urban *shayar*, *Pyaasa*'s Vijay and *Namak Haraam*'s Alam, I argue that *Gully Boy* departs from the politics of those films by adhering to a neoliberal order. Murad is a *shayar* true to his age, just as Vijay and Alam were to theirs, and his version of the *shayar* must be understood in his historical context. He is meant to represent the aspirations of citizens in a neoliberal political economy of which Mumbai is an important infrastructural and emblematic node.

Though Murad is a *shayar*, his trajectory is one that accords him agency and upward mobility, as he is embraced and rewarded by the market. Unlike his onscreen predecessors, Murad's words are easily co-opted by the capitalist system of injustice and inequality that he rails against, a sign that his confrontations themselves are now palatable and profitable. Mirroring the co-option of a proletarian art form like *gully* rap by the music and film industries, *Gully Boy* departs from older characterisations of poetry as a mode too radical to allow the character wielding it to thrive within the confines of the Hindi film. Whereas the older *shayars* rail against and resist a system that they recognise as being inherently flawed and configured to exploit the oppressed, Murad's poetry catapults him to the world stage, making a case for poetry (through music) as compatible with the neoliberal order in which an individual can rise above structural oppression by sheer grit and talent.

A comparison with older *shayars* shows how Murad is an era-appropriate manifestation of the *shayar*. In *Pyaasa*, the gifted but unsuccessful poet Vijay, asked, '*Yeh duniya agar mil bhi jaaye toh kya hai?*' ('So what if the world were mine?'); the song was written by Sahir Ludhianvi, 'master of the technique of the classical ghazal and of the film lyric' (Masud 2005). Though Vijay too faces poverty and rejection as an artist in the big city, his story is a tragic unfurling of the immoral forces of capital and power vanquishing an authentic artist. In rejecting the world of material success that only wants to profit off his words, Vjiay maintains his artistic integrity. Compare the iconic scene in which Vijay appears singing this song towards the end of *Pyaasa*, framed in silhouette against the doorway facing the stage with the vast audience's back to him, with Murad's triumphal performance of '*Apna Time Aayega*' at the end of *Gully Boy* where he commands the stage, facing his admirers. There are similarities: whereas the former sequence is composed of a triangulated intercutting between close-ups of a stricken Vijay, his lovers, treacherous friends and nemeses and long shots of his audience as he is dragged out of the auditorium, the latter features Murad's girlfriend Safeena (Alia Bhatt), loyal friends like MC Sher and Murad's competitors nodding along interspersed with mid-shots of his audience. The righteous rejection of Christ-like Vijay is stark when juxtaposed with Murad standing on the precipice of attaining the world – the *duniya* (world) Vijay repudiates is Murad's for the taking.

Informed by the Nehruvian socialism of the 1950s, a time replete with a postcolonial socialist sensibility, *Pyaasa*'s leftist poet does not consider popular or commercial appreciation of his poetry to be worth the suffering he has endured, instead finding solace in retreating from the urban public he once so craved to be recognised by. In contrast, Murad finds himself profiting off his own words; in the end he wins the rap battle and along with it Rs. 10 lakh, ADIDAS classic sneakers and a ticket to global stardom. Murad lives in an age when India has long embraced the free market and its celebration of individual accomplishment.

My second point of comparison with *Gully Boy* is *Namak Haraam*. That film's character Alam writes verses like '*Nadiya se darya, darya se sagar, sagar se gehra jaam / Jaam mein doob gayee hai yaaron meri jeevan ki har shaam*' ('From stream to river, river to sea, deeper than the sea a drink / Friends, drowned in drink are each of my life's evenings'). A young alcoholic kitemaker, Alam belongs to a similar world as Murad, composing poetry from a proletariat perspective and performing despair for Somu (Rajesh Khanna), a friend of Vicky (Amitabh Bachchan) the factory owner, who infiltrates Alam's community to destroy them from within. Sometime before dying surrounded by a *mehfil* (intimate poetry recital) of friends, Alam bequeaths his poetry to Somu, now sympathetic to this community, his words becoming a souvenir of the pain of poverty and marginalisation that he has carried all his life. Somu's status as a sort of intermediary between the ruling class and the proletariat allows him to 'carry' this pain to his friend, eventually converting Vicky to Somu's side in a death scene that echoed Alam's, a victim of the system once he fully accepted the mantle of a proletariat consciousness.

Alam's verse is dark and pessimistic, as befits the 1970s, an era of workers' agitation and political disillusionment with the status quo. By contrast, Murad's rap is hopeful and celebratory: '*Apna Time Aayega*', '*Mere Gully Mein*' and even Murad's political anthem '*Azadi*' ('Freedom') are fuelled by righteous anger rather than depressed resignation. Unlike Alam's resignation to death dictated by his structural powerlessness, Murad's confrontational optimism manages to change his circumstances and effect the leap to a better life, not an ignominious death. It is interesting to note, however, that Murad is constantly aware of the spectre of ruin by the presence of his friend Moeen (Vijay Varma), the mechanic-cum-carjacker with a heart of gold whose life represents what Murad's might be if he isn't careful. Cynical and caustic, it is Moeen who captures some of Alam's angst and serves as an alter ego and reminder for Murad as he occupies the gap between two worlds. In doing so, the film shifts the burden of diegetic nihilism from the poet-as-citizen to the citizen-as-criminal: the poor poet might find his way to a better life but the negotiation between the citizen and the city is not without danger.

Another small but significant difference between Murad and his predecessors is that unlike with Vijay and Alam, there is nothing mysterious about his craft; the materiality of his labour of language is on display, tying it into his physical conditions. In one montage, we see Murad's process of toiling over his poetry: working in collaboration with MC Sher, marking rhythm in his notebook, rapping into a sieve for the right acoustic effect and practising rapping in front of a mirror with hand gestures and wearing a borrowed hoodie. We often catch him in the act of writing down his words that we later hear as fully formed songs. '*Apna Time Aayega*' is an example of a song that provides an invisible thread through Murad's journey, in a sense running parallel to him.

Figure 6.1 Murad is shown toiling over his writing, dispelling its mystery.

Relevant here is the broader history and evolution of hip-hop and rap music from its origins in the Bronx of the 1970s, inhabited by the Black community and other disenfranchised racial minorities, to its current mainstream avatar as a multibillion-dollar industry (Price 2006). In *Gully Boy*'s opening sequence, while assisting Moeen during an auto theft, Murad criticises the Punjabi rap tracks ubiquitous in Bollywood films for being about superficial, material pleasures like 'my ride, my shoes, my liquor, my chicks'. Ironically, while initially there is an ostensible commitment to the possibility of radical popular art (as this bit of dialogue shows), by the end of the film, the expressive depth in Murad's rap is on its way to being co-opted by the entertainment industry.[4] Consider how the original track '*Azadi*' (a remix of a leftist student leader's chant in response to a state crackdown on a university in 2016) was edited for *Gully Boy* by removing its references to the structural problems of Indian society and the violence of Hindutva unleashed by the Indian government.[5] The commercialisation of Murad's art in the free market and the acquisition of associated capital is underway. This is also a valid interpretation of the real stories on which *Gully Boy* is based and points to how the music industry has historically been able to enervate the radicalism that powered the art of the marginalised and made it consumable by the masses.[6] Instead of standing up against the capitalist machinery that is the cause of his suffering, Murad is on the brink of being absorbed by it when the film ends.

Tracking the figure of the *shayar* across half a century, from *Pyaasa*'s Vijay to *Namak Haraam*'s Alam to *Gully Boy*'s Murad, the distinctions in political attitudes are revealed. The shift in the *shayar*'s journey from melancholia to optimism signals an alignment with a neoliberal-bourgeois order that is inimical to the interests of the working classes and oppressed castes. This is important in the context of Murad's class/religious location in Mumbai which genealogically connects him to another classic Hindi film character type: the *tapori*. Where Vijay and Alam reject the materialism of the world and fight the status quo, Murad embraces it, for as much as he is a *shayar*, he also carries the baggage of the *tapori* whose 'style is individual and his resistance relies on an ambiguous relationship to issues of lifestyle and consumption' (Mazumdar 2001: 4876).

SHAYAR AS TAPORI, TAPORI AS SHAYAR

As the previous section shows, though the film ultimately succumbs to Bollywood's neoliberal tendencies with Murad's success coded in terms of consumerism and global capital, there are brief moments when the lingual becomes subversive, rejecting the system that keeps artists like Murad oppressed. This is made possible by the adding of the *tapori*'s features to the characterisation of Murad, making him wield language rooted in his city to talk about the despair of living in it.

While Murad is a working-class Muslim man whose parents worked hard to make sure he could get an education, his class location, polyglossal dexterity and distance from 'pure' Urdu together allow him to fit into the lineage of another Bollywood figure – the *tapori*. From *Awaara*'s Raj (Raj Kapoor) to *Ghulam*'s (Vikram Bhatt 1998) Siddhu (Aamir Khan), the *tapori* has had a long career in Hindi cinema and can be theorised thus:

> The tapori's imagination has emerged out of a complex web of linguistic, spatial and imaginary journeys. He speaks to a structure of feeling that is located both in the everyday and the spectacles of cataclysmic transformations that a city witnesses. Using the popular Bambaiyya language as his weapon against an unequal world, the tapori creates a space through insubordination – of subcultural practices that endow him with certain dignity in the cinematic city. (Mazumdar 2001: 4872)

The *tapori*'s deft navigation of Mumbai and distinctive use of language are qualities that allow Murad to occupy an intermediary space where he navigates multiple spaces of the city by toggling between the elite performative register indicated by *shayari* and the subaltern one indicated by *tapori Bambaiya*.

There is a broad context to the *tapori*-esque characterisation of Murad in *Gully Boy* which in the first section I showed to be a film that is invested in showing Mumbai and its class intersections through its male protagonist. After a long absence through the 2000s and 2010s, the return of this type of male persona is tied to a response to two phenomena: the dominance of Mumbai as a global city and the rise of North India as the setting for Hindi films during these decades. Along with the increase of narratives set in foreign locales with the commercial clout of the South Asian diaspora viewership in the 1990s, Mumbai started being presented onscreen in the 2000s and 2010s through the neoliberal logic of global capital that excludes its most vulnerable occupants. The modernity of Mumbai, when relevant, has become externalised through the markers of a 'global city', as opposed to the small town which represents 'the shadow-regions of the urban order . . . visually chaotic and performatively excessive' (Kumar 2019: 63–4). Almost in opposition to the overdetermined globality of Mumbai that dominated Hindi cinema in the post-New Economic Policy (1991) era, in the past fifteen years there has been an emergence of Delhi, a city widely associated with feudal orthodoxy, as well as the northern Indian small town as the space of the 'local' in the narratives of Hindi films. Tracing it to the deployment of local language as a signifier of place in Mumbai gangster films, Kumar has termed this phenomenon the 'provincializing' of Bollywood:

... cinematic Delhi emerged not as a competing metropolis but as a north-Indian congregation sitting on the tricky boundary between urban and elsewhere ... become[ing] the synecdoche for north-Indian small-towns by hosting the urban-provincial, a performative counterpoint which finds resonances within the urban. This, indeed, has its precedents in the provincial turn to vernacular Mumbai, later overwhelmed by the north-Indian dislocation. (2013: 71–2)

Language in *Gully Boy* is a marker of the 'local' in the context of a city that is constantly positioned as 'global', a node that connects India to the international market. The *tapori* embodies this through his language and urban connections. 'Through his linguistic performance, the tapori shifts the course of a well-defined language system [and] enters a space where a multilingual street culture inflected with diverse regional accents can be captured' (Mazumdar 2007: 44). Through Murad's use of *Bambaiya*, *Gully Boy* imparts to him the spirit of the classic Mumbai masculinity of the *tapori*. Incorporating the provincial in terms of language, notably without centring crime and violence as the prominent feature of life-worlds by choosing, instead, to foreground poetry, *Gully Boy* brings into visibility the Mumbai Muslim proletariat after three decades of absence from the screen.[7]

Despite going to college and writing poetry, Murad nevertheless embodies the *tapori*'s urban subaltern masculinity, 'the performative desires of marginalized groups' (Mazumdar 2007: 78). He is 'the voice of the streets', as *Gully Boy*'s trailer announces, that he brings to the national and global stage, transforming the street into both. United by the quality of lingual dexterity, the *shayar*'s political angst is fused with the *tapori*'s proletarian mobility, allowing the titular *Gully Boy* to move between the local street and the global stage. Akhtar has framed her own interest in bringing the story of *gully* rap's young poster boys to the screen in terms of exploring how class limits artistic ambition and creativity (Akhtar 2019b). She has downplayed the importance of Murad's Muslim identity in favour of emphasising the film's focus on class,[8] presenting it as a commentary on how an unjust economic system has 'colonised dreams' (Akhtar 2019b).

This 'provincial turn to vernacular Mumbai' in *Gully Boy* is confirmed by Vijay Maurya, the film's dialogue writer. Working in collaboration with young rappers to update his *Bambaiya* vocabulary (Iyengar 2019) and drawing on his own lingual reserves as a Mumbai native who grew up in a *chawl* and internalised the city's multilingualism, Maurya 'transcreated' the script from Zoya Akhtar and her co-writer Reema Kagti's English original (Kharude 2019). Words like *altarpanti* (messing around), *bahot hard* (very cool), *tod-phod* (sexy) rub up against *dozakh* (hell) or *baahargaon* (foreign), creating a lingual map, seamlessly pinning character to location or cluing viewers in to context and tone. One of the most memorable lines in the film is uttered by Murad's girlfriend Safeena, who justifies her assault of a romantic rival thus: '*Mere boyfriend se gulu-gulu karegi toh dhoptoyengi na usko*' ('If she coochie-coos with my boyfriend, sure I'll whack her'). It is Maurya who brought in the word *dhoptoyengi*, a *Bambaiya* word with Marathi origins. He discusses his own process as one that involves being tuned into everyday language in the city: 'I try to use what I observe and hear on the street in rhyme. Now I realize maybe I was Murad' (Iyengar 2019). Indeed, as Kumar notes in the context of *Gully Boy*, 'The true protagonist of *Gully Boy* is the linguistic community of Mumbai subalterns, whose rebellion against their political inexistence is not just rap music but how it is provincialized in Mumbai swagger' (2019).

This amalgam of city and language in the figure of the *tapori* is key to understanding how the lingual becomes subversive in *Gully Boy* when combined with the *shayari* of protest. It is in the melding of the cinematic imprints of the cultural form of protest poetry represented by the *shayar* and that of Mumbai's everyday proletarian lingual (and by extension performative) legacy exemplified by the *tapori* that the film, like Murad, briefly challenges the dominant socio-political order before succumbing to its ideological underpinnings.

CONCLUSION

Through its use of language and its relationship with the city, *Gully Boy* captures a fraught dynamic within the framework of popular cinema, with all its ideological limitations and conservatism, at once positing the possibility of a radical politics but necessarily effacing it in favour of industrial cinema's appropriation of subaltern angst. From carjacker to celebrity, Murad's journey as *shayar/tapori* is framed as aspirational for those watching in his neighbourhood, and the film seems to end on a predictably conformist note, with socio-economic ascent accomplished and the hero's problems with love and family surmounted. But sandwiched between *Gully Boy*'s ending, the final stage of the contest and his opening act for Nas, is Murad moving through the local stations of Mumbai and bylanes of Dharavi 17. He will always be moving between two worlds, a successful artist but also one whose art is entirely driven by the place he comes from – we have invested too much in the detail and drama of that odyssey for it to be entirely erased by Bollywood's corporatist gaze. Kumar writes:

> Even though the narrative of the film is derailed via false boundaries, the performative essence of living amidst soul-crushing contrasts and the desire to break free of glass ceilings continues to linger ... While the film may want you to exit the environs as he exits them, only to briefly revisit as a 'star', we know almost intuitively, that Murad would

still remain suspended in the cracks between vertical integration and horizontal sprawl. (2019)

The anecdote about Javed Akhtar's suggestion to Divine and Rishi Rich to change *sabka* to *apna* captures the film's attitude towards Murad's movement between two worlds. Playing with the word *apna*, which could mean both 'mine' and 'ours', *Gully Boy* presents the journey through the city-as-spatial-metaphor for success through a *tapori* brand of *shayari*. Like language, this journey is something individual but also shared by a community of citizens. The tension between city and citizen key to the equilibrium of *Gully Boy* is ultimately negated by the predictably reactionary commitments of Bollywood. However, the staging of the tension itself is one of the functions of popular cinema and, in doing so, *Gully Boy* presents a tantalising vision of the possibilities of a creative life in a deeply unequal society.

NOTES

1. The song sequence is based on the actual music video recorded by Naezy and Divine.
2. The documentaries *Bombay: Our City* (Anand Patwardhan 1985) and *A Night of Prophecy* (Amar Kanwar 2002) are important points of reference in discussing the subaltern poet in Indian cinema.
3. The contemporary *lokshahir* (people's poet) movement emerged in pre-Independence Maharashtra from an existing medieval itinerant balladeer tradition combining 'familiar refrains' with 'colloquial speech-song' (Damodaran). In Urdu poetry, a language that dominated Hindi film song lyrics since its earliest years, there is a strain of political and explicitly dissident sentiment from the eighteenth century to the present day (Jalil).
4. Looking at the role of art in revolution, Pope (2005) uses Herbert Marcuse's distinction between 'life art' and 'contrived art' to describe the devolution of hip-hop music into twenty-first- century 'party rap' (81). He tracks how a genre that grew out of a radical political consciousness about poverty and race became one that celebrates capitalism which only perpetuates systemic racial violence, thereby transforming 'from a mode of expression . . . to entertainment . . .' (87).
5. 'The fact that the track is now owned by Zee Music Company, part of Zee News, which was instrumental in spreading false narratives about the JNU protests, is a haunting example of how movements can be co-opted and profited from' (Kapur 2019).
6. Continuing with Marcuse's model, Pope (2005) attributes the deradicalisation of hip-hop music from the 1970s to the 2000s to two factors: the economics of the mass market system (87) and the change in audience (91).
7. The last major Hindi film to focus on the Muslim proletariat was *Salim Langde Pe Mat Ro* (Saeed Mirza 1989), which featured a protagonist who is a petty criminal bribed into stirring up a communal riot in his neighbourhood, leading to his tragic death.
8. Though there is no explicit reference to it, Murad's Muslim identity and the film's subtle acknowledgement of his religious culture is significant in the context of India's current political climate of Hindu majoritarianism and the long absence of a Muslim male protagonist from Hindi cinema.

WORKS CITED

Akhtar, Zoya (2019a), 'Zoya Akhtar interview with Anupama Chopra'. Interview by Anupama Chopra. *Film Companion*, 6 February 2019. Video, 22:53. Available at <http://www.youtube.com/watch?v=Zs_58AocYi4>

—— (2019b), 'Zoya Akhtar | *Gully Boy* postmortem'. Interview by Anupama Chopra. *Film Companion*, 15 February 2019. Video, 29:49. Available at <http://www.youtube.com/watch?v=o8V7Z4n5hko>

Bose, Nandana (2017), 'Globalization, reflexivity, and genre in Zoya Akhtar's films', in Aysha Iqbal Viswamohan and Vimal Mohan John (eds), *Behind the Scenes: Contemporary Bollywood Directors and Their Cinema*, New Delhi: Sage, pp. 215–26.

Damodaran, Sumangala (2020), '"Yeh Gulab Nahin, Inquilab Hai": The tradition of protest music in contemporary India', *The Wire*, 5 March 2020. Available at <https://thewire.in/culture/yeh-gulab-nahin-inquilab-hai-the-tradition-of-protest-music-in-contemporary-india>

Iyengar, Shriram (2019), 'In a way, I am Murad. Words liberated me: Vijay Maurya on crafting the magic of *Gully Boy*'s dialogues', *Cinestaan*, 17 March 2019. Available at <https://www.cinestaan.com/articles/2019/mar/17/19292>

Jalil, Rakhshanda (2017), 'Why it is impossible to think of Urdu poetry without thinking of India's journey to (and after) 1947', *Scroll.in*, 15 August 2017. Available at <https://scroll.in/article/846902/why-it-is-impossible-to-think-of-urdu-poetry-without-thinking-of-indias-journey-to-and-after-1947>

Kappal, Bhanuj (2019), 'The voice of the Gully', *Livemint*, 12 February 2019. Available at <https://www.livemint.com/mint-lounge/features/the-voice-of-the-gully-1549620977670.html>

Kapur, Uday (2019), '*Gully Boy*: Ranveer Singh and Alia Bhatt's "apolitical" views and edited Azadi song betray the film's authenticity', *Firstpost*, 18 February 2019. Available at <https://www.firstpost.com/entertainment/gully-boy-ranveer-singh-alia-bhatts-views-edited-azadi-song-betray-films-authenticity-6105651.html>

Kharude, Dipti (2019), 'The man behind the "Tod Fod" dialogues of Ranveer-Alia's *Gully Boy*', *The Quint*, 20 February 2019. Available at <https://www.thequint.com/entertainment/bollywood/gully-boy-dialogues-vijay-maurya-interview-ranveer-singh-alia-bhatt-zoya-akhtar>

Krstic, Igor (2017), *Slums On Screen: World Cinema and the Planet of Slums*, Edinburgh: Edinburgh University Press.

Kumar, Akshaya (2019), 'Geek out: We're going all film theory on Ranveer Singh and *Gully Boy*', *Huffington Post*, 9 March 2019. Available at <https://www.huffingtonpost.in/entry/geek-out-we-re-going-all-film-theory-on-ranveer-singh-and-gully-boy_in_5c825a83e4b0ed0a00125811f>

—— (2013), 'Provincialising Bollywood? Cultural economy of north-Indian small-town nostalgia in the Indian multiplex', *South Asian Popular Culture*, 11: 1, pp. 61–74.

Masud, Iqbal (2005), 'Muslim ethos in Indian cinema', *Screen*, 4 March 2005. Available at <http://www.screenindia.com/fullstory.php?content_id=9980>

Mazumdar, Ranjani (2019), 'The Mumbai slum: Aerial views and embodied memories', *Mediapolis: A Journal of Cities and Culture*, 4: 3. Available at <www.mediapolisjournal.com/2019/11/the-mumbai-slum/>

—— (2007), *Mumbai Cinema: An Archive of the City*, Minnesota: University of Minnesota Press.

—— (2001), 'Figure of the "Tapori": Language, gesture and cinematic city", *Economic and Political Weekly*, 36: 52, pp. 4872–80.

Mohanty, Aditya (2019), '*Gully Boy* and its silent mutinies', *EPW Engage*, 54: 8. Available at <https://www.epw.in/engage/article/gully-boy-and-its-silent-mutinies>

Nerlekar, Anjali and Laetitia Zecchini (2017), 'Introduction: The worlds of Mumbai poetry', *Journal of Postcolonial Writing*, 53, 1–2, pp. 1–11. Available at <https://doi.org/10.1080/17449855.2017.1298505>

Nowell-Smith, Geoffrey (2004), 'Cities: Real and imagined', in Mark Shiel and Tony Fitzmaurice (eds), *Cinema and the City: Film and Urban Societies in a Global Context*, Hoboken: Wiley-Blackwell, pp. 99–108.

Pope, H. Lavar (2005), 'Protest into pop: Hip-hop's devolution into mainstream pop music and the underground's resistance', *Lehigh Review*, 13, paper 5, pp. 79–98. Available at <http://preserve.lehigh.edu/cas-lehighreview-vol-13/5>

Price, Emmett G. and Jorge Iber (2006), 'The rise and spread of hip hop culture', in *Hip Hop Culture*, California: ABC-CLIO, pp. 1–19.

Ramnath, Nandini (2019), 'Designing *Gully Boy*: "When nobody knows what's a set and what isn't, that is the best compliment"', *Scroll.in*, 3 March 2019. Available at <https://scroll.in/reel/915126/designing-gully-boy-when-nobody-knows-whats-a-set-and-what-isnt-that-is-the-best-compliment>

CHAPTER 7

Queer Love: He is Also *Made in Heaven*

Iqra Shagufta Cheema

Homosexuality, despite being represented conservatively and in dichotomous opposition to heterosexuality, is not an entirely unfamiliar territory for Indian popular and independent cinema. Indian cinematic queer representations range from homosocialism and homoeroticism in films like *Sholay* (Ramesh Sippy 1975), *Kal Ho Na Ho* (Nikhil Advani 2003), *Masti* (Indra Kumar 2004), *Dostana* (Tarun Mansukhani 2008) and *Dedh Ishqiya* (Abhishek Chaubey 2014) to movies with homosexual characters like *Fire* (Deepa Mehta 1996), *The Pink Mirror* (Sridhar Rangayan 2004), *My Brother, Nikhil* (Onir 2005), *Honeymoon Travels Pvt. Ltd* (Reema Kagti 2007), *I Am* (Onir 2010), *Bombay Talkies* (2013), *Ek Ladki Ko Dekha Toh Aisa Laga* (Shelly Chopra Dhar 2019) and *Shubh Mangal Zyada Savdhan* (Hitesh Kewalya 2020). Despite these diverse representations, homosexuality is culturally so controversial that, for example, cinemas playing *Fire* were attacked by members of the right-wing Shiv Sena because the film depicts lesbian love scenes between two Hindu women named Radha (Shabana Azmi) and Sita (Nandita Das),[1] and the Indian Censor Board banned *The Pink Mirror* and *Unfreedom* (Raj Amit Kumar 2014).[2] Among all of the above described portrayals, *Made in Heaven* (Zoya Akhtar and Reema Kagti, 2019), a series streaming on Amazon Prime, stands out for its vocal politics, representational nuance and global reach in representing homosexuality in India.

Homosexuality as a category did not exist in the Indian subcontinent until 1861, when the British Colonial Government introduced Section 377 in the Indian Penal Code, which declared 'unnatural offenses', like homosexuality, 'against the order of nature'.[3] Thereby, it made non-procreative sex a crime and encouraged homophobia. Despite the fact that the statute had criminalised both anal and oral sex, Section 377 mostly affected India's reported 2.5 million homosexual individuals.[4] The efforts to repeal Section 377 started in 2001 and the Delhi High Court declared consensual homosexual sex legal in 2009; this decision was overruled by the Supreme Court of India in 2013, deferring the legislative amendment to the Parliament of India.[5] Eventually, in 2018, a five-judge bench of the Indian Supreme Court overturned the 2013 ruling and decriminalised homosexuality.[6]

In its representation of queer sexualities, Bollywood cinema gradually moved from homosocial to homoerotic and then to homosexual in accidental, intentional or political ways, as is evident in the films listed above. Bollywood films started engaging in more political portrayals of queer sexualities only in the last decade, which is the decade of the legalisation of homosexuality. Yet most of the above-mentioned films prototypically either downplay homosexual desire or portray homosexual love subtly, humorously and connotatively; have diasporic gay characters whose sexuality is only captured passingly and show homosexuality either in competition with or in opposition to heterosexuality. However, the portrayal of homosexuality in *Made in Heaven*, through the character of Karan Mehra (Arjun Mathur), is unlike any of the representations in other films.

In *Epistemology of the Closet* (1990), Eve Sedgwick points out an internal contradiction in homo/heterosexual definitions. She calls it the contradiction between 'a minoritizing view' – wherein issues of homosexuality are considered significant only for a 'small, distinct, relatively fixed homosexual minority' – and 'a universalizing view' – wherein homosexuality is 'an issue of continuing, determinative importance' for people 'across the spectrum of sexualities' (1). In this chapter, I will show that Karan Mehra's character is, borrowing Sedgwick's terminology, neither minoritised nor universalised – rather he is parallelised with heterosexual portrayals of love. The term 'parallel' connotes a resolution of the contradiction identified by Sedgwick. Devoid of any stereotypical queer behaviour and mannerisms and trapped in the relatable socio-economic struggles of the upper middle class, this parallelisation in the series complicates and challenges the normative interconnections of desire, sexuality and security in India. To contextualise this argument, I review the interconnections of homosexuality, sociality and eroticism in Indian films with the background of legislative changes. Using *Made in Heaven* as a point of departure, I further discuss the rise of streaming services like Amazon Prime Video in India and their role for Indian democracy in an increasingly globalised world.

Since streaming services are changing viewership patterns, this chapter examines this significant shift in Indian TV and film and its political repercussions. Globally streamed *Made in Heaven*, along with the annulment of Section 377, solidifies and facilitates India's image as a secular and increasingly progressive country in the era of neoliberal globalisation. The series, as opposed to previous cinematic conversations, depicts that India legally accepts and recognises its queer community. Additionally, it shows that the younger generation is much more accepting of non-normative sexualities. Considering that the 2018 decriminalisation of homosexual relationships does not end socio-cultural challenges for the Indian gay community, I posit that the documentation of gay rights' activists in a popular visual medium like *Made in Heaven* is an act of socio-cultural narrative (re)formation in itself. Overall, the series' depiction of a homosexual man in India represents a shift in cinematic discourses of queer subjectivities, which sets the precedent for a more accepting and tolerant social, historical and global representation and existence for India's queer community.

LGBTQIA+ IN BOLLYWOOD

The long tradition of homosocial and homoerotic friendships in popular Hindi cinema goes as far back as the 1960s and extends to the 2010s, when Bollywood films started portraying homosexual, albeit subtle or peripheral, characters in the above-listed films as well as in other massively popular films like *Chaudvin Ka Chand* (M. Sadiq 1960), *Anand* (Hrishikesh Mukherjee 1971), *Zanjeer* (Prakash Mehra 1973), *Dostana* (Raj Khosla 1980), *Hum Aapke Hain Kaun* (Sooraj Barjatya 1994) and *Raja Hindustani* (Dharmesh Darshan 1996). Scholars have rigorously explored the 'trope of homosocial triangle' (Dasgupta and Baker 2013: 91) and homosocial concepts like *yaar, dosti, yarana* (friendship) in these films (Ghosh 2007, Kavi 2000, Rao 2000, Gopinath 2005, Parasad 1998, Dasgupta and Baker 2013). In Hindi, Urdu and Punjabi, the words *dost* and *yaar* mean friend or lover; these are also the crucial words for reading homosocial and homoerotic undertones in these films. R. Raj Rao notes that a man may use *yaar* to refer to a male friend, but a husband will also use *yaar* to refer to his wife's lover (2000: 306); or it could refer to the male lover of any woman who is having an illicit or socially impermissible affair. Even in the context of male friendship, Rao observes that the word *yaar* is 'much more than a friend' (305). He further quotes Raj Ayyar: 'a *yaar* is an individual with whom one feels a deep almost intangible connection' (306). The suggestive ambivalence of these words leaves plenty of room for stealthy sexual slippage from a friend into a *yaar* when reading male relationships.

Homosocialism and homoeroticism markedly take centre stage in Amitabh Bachchan's exceptionally popular 'buddy films', where a female heroine is reduced to a mere prop or a device. *Zanjeer*, Rao writes, was the turning point that replaced the female heroine with a male best friend (2000: 300). Rama Srinivasan also comments that buddy films 'de-legitimize[d] the female body' (198) and 'literally drip[ped] with homoeroticism' (2013: 197). Rao posits that homosexuality 'thrive[s] in covert yet cognized places' in India 'under the auspices of normative patriarchal culture' (299). He traces the 'subtler forms of homosexuality' in the ways these films construct male friendship and love within both Indian cinema and male audience. Shohini Gosh also argues that Indian cinema uses 'similar, even identical' devices to represent love and friendship (2005); song sequences in films are an appropriate example of that. Gosh uses the songs '*Choli Ke Peechay Kya Hai*' ('What are you hiding behind your blouse?') from *Khal Nayak* (Subhash Gai 1993) and '*Didi, Tera Devar Deewana*' ('Sister, your brother-in-law is crazy') from *Hum Aapke Hain Kaun* as examples that suggestively rupture heteronormativity (2002: 211). Similarly, Rao equates the song lyrics in *Sholay*, *Dostana* and *Namak Haram* to wedding vows since the songs contain the promises of lifelong friendship and living in each other's hearts forever (2000: 300–2).

In cinemas, these promises would warm the hearts of audiences for their *friends* too. In the 'cramped' and 'sleazy atmosphere' of cinema halls, two onscreen male best friends being viewed by an all-male audience would turn an Indian cinema hall into a homoerotic zone where one was 'likely to find young men all over each other, clasping hands, putting arms around shoulders and waists, even a leg on a leg' (303). Rao himself shares how he often sought sexual encounters in cinemas and 'rarely came back disappointed' (304). Though homoerotic desire remained tacitly veiled in homosocial interactions, the subtle portrayals of queer sexualities in films became more intentional and political with changing legislation.

Prior to the annulment of Section 377 of the Indian Penal Code in 2009, Kaustav Bakshi and Parjanya Sen trace two key Bollywood films,[7] *Fire* and *Dostana* (2008), that made lesbian and gay sexual relations visible in India (2012: 168). Rohit Dasgupta and Steven Baker describe *Dostana* as the first film to study the 'traffic between discourses of sexuality, Indian-ness, diaspora and performativity' (2013: 90). Bakshi and Sen contend that the diasporic position of *Fire*'s director Deepa Mehta, who is settled in Canada, made her 'critique of nationalist masculinity' feasible (2012: 170). *Fire* is the story of the women married to two brothers: Sita is married to unfaithful Jatin (Javed Jafrey), whereas Radha is married to celibate Ashok (Kulbhushan Kharbanda). Trapped in the same house and stuck in unhappy marriages, Sita and Radha fall in love. Sibaji Bandyopadhyay comments that 'it was as if the release of *Fire* had also released the "homosexual" from the depths of the "communal unconscious"' and made it into 'a full-blown conceptual category' that 'challenge[s] the national masculinity' (2007: 19).

Building on Bandyopadhyay's argument, Bakshi suggests that *Fire* 'effectuates a rupture within the founding ethos of a heteropatriarchal ideal of nationalist masculinity' (2007: 170). *Fire*'s effect was two-pronged: it provided an 'inaugural moment' for woman–woman desire by invoking the trope of lesbianism (but erased other possibilities of woman–woman desire in doing so) and it undermined the Hindu middle-class family, which is the 'fundamental functional unit' of Indian patriarchy (Bakshi 2007: 170). Ghosh, while arguing that the film posed a threat to heteropatriarchal Indian social structure, refers to Ruth Vanita and Saleem Kidwai's argument that *Fire* unleashed lesbian desire in the 'midst of an ordinary household among mundane domestic chores' (2010: 99). In addition to that, Srinivasan also reads 'countless queer ruptures' and 'repeated queer onslaughts on patriarchal heteronormativity' in films like *Fire* and *I Am*.[8] He maintains that these films expand the 'discursive field around the expression of non-normative desires' and affirm the shift from 'incidental portrayals and defiant readership to direct references to queerness' in cinema (2013: 193–4). While non-heteronormative subjects in most films solely 'provide comic relief or are punished and killed in predictable ways' (Gopinath 2000: 295), *Fire* and *I Am* treat non-heteronormative sexualities as 'political identit[ies]' (Srinivasan 2013: 194) rather than 'laugh[ing] [them] off as an aberration' (Bakshi and Sen 2012: 173).

Bakshi and Sen argue that Bollywood makes a 'discursive shift from the "homosocial" to "homosexual"' from *Dostana* (1980), a story about two male friends who fall in love with the same woman, to *Dostana* (2008), a story about two men who pretend to be gay first to rent a room in an apartment whose female owner has a 'no boy roommate' policy and then to help one get the American residence permit and who, by falling in love with the same woman, actually become close friends (Bakshi 2012: 172). *Dostana* (2008) brings 'the implicit homoeroticism out of the closet' and 'foregrounds the very ethos of a male homosocial masculinist culture' that 'legitimizes' and 'validates' different forms of 'homoerotic desire' (Bakshi 2012: 170). The identical titles of these films, meaning 'friendship', are evidence of the existence of homoerotic desire in homosocial spaces throughout the decades. In addition to these, *Kal Ho Na Ho* (2003), where the two male characters Aman (Shah Rukh Khan) and Rohit (Saif Ali Khan) fall in love with the same woman, Naina (Preity Zinta), and Rohit marries Naina to fulfil Aman's last wish before he dies of cancer, also 'prefigures [this] moment of transition' from homosocial to homosexual (Bakshi 2012: 173). Rohit and Aman's friendship foregrounds 'the presence of male–male homoeroticism within male–male homosocial spaces', note Bakshi and Sen (2012: 173), whereas Naina becomes a mere device to commemorate their friendship.

Films like *Dostana* and *Kal Ho Na Ho* were big steps towards 'de-closeting homosexuality' as the male Indian friends 'drift effortlessly' between homosocial and homoerotic, and constantly border on homosexual categories (Srinivasan 2013: 194).[9] But both of these films, like most other homoerotic Bollywood films, usually have non-heteronormative Indian diasporic characters and/or are set in the West, which positions the critique of heteronormativity outside of India. Hence, these films create a safe distance between the heteronormative Indian home and the threat of homosexuality. These films might appear 'non-transgressive in their native Indian context' but they 'acquire subversive value' when viewed from a non-nationalist and diasporic point of view, posits Gayatri Gopinath. She describes 'queer diasporic viewing practice' as a lens 'removed from patriarchy, sexism, and homophobia' (2000: 283).

The decision of the Delhi High Court to declare consensual homosexual sex legal (a decision that was made in 2009 and repealed in 2013) brought the queer community further 'out of the closet' (173) and 'necessitated a discursive construction of the [Indian] queer subject' (Bakshi and Sen 2012: 179–80). It rendered this community visible and gave them a name and recognition, which also affected queer representation in Bollywood. Since homosexuality could no longer be elided or silenced, films started making a more active effort to acknowledge and understand it (Ghosh 2007: 433). Bakshi and Sen suggest that the Delhi High Court's decision came as the 'aftermath of increasing globalization and neo-liberalization', and that is why it should be located 'within an emerging ethos of neo-liberal globalization' (2012: 172).

In addition to the Court's decision, India's status as the world's largest democracy and its emerging recognition as the next economic superpower in Asia further encouraged a reconsideration of its queer subjects. Indian cinema also received global attention because of an influx of multinational capital, urbanisation, consumer economy and globalisation. In turn, both Western media and Indian cinema highlighted India as a 'significant global nation', 'a force to be reckoned with' and a 'democratic, tameable alternative to red China' (Dasgupta and Baker 2008, Mehta 2010). Increasingly more Western democracies have legalised homosexuality and gay marriages, which further contributed to the Delhi High Court's decision. The combination of these legislative and global influences directed the changes in legal rights, identity politics and representation of queer communities in India. Globalisation also brought an 'influx of Hollywood film and American television' to India, in which 'changing perceptions' of gender and sexuality are popular themes; this in turn made the queer subjects more visible and led to their acknowledgement in Bollywood (Holtzman 2010: 111–12). As a result, the 'new Bollywood' became 'the face of post-global India' (Mehta 2010: 2).

But these changes highlight the discordance between India's ambitions and local Indian traditions. Films like *Fire* and *Dostana* (2008) show India's 'national, cultural anxiety' about its 'integration into global economy dominated by Western popular culture' (Holtzman 2010: 112). The reception of the films with queer characters (for example, previously mentioned attacks on cinemas that were showing *Fire*) manifests 'a desire to maintain a sense of national identity rooted in Hindu hegemony despite the nation's new status' (Holtzman 2010: 117). Woman–woman eroticism or sex (as is the case in *Fire*) poses a bigger threat to the nation state than male–male eroticism and sex because women, as mothers and wives, are burdened with holding the heteropatriarchal family together. It is noteworthy that most of the above-mentioned films represent male queerness, while there are far fewer films about lesbian love. Dozens of Bollywood films, starting from the 1960s onwards, explore themes of male homosocialism, homoeroticism and homosexuality, whereas *Fire*, *Girlfriend* (Karan Razdan 2004), *Dedh Ishqiya*, *Ragini MMS-2* (Bhushan Patel 2014), *Unfreedom* and *Ek Ladki Ko Dekha Toh Aisa Laga* are the only films and *Four More Shots Please!* (Rangita Pritish Nandy, 2019–20) the only series that explore female queerness, with very few other subtle or passing nods to lesbian love.[10]

Because of this discriminatorily gendered 'national, cultural anxiety', a woman's role as the upholder of a heteronormative Hindu family is emphasised via Indian satellite TV soap operas. Soap operas of the 2000s, like *Kyunki Saas Bhi Kabhi Bahu Thi* (2000–8), where Tulsi (Smriti Malhotra-Irani) and Mihir (Ronit Roy) had a love marriage despite the disapproval of Mihir's family, but the ideal daughter-in-law Tulsi wins over her husband's family's hearts; *Kahaani Ghar Ghar Ki* (2000–8), the story of married couple Parvati (Sakshi Tanwar), the perfect daughter-in-law, and Om Agarwal (Kiran Karmarkar), the perfect son; and *Kasauti Zindagi Ki* (2001–8), the story of two heterosexual lovers, Anurag (Cezanne Khan) and Prerna (Shweta Tiwari), who could only meet after death, became extremely popular both with local and diasporic Indian audiences. Against the backdrop of India's economic liberalisation, these TV soaps used 'aspirational lifestyles' and Bollywood-style 'catchy title songs', but 'espoused' family and tradition (Munshi 2010: 1). These soap operas were set in heteronormative joint family systems and their dominant themes were the dichotomy of good and bad women and the significance and sanctity of a home. Tulsi and Paravati, the main characters of *Kyunki Saas Bhi Kabhi Bahu Thi* and *Kahaani Ghar Ghar Ki*, became 'ideal wives' and *bahus* (daughters-in-law) for every household (Munshi 2010: 1). These TV soap operas weaved together the economic and socio-cultural dreams of most Indians and gained incredible popularity among middle-class and lower middle-class audiences. According to the Television Audience Measurement (TAM) Report (2015), 167 million Indian households have terrestrial TV and 161 million have satellite TV. I suggest that TV soaps encouraged heteronormative family structure and simultaneously marketed economic liberalisation, thus becoming a cheaper and more accessible alternative to Bollywood cinema. Instead of going to a cinema for a film, millions of Indian housewives could watch their dream houses and ideal families on TV. This sparked a comparison between the soap opera world and the real world of female audiences and inspired them to model the traditional heteronormative prosperous family of soap operas in their own houses. Thus, satellite TV soap operas compensated for the representational shifts in Bollywood films.

Soap operas on popular satellite TV keep the heteropatriarchal joint family central to their plots, as opposed to more recent films that 'project ambivalence on the possibility that Indians may begin to identify with Western forms of queerness' (Holtzman 2010: 127). But instead of 'vilify[ing] homosexuality' (Holtzman 2010: 127), these films 'either rework or subvert' the 'older traditions/tropes of representation' to fit into a 'globalized discourse of identity' 'towards a neo-liberal inclusion of the "gay" citizen subject' (Bakshi and Sen 2012: 167). Films like *Dostana* (2008) and *Kal Ho Na Ho* openly play with the trope of homosexuality and make it visible, but, ultimately, they keep heterosexuality intact. Collectively, globalisation, urbanisation and a consumerist economy not only anticipated and encouraged the streaming services revolution in India, but also made a series like *Made in Heaven* possible.

STREAMING SERVICES AND THEIR IMPACT

Netflix and Amazon Prime Video have revolutionised Indians' TV consumption patterns. Such is the exponential growth of streaming services that India had thirty streaming services in 2019, as opposed to nine in 2012. In 2019, Amazon Prime Video had 13 million subscribers while Netflix had 11 million subscribers in India (Rao 2019). Over the last few years, Amazon Prime and Netflix have drastically increased their investment in India, the largest market in the world. With a Gross National Income per capita of $7,680 in 2018 (World Bank),[11] a cheap mobile phone with internet is the first personal gadget for most Indians and simultaneously serves as a TV, phone and laptop (Agrawal 2019). Amazon has targeted Indians aged 18–24 years old, who make up more than half of India's population, and who subscribe to Amazon Prime for their cheapest video-streaming services (Agrawal 2019). Amazon Prime also attracted 50 per cent new subscribers from small cities in India (Shrivastava 2019). This significant consumer increase from smaller cities and younger populations points to the outreach of streaming services. Streaming services are capitalising on this and developing projects that would be of interest to both local and global audiences.

Streaming services like Amazon Prime and Netflix facilitate a more equitable representational space for an increased portrayal of taboo or controversial subjects. For example, *Unfreedom*, which was banned in Indian cinemas, was subsequently released on Netflix India. This release anticipated the different and freer nature of streaming services. While the Amazon Prime series *Made in Heaven* received good reviews and had a positive impact, leading some viewers to share stories of coming out to their families after watching the show, responses to the Bollywood film *Ek Ladki Ko Dekha Toh Aisa Laga* about the struggle of a young lesbian woman, Sweety (Sonam Kapoor), were less positive. One of the film's writers, Ghazal Dhaliwal, watched the film in cinemas four times and reported that she witnessed up to '10 couples or families' leave the cinema when they saw Sweety come out as a lesbian (Sarivastava 2019). While *Ek Ladki* and *Made in Heaven* both faced the same homophobia that still exists despite the annulment of Section 377, the latter had a different reception because of its viewing platform.

Streaming services make the viewing experience more independent and personal. A viewer might not be comfortable accepting a non-normative sexual representation onscreen in the presence of their family, friends, partner or other cinemagoers, but digital streaming services create a space for a private viewing experience. This viewing experience is comparatively more equitable, democratic and both cost- and time-effective, as evidenced by the growth of Amazon Prime subscribers from small Indian cities. Directors also have more creative freedom when making originals for streaming services like Amazon Prime and Netflix because of limited regulatory restrictions on their content. This has allowed for shows like *Made in Heaven* not only to talk about themes like gay rights, but more explicitly to make reference to and depict both gay and heterosexual sex scenes; something that, as discussed earlier, would be censored in industry films.

One of the other benefits of the streaming platform is its larger global reach. American companies like Amazon Prime or Netflix, with their global consumer base, have not only brought more programmes to India, but have also brought Indian programmes to the world. Reportedly, two out of every three consumers of the Hindi-language Netflix original *Sacred Games* (Vikramaditya Motwane 2018–19) were outside of India. When comparing the digital streaming platform with Hindi cinema, actor Arjun Mathur, who plays Karan Mehra in *Made in Heaven*, shared his preference for the digital medium because of its wider impact. He considers Hindi cinema 'narrow' because for a brief period the films are shown in cinemas only to the local Indian population. In contrast, digital platforms like Amazon Prime or Netflix are available in around 280 countries to be watched whenever the audience prefers (GQ Staff 2019). Streaming services are transforming the viewing experience and its consumption and politics in India; Bollywood will have to get bold and experimental to compete against streaming services, which only benefits the Indian consumer and improves their options.

KARAN IS *MADE IN HEAVEN*

The digital longevity of streaming services that Mathur refers to in terms of distribution and audiences also renders more visibility to actors and allows for a greater character development than does a film. Commenting on his performance as Karan Mehra, Mathur shared that the directors wanted an 'alpha male who they couldn't tell is gay just by looking at him' (GQ Staff 2019). As a result, his character departs from previous comic, diasporic, playful or stereotypical portrayals of queer characters and becomes a 'regular' Indian man who is not reduced only to his sexuality, rather his sexuality only forms one part of his identity. Borrowing Bakshi and Sen's terminology, the series 'incorporates the homosexual within the ambit of liberal human rights' and sets up a category of the homosexual in need of 'recognition as a universal citizen-subject' (175).

Unlike the Bollywood films mentioned previously, *Made in Heaven* neither portrays homosexuality as a minor or universal issue nor portrays it in a humorous or derogatory manner; rather it parallels homosexuality with heterosexuality, thus rendering it a valid and visible part of the identity of homosexual individuals. The series addresses internalised homophobia, homosexual sex, stereotypes about gay performativity and struggles of queer community, and as such *Made in Heaven* masterfully complicates and addresses these sociocultural and legal issues of queer identity in a way that Indian cinema has not done before. In doing so, it serves as a step forward in addressing homophobia and normalising homosexuality in India.

Made in Heaven uses a wedding-planning company, named Made in Heaven, as its central setting to advance separate plots for its nine episodes; each episode focuses on a different client. The company is founded by Karan Mehra, a homosexual man who is financially struggling due to his previously failed business, and Tara Khanna (Sobhita Dhulipala), Karan's close friend whose rich husband (Jim Sarbh) has invested in their company. At every *Made in Heaven* wedding, Karan and Tara run into multiple political, economic and socio-cultural problems, meanwhile also navigating the complex maze of their own lives.

Through the development of Karan's character, we get insight into the performativity and politics of homosexuality in India. Karan is closeted, debt-ridden and struggling for work with his wedding-planning company. He is legally and socio-culturally a sexual outcast, but that is not obvious when the audience first encounters him. The audience is first introduced to other aspects of his character, like his insufficient income, his close friends, his professional struggles and his entanglement with moneylenders before learning about his sexuality. Using this intentional order, the creators of the show invite the audience's emotional investment in Karan's relatable socio-economic struggles. The audience gets no hint about his sexuality at all because of an absence of stereotypical queer mannerisms such as flamboyance, effeminacy or aesthetics, all characteristics which appear inseparable from characters in most other queer portrayals in Indian cinema.[12] This normalising portrait of homosexuality humanises Karan for the audience.

Karan's personal struggles are thus introduced not as centred around his sexuality, but rather as the result of a number of other socio-economic factors. When his sexual identity is finally revealed, it is just another part of his life. Right after asking for a loan from his business partner, Tara, Karan leaves to meet a man, Utsav (Anhad Singh), at a dimly lit bar. So far, the audience is ignorant of Karan's sexual identity. Later that night, Karan opens a door into his rented apartment, which is like a door to invite the audience into the privacy of his sexuality. The camera pans between Karan and Utsav, their faces momentarily lit up, before they are devoured by the darkness of the room again. In this significant scene, the show of light and dark symbolises their indecision about whether to come into the light with their homosexuality or hide it in the dark. Then the camera captures Utsav and Karan's first kiss, which is also the first kiss in the series. With the suggestive sound of opening zippers, Utsav drops down in front of Karan while Karan's face is pre-euphoric. The next shot is of them asleep in bed the next morning, interrupted when Karan's landlord, Ramesh Gupta (Vinay Pathak), knocks on his door to tell Karan that he has purchased a new Honda City car. In these scenes, the series shows two simultaneous situations: homosexual Karan and his one-night stand in the upstairs rented apartment, and the heterosexual landlord's middle-class family downstairs.

This morning sequence, played out between Karan and his landlord Ramesh's family, highlights the epistemological anxieties of both homosexual individuals and the heterosexual couple. Ramesh is a married but closeted gay man. From her house, Ramesh's wife, Renu (Ayesha Raza), witnesses Karan bid goodbye to Utsav in the street. Unaware of both her husband and Karan's secret, Renu feels apprehensive about the homosocial interaction that took place between Karan and Utsav. She pointedly tells Ramesh to do something about Karan's *friends* [emphasis added] since they have a 'young daughter in the house', a daughter who, as we learn later, is unbothered by Karan's sexual identity. As the series progresses, Karan is watched by both the landlord and his wife, albeit for different reasons.

In a later episode, having secretly installed a surveillance camera in Karan's bedroom, Ramesh watches Karan have sex. The camera shows two male bodies intertwined on the bed in the dim, romantic light – bodies contorting in pleasure, unaware that they are being watched and recorded. This scene portrays the men as homosexual objects of desire for the voyeuristic pleasure of the married landlord. The camera, from the beautifully shot scene of queer desire, pans over to the hidden face of the landlord, gradually exposing his face both visually and metaphorically. The landlord is unblinkingly staring at his laptop screen where Karan is having sex with a man. The camera then zooms out to show the landlord masturbating to the homosexual sex. It is important to remember that this is the first scene where the landlord, despite having his wife in the house, is shown engaged in any sexual or romantic activity.

Renu discovers the recording on her husband's laptop and her apprehensions about Karan now turn into a real threat; Karan's homosexuality has the potential to uproot the heterosexual nucleus of her middle-class family. To placate his wife, Ramesh calls Karan a 'dirty man' and says he recorded his sex to 'collect evidence'. Despite not accusing her husband, it is evident that Renu is implicitly aware of his homosexuality. With accusatory glances, she asks him to give the video footage to the police. It turns out, then, that it is not their daughter she is worried about, but the disturbance of the heteropatriarchal order by any non-heteronormative sexuality. To her mind, their daughter symbolises the reproductive machine who will continue the cycle of heterosexual desire and production for the heteropatriarchal Indian society. Hence, they must save her by trying to eliminate or at least render invisible non-normative sexualities and the perceived threats associated with them.

The young daughter (Yashaswini Dayama), however, confronts her father about setting a surveillance camera in Karan's bedroom, which, according to the landlord's lie, was his office security camera. He, once again, calls Karan a 'dirty, disgusting man' whom he reported to the police to protect his daughter. But the daughter responds: 'Protect me? He is gay. He is actually one of the few men I am safe with in Delhi.' Upon hearing his daughter say 'there is nothing wrong with being gay' and 'it's okay to love who you love', Ramesh has an epiphanic facial expression as if he realises the normalcy of his own homosexual desire that he had denied and then projected onto Karan.

Karan faces the same homophobic treatment of denial and projection from his mother in his childhood and a policeman in jail after he is arrested when Ramesh reports him for his homosexuality. While Karan sits in a dirty prison cell, a policeman tries to convince and then force himself on him for sex. Upon Karan's refusal, the policeman beats him up. Karan's homosexuality had brought this violence upon him in the past too. In a flashback, we see that Karan's mother (Preeti Mamgain) pushes open the bathroom door to walk in on a young Karan having sex with his classmate. She blames the other boy for corrupting Karan and asks him to leave the house. Afterwards, she picks up a cricket bat and beats Karan. She learns that Karan is gay but it remains an open, unacknowledged secret between Karan and his mother. This traumatic experience forces Karan to deny his sexuality and even act like a homophobe and make fun of the friend with whom he was caught in the bathroom. The punishment for Karan's homosexuality leaves emotional and physical marks on him in the form of his mother's cricket bat and the policeman's kicks.

While Karan recurrently experiences his sexual identity as a burden, other closeted gay men make different choices. In an early episode, Karan's company Made in Heaven gets hired to organise a wedding. To Karan's and the audience's surprise, the groom is Utsav, the man who was Karan's first gay encounter in the series. Interestingly, the groom tries to hook up with Karan in the bathroom and later even at Karan's house, while Karan continues to plan the groom's heterosexual wedding. Utsav also pleads with Karan not to share the secret of his sexuality with anyone. Karan, riddled with guilt, tells the bride, who is an old friend of his. Instead of breaking off the wedding, she fires Made in Heaven as the wedding planner and hires their rival, Harmony.

Later on, when Karan is released from prison, the landlord compliments him for his bravery for coming out as homosexual by saying *'yahan tau umer guzr jati hai apnay aap ko chupatay'* ('some people waste their whole lives trying to hide their truth'). All of these incidents validate R. Raj Rao's comment regarding homosocial and homoerotic interactions to say that homosexuality exists in hidden yet cognisant ways in India as something that is known but not openly acknowledged (2000).

Paradoxically, Karan attempts to minimise his intrusion or interaction with Ramesh's heterosexual family, but it is the 'ideal', 'safe' heterosexual community that consistently attempts to voyeuristically and physically invade, decipher and disrupt Karan's sexuality: the landlord's wife keeps an eye on Karan from her window, the landlord fixes a spy camera in Karan's bedroom to watch him have sex, a teenage Karan's mother walks in on him in the bathroom and catches him with a boy, a policeman intrudes when Karan is kissing a man in his car, another policeman tries to force himself on Karan in prison. Numerous incidents of heterosexual invasions of and attacks on Karan's gay identity challenge the popular notion that homosexuality is an existential threat to heterosexuality.

Although homosexuality is still problematised in India, it is the heterosexual relationships in the show that fall apart without any external threats to their sexual identity. Faiza (Kalki Koechlin) is divorced, Tara's marriage is failing as her husband Adil is cheating on her and Renu is scared that the gay man living in their property will threaten her marriage. Karan, as a friend and wedding organiser, tries to save the heterosexual marriages. The already married and those just getting married are all anxious, worried and painfully unhappy. Even heterosexual sex is represented as riddled with anxiety, for example Tara and Adil have sex only for reproduction. Likewise, Adil and his mistress Faiza (who is also Adil's wife's best friend) are afraid of getting caught in the act, the landlord and his wife seemingly do not have sex anymore, the bride Harsimran sleeps with a famous actor on the night of her wedding, a wife who is chosen via a beauty pageant finds out that her Indian-American husband is impotent but he blames her for her sexual naivety and Jaspreet 'Jazz' Kaur (Shivani Raghuvanshi) goes back to her lover after getting fired from work and has sex with an absent-looking facial expression; other episodic heterosexual romances also appear devoid of unbridled sexual pleasure.

Meanwhile, *Made in Heaven* enlivens the gay sex scenes and makes them sensual for the audience. Pankhari Shukla credits the show's writing of Karan's complex character and calls his relationships with other men 'refreshing, unabashed, multi-dimensional' (2019). Most of Karan's interactions with men in his apartment are shown in the dark. There is never enough light to see their facial expressions, but the first gay scene in the show is in the best light. Karan wakes up after making love to Utsav and is bathed in sunlight, clearly showing his face and leaving no question about his sexuality.

QUEER LOVE 139

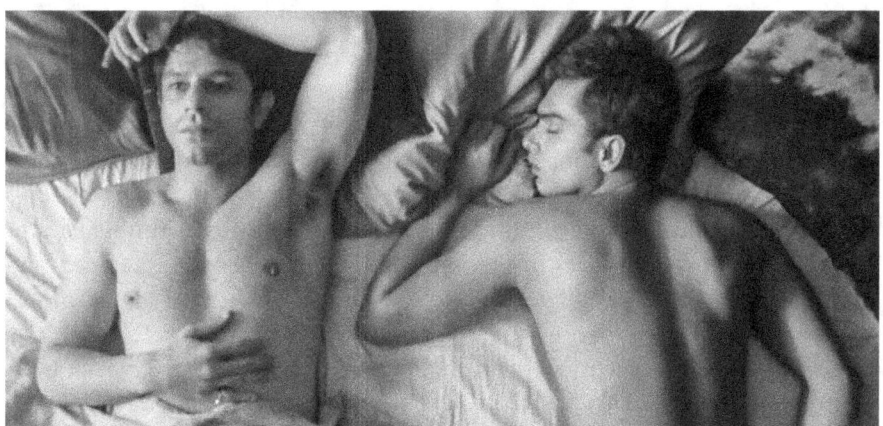

Figure 7.1 Karan and his lover in the light.

While Karan struggles for validation of his own sexual identity, professionally he weds heterosexual couples and brings lovers together. In this nuanced and comprehensive commentary on rich people's weddings, the series exposes the problematic basis of heteropatriarchal families. These marriages provide the audience with an insider's view on issues like demands for dowry, loans for the (in)famous big Indian wedding, forced marriages for political advancement, the persistence of obsolete traditions at the expense of women, prejudice against inter-class or inter-religion marriages or the unchallenged power of wealthy patriarchs that get away with all offences, even rape. It is these issues that represent a threat to the heterosexual patriarchal order, not Karan's homosexuality. Ironically, it is Karan who, as a wedding planner, must fix these problems and restore the order to ensure a smooth wedding to help maintain heteronormativity.

But this heteronormative order consistently threatens Karan himself, both socio-culturally and legally. The policeman, while manhandling Karan, says, 'We have an arrest warrant for you under Section 377.' When Tara and Adil go to jail for Karan's bail, the police officer in charge informs them 'there is a complaint against Karan. Article 377. Homosex.' Even their lawyer informs them 'it is very difficult to get bail on Article 377. It is actually an unbailable offence.' Hence, the annulment of Section 377, which happened after the series takes place, has rendered homosexuality visible, and legitimised it as a category of identity.

Karan, after getting bail, decides to file a Public Interest Litigation against Section 377.[13] He shares: 'If I hadn't gotten arrested, I might have never filed a PIL.' After realising the importance of individual action for collective rights, he also appears on TV to discuss the PIL and the rights of the gay community.

During his debate on TV, Karan shares that Section 377 criminalises 11 per cent of the Indian population. But he, looking directly into the camera to address the audience, expresses his faith that the 'Indian judiciary will uphold that Citizens of India are truly free to love and have sex with consenting adults of all genders'. Though Section 377 was revoked, the gay community still faces socio-cultural homophobia, but they no longer have to face any legal repercussions for their identity. With legal protection in place, and portrayals like the one in *Made in Heaven* growing in importance and impact, the gay community has gained more acceptance and protection. Legalisation of gay sex, then, sends out the message that India accepts its queer citizens and is committed to protect them, which eventually helps to improve further India's image on the global map as a secular, inclusive and democratic power.

Made in Heaven addresses the issue of the legalisation of gay sex in a global context in the scene where Karan is interrupted while kissing a foreigner in his car. While they are kissing, a policeman knocks on the car window, whereupon the male foreign visitor panics. But Karan promises that he will take care of it and tries to bribe the policeman. The policeman, in turn, attempts to extort more money from Karan by threatening to charge him with both drinking and homosexuality. Though Karan was harassed and extorted, he apologises to the foreigner who had to go through this experience for kissing a man in India. When they go back to Karan's apartment, the male foreign visitor expresses his concerns:

> The Foreigner: How do you live like that here?
> Karan: It's not all that bad.
> The Foreigner: We almost got arrested and it is my second day here.
> Karan: Nothing happened.
> The Foreigner: What if you couldn't afford to bribe them? We would be in jail right now.

This dialogue captures the reality that India's legalisation of gay sex and acceptance of its gay citizens will help enhance its image as the protector of human rights in a globalised world. Thus, it positions India as an important, progressive and liberal economic power. Another notable point here is that this scene shows a foreigner's experience in India as opposed to previous movies where gay Indian men always live in Western countries and visit their homes briefly, as in *Kapoor and Sons* (Shakun Batra 2016).

While many of the gay characters in previous films were diasporic, Karan's character is rooted in his home country. Multiple people offer to whisk him away from homophobic India, where he faces police brutality and invasion of privacy just for being gay. Despite having the option to leave India and go to a Western country where gay sex and marriage are legal, Karan chooses to stay.

His decision to stay in India is a reclamation of his space and home as an Indian citizen. Additionally, it encourages alternative ways of thinking about nationhood and its relation to personhood.

Along with shifting the onscreen representation of the gay community, *Made in Heaven* also inaugurates a new era for viewership practices in India. Appropriating Bakshi and Sen's discussion of Bombay cinema as a significant 'cultural referent' that could 'affect public opinions on different issues' (2012: 181), I suggest that streaming services like Amazon Prime are quickly becoming the new 'cultural referent' which is more suitable for contemporary India and for the large population of local and diasporic Indians and non-Indians. While most other films posit gay relationships against heterosexual marriages where one threatens the other, *Made in Heaven* shows the possibility of coexistence, where both heterosexual and homosexual relationships go through their own challenges. It is not too early to say that *Made in Heaven* forecasts a brighter, better and more equitable future for gender and sexual identities in India.

NOTES

1. The Shiv Sena, a Hindu militant organisation, attacked cinemas and declared the lesbian sex scene in the film *Fire* an attack on 'Hindu culture and civilisation'. See BBC News (1998).
2. The Censor Board banned *Unfreedom* due to its homosexual and religious content, which, the Board said, might 'ignite unnatural passions' and Hindu–Muslim fights. It was later released on Netflix India. See Pathak (2015). Similarly, *The Pink Mirror* was banned for transsexual and homosexual content. See Smith (2004).
3. Section 377 states: '"Unnatural offences" – Whoever voluntarily has carnal intercourse against the order of nature with any man, woman or animal, shall be punished with I[imprisonment for life], or with imprisonment of either description for a term which may extend to ten years, and shall also be liable to fine.' See Rao, T. S. S. and K. S. Jacob (2014).
4. According to this 2012 report, the Indian government reported 2.5 million homosexual people in India, 7 per cent of whom are affected by AIDS. Available at <https://www.bbc.com/news/world-asia-india-17363200>
5. Section 24 (I) delegalised Section 377 of the Indian Penal Code on 2 July 2009. The decision declares that Section 377 'unfairly targets the homosexual or gay community. It also unreasonably and unjustly infringes upon the right of privacy, both zonal and decisional. It also conveys the message that homosexuals are of less value than other people, demeans them, and unconstitutionally infringes upon their right to live with dignity' (Section 24 (I): 22).
6. See 'India court legalises gay sex in landmark ruling' (2018).
7. Since *Fire* is directed by Deepa Mehta, an Indo-Canadian director, it is a stretch to include this film under the Bollywood umbrella, but there are important continuities between *Fire* and conventions of Bollywood melodrama: (1) trials and tribulations of difficult love, (2) conventions of romantic love, (3) drag performances . . . for the play of forbidden love and transgressive desire, (4) privileging romantic love . . ., (5) lovers are always united (Srinivasan 2013: 201).

8. *I Am* is an anthology film based on real events. 'Omar', one of the four films in the anthology, is based on resources from online portal *Gay Bombay* and tells the story of a homosexual man from whom the police extort money by trapping him in a planned homosexual encounter.
9. It is notable that Karan Johar, who co-produced both of these films with his father Yash Johar, has worked towards initiating a debate on homophobia in popular cinema via a series of films. For more, see Sahni (2017). 'The evolution of homosexuality in Karan Johar's films has been slow but worth appreciating', *ScoopWhoop*, March 2017. Available at <https://www.scoopwhoop.com/the-evolution-of-homosexuality-in-karan-johars-films/>
10. *The Journey* (Ligy J. Pullappally 2004), a Malayalam-language film, and *Heroine* (Madhu Bhandarkar 2012) subtly explore lesbian desire. A few Indian diasporic directors also explore lesbian love, like in *Nina's Heavenly Delights* (Partibha Parmar 2006) and *Chutney Popcorn* (Nisha Ganatra 1999), but their work does not fall in the category of Bollywood films, and neither is it popular in India.
11. Measured in PPP (purchasing power parity) dollars.
12. Some films, like *Kapoor and Sons*, depart from this stereotypical portrayal of gay men, but they keep the homosexual identity of their characters at the margins.
13. Public Interest Litigation 'is not defined in any statute or act'. Rather, judges interpret it to 'consider the *intent of public* at large'. It can be filed against the government in the case of (a) public injury and (b) public wrong for the enforcement of basic human rights of weaker sections. See Desai and Bali (2013).

WORKS CITED

Agrawal, Ravi (2019), 'The great Indian streaming wars', *Foreign Policy*, 2019. Available at <https://foreignpolicy.com/2019/09/27/the-great-indian-streaming-wars/>

Arora, Priya (2019), 'In 2019, Netflix and Amazon set their sights on India', *New York Times*, 30 December 2019.

— (2019), 'An Indian TV show points the way for a new generation', *The New York Times*, 9 April 2019.

Bakshi, Kaustav and Parjanya Sen (2012), 'India's queer expressions on-screen: The aftermath of the reading down of Section 377 of the Indian Penal Code', *New Cinemas: Journal of Contemporary Film*, 10 :2, pp. 167–83.

Bali, Mahabal Kamayani and Mihir Desai (2013), 'Introduction to Public Interest Litigation', Accessed 29 July 2020. Available at <https://web.archive.org/web/20131005010030/http://www.karmayog.org/pil/pil_10720.htm>

Bandyopadhyay, Sibaji (2007), 'Approaching the present: The pre-text – the *Fire* controversy', in Brinda Bose and Subhabrata Bhattacharya (eds), *The Phobic and the Erotic: The Politics of Sexualities in Contemporary India*, New Delhi: Seagull.

BBC News (1998), 'World: South Asia Hindu militants stage lesbian film attacks', BBC, 3 December 1998.

— (2018), 'India court legalises gay sex in landmark ruling', 6 September 2018. Available at <https://www.bbc.com/news/world-asia-india-45429664>

Bhandari, Aparita (2019), 'Amazon's *Made in Heaven* pulls back the veil on "Crazy-Rich" Indian Weddings', *NOW*, 12 March 2019.

Dasgupta, Rohit K. and Steven Baker (2013), 'Mistaken identities and queer framing in Bollywood: "Dosti," "Yaarana" and "Dostana"', *The Quint: An Interdisciplinary Quarterly from the North 91*, 4: 4, pp. 90–107.

Devasundaram, Ashvin I. (2016), 'Bollywood's soft power: Branding the nation, sustaining a meta-hegemony', *New Cinemas*, 14: 1, pp. 51–70. Available at <https://doi.org/10.1386/ncin.14.1.51_1>

Gokulsing, K. Moti and Wimal Dissanayake (2013), *Routledge Handbook of Indian Cinemas*, Oxon and New York: Routledge. Available at <https://doi.org/10.4324/9780203556054>

Gopinath, G. (2000), 'Queering Bollywood: Alternative sexualities in popular Indian cinema', *Journal of Homosexuality*, 39: 3–4, pp. 283–97. Available at <https://doi.org/10.1300/J082v39n03_13>

Gosh, Shohini (2005), 'The closet is ajar', *Outlook India*, 30 May 2005. Available at <https://www.outlookindia.com/magazine/story/the-closet-is-ajar/227507>

— (2002), 'Queer pleasure for queer people: Film television and sexuality in India', in Ruth Vanita (ed.), *Queering India: Same-Sex Love and Eroticism in Indian Culture and Society*, New York: Routledge.

— (2010), *Fire: A Queer Film Classic*, Vancouver: Arsenal Pulp Press.

GQ Staff (2019), 'Arjun Mathur talks about his role as Karan Mehra from *Made in Heaven*', *GQ India*, 3 April 2019. Available at <https://www.gqindia.com/content/arjun-mathur-made-in-heaven-gay-character-karan-mehra-reveals-what-it-was-like-playing-a-homosexual-character-three-times-in-his-career-preparing-for-made-in-heaven-season-2>

Holtzman, Dinah (2010), 'Between yaars: The queering of Dosti in contemporary Bollywood films", in Rini Mehta and Rajeshwari Pandharipande (eds), *Bollywood and Globalization Indian Popular Cinema, Nation, and Diaspora*, London and New York: Anthem Press, pp. 111–28.

IANS (2019), '*Made in Heaven* review: Possibly the best Indian web series so far', *The New Indian Express*, 8 March 2019.

Mehta, Rini Bhattacharya and Rajeshwari V. Pandharipande (eds) (2010), *Bollywood and Globalization: Indian Popular Cinema, Nation, and Diaspora*, London and New York: Anthem Press.

Munshi, Shoma (2010), *Prime Time Soap Operas on Indian Television*, New Delhi: Routledge.

Pathak, Ankur (2015), 'Board bans film on gays, claims it'll ignite "unnatural passions"', *India Times*, 28 March 2015. Available at <https://mumbaimirror.indiatimes.com/entertainment/bollywood/Board-bans-film-on-gays-claims-itll-ignite-unnatural-passion/articleshow/46720831.cms>

— (2019), '*Made in Heaven* review: Zoya Akhtar's show exposes our vulgar obsession with social perceptions', *Huffington Post*, 12 March 2019. Available at <https://www.huffpost.com/archive/in/entry/made-in-heaven-review-zoya-akhtars-show-exposes-our-vulgar-obsession-with-social-perceptions_in_5c81327ae4b06ff26ba665a7>

Qureshi, Bilal (2019', '*Made in Heaven* offers a groundbreaking look behind Big Fat Indian Weddings', *The Washington Post*, 4 April 2019. Available at <https://www.washingtonpost.com/entertainment/made-in-heaven-offers-a-groundbreaking-look-behind-big-fat-indian-weddings/2019/04/03/7d4d3a68-561a-11e9-814f-e2f46684196e_story.html>

Rao, R. Raj (2000), 'Memories pierce the heart: Homoeroticism, Bollywood-style', *Journal of Homosexuality*, 39: 3–4, pp. 299–306. Available at <https://doi.org/10.1300/J082v39n03_14>

Rao, Rukmini (2019), 'Long road for Netflix to catch up with rivals in India', *Business Today*, 23 July 2019. Available at <https://www.businesstoday.in/technology/news/long-road-for-netflix-to-catch-up-with-rivals-in-india/story/367082.html>

Rao, T. S. Sathyanarayana and K. S. Jacob (2014), 'The reversal on gay rights in India', *Indian Journal of Psychiatry*, 56: 1. Available at <http://www.indianjpsychiatry.org/text.asp?2014/56/1/1/124706>

Sahni, Devika (2017), 'The evolution of homosexuality in Karan Johar's films has been slow but worth appreciating', *ScoopWhoop*, 7 March 2017. Available at <https://www.scoopwhoop.com/the-evolution-of-homosexuality-in-karan-johars-films/>

Sedgwick, Eve Kosofsky (1990), *Epistemology of the Closet*, Los Angeles: University of California Press.

Sharma, Sanjukta (2019), '*Made in Heaven* review: Strong performances and sharp writing, but the weddings get in the way', *Scroll-In*, 9 March 2019.

Shrivastava, Aditi (2019), 'Amazon Prime doubles India subscribers in 18 Months, 50% new members from smaller cities', *Economic Times*, 25 June 2019. Available at <https://tech.economictimes.indiatimes.com/news/internet/amazon-prime-doubles-india-subscribers-in-18-months-50-new-members-from-smaller-cities/69937471>

Shukla, Pankhari (2019), '*Made in Heaven*: A milestone in depiction of gay characters', *The Quint*, 12 March 2019. Available at <https://www.thequint.com/entertainment/hot-on-web/made-in-heaven-a-milestone-in-depiction-of-gay-characters>

Smith, Neil (2004), 'UK premiere for Indian drag film', *BBC News Online*, 6 May 2004. Available at <http://news.bbc.co.uk/2/hi/entertainment/3689509.stm>

Srinivasan, Rama (2013), 'Queer times in Bollywood', in K. Moti Gokulsing and Wimal Dissanayake (eds), *Routledge Handbook of Indian Cinemas*, London and New York: Routledge, pp. 193–205.

Srivastva, Soumya (2019), '*Made in Heaven* review: The best Desi original by Amazon Prime, it unmasks the shiny lies of Big Fat Indian Weddings', *Hindustan Times*, 9 March 2019. Available at <https://www.hindustantimes.com/tv/made-in-heaven-review-zoya-akhtar-does-it-again-gives-amazon-prime-its-best-desi-original-yet/story-YONqoQxcOSwHiLx7ftJb2J.html>

TAM (2015), 'TAM Annual Universe Update – 2015'. Accessed 31 July 2020. Available at <https://web.archive.org/web/20150702013518/http://www.tamindia.com/ref_pdf/Overview_Universe_Update_2015.pdf>

Vanita, R. and S. Kidwai (2000), *Same-Sex Love in India: Readings from Literature and History*, New York: Macmillan.

PART III

A New Era of Gendered Politics

CHAPTER 8

Conflicted and Confused: The Changing Complexity of Masculinity in Zoya Akhtar's Films

Amber Shields

THE YEAR OF THE MAN, AGAIN

In 2018, India and the Hindi film industry underwent their #MeToo Movement. Starting with actress Tanushree Dutta's accusation of sexual harassment against actor Nana Patekar, several women came forward with their stories of sexual harassment and assault. Though these high-profile discussions resulted in some action, such as director Sajid Khan being forced to step down from *Housefull 4* (Farhad Samji 2019) and a topical fictional account with the film *Section 375* (Ajay Bahl 2019),[1] the spotlight on gender inequality and violence resulted in neither immediate nor powerful change. A large part of the industry quickly moved away from these conversations, as exhibited by the productions that came out in their wake. The fifteen highest-grossing Indian releases the following year were all dominated by one or more male protagonists and, with the exception of *Mission Mangal* (Jagan Shakti), which had an all-star female cast alongside superstar Akshay Kumar, provided sparse glimpses into the lives and experiences of the female protagonists.[2] Reflections on shifting perceptions of men and masculinity, central to the #MeToo Movement, were also limited as many of the action and comedy hits of 2019 provided little space for introspection. Among these films, the dramas *Gully Boy* (Zoya Akhtar) and *Kabir Singh* (Sandeep Reddy Vanga) stand out as cases that, through the distinct struggles of their male protagonists, highlight some of the greater gender discussion and conflicts of the time.

The differences between the two expose the multiple issues at stake as a new generation struggles to define not only their identity but their masculinity. *Gully Boy*'s Murad (Ranveer Singh) is poor and Muslim, left out of his country's economic growth and Hindu-dominated politics. His demure manner reflects his ostracised position, and he struggles to reconcile his dreams with his nation's and family's expectations. *Kabir Singh*'s Kabir (Shahid Kapoor) is rich, smart and privileged in every way. He is not only driven by but easily acts on his emotions and desires, able to evade consequences either through his own charm or his family's financial and legal intervention. Murad must learn to find his voice through his personal journey. Kabir must learn to tame his voice but has no desire to do so – he knows exactly what he wants and violently pursues his desires, physically and emotionally abusing those he loves and himself to follow his whims. While Murad shows a confrontation with different aspects of identity in a period of change, and the subsequent potential for growth, Kabir's lack of introspection as well as society's concession to and almost celebration of his behaviour (it was 2019's second-highest-grossing Indian film) represents a toxic masculinity that makes #MeToo a movement rather than a singular case.

While these presentations of masculinity show that men still clearly dominate Hindi cinema, their portrayal is varied, representing a point of reflection and inflection in which past assumptions and privileges of masculinity are 'challenged' (Dasgupta and Gokulsing 2013: 12). The questions that these protagonists, as well as society through the cultural marker of cinema, find themselves confronting are: How does one reconstruct an identity and masculinity that can find a place in the changing world? What does this mean not only for men, but society as it negotiates new gender identities and roles?

Throughout her career, Zoya Akhtar has portrayed men negotiating these changes as they find their masculinity and identity being reshaped by societal shifts. While Akhtar has stated, 'I feel men are easier to depict than women. Women are way more complicated, more unpredictable and more layered' (Chaturvedi and Kumar 2015: 136), her portrayal of conflicted and complex male characters paints a different picture. By depicting masculinity in the midst of change, Akhtar's films and streaming series actually contribute to highlighting the complexities of men and the challenges they face, as well as the resulting tension and violence these can animate. Her work thus highlights a layered vulnerability in masculinity that needs to be examined. Akhtar's films and male protagonists embrace the complications of this change and give space to negotiate its nuances. Looking at the male characters in her films *Zindagi Na Milegi Dobara* (2011), *Dil Dhadakne Do* (2015), *Gully Boy* and her streaming series *Made in Heaven* (2019), this chapter will explore how Akhtar's male protagonists navigate neoliberal challenges to identity creation by negotiating changes in values, generations, class and politics as they form new masculine identities. Further, it will emphasise how Akhtar's portrayal of these journeys is unique as she allows for a rare glimpse at and acceptance of male vulnerability that is often foregone in 'hero'-centred narratives. Drawing on a close reading of her works and regarding their position as part of a larger, multi-faceted social dialogue, it will position Akhtar as a critical writer and director examining multiple aspects of the evolution of gender roles in an era marked by change.

THE MALE HERO: FROM SCREEN TO SOCIETY

Cinema has been a space to create identity in a nation that spent the latter half of the twentieth century reimagining itself after colonial rule,[3] as well as to 'negotiate notions of traditional and modern India' (Thomas 1995: 158). At the centre of several studies underscoring the strong relationship between cinema and the country's socio-historical development is the male hero and his larger-than-life status both onscreen and off. Sumita Chakravarty emphasises this influential role, describing how in Hindi cinema, 'the male hero [is] the center and source of narrative meaning' and the male star, as he successfully moves between films, becomes 'a popular cultural icon, a receptacle, like a wax mold, into which may be poured the social collectivity's needs and desires of the moment' (2008: 94, 86). Beyond the character, it is the male body itself which is 'idealized' in Hindi cinema and 'symbolically aligned with the changing aspirations of the nation' (Mubarki 2018: 2).[4]

More recently, these identity negotiations have been heavily influenced by one of the biggest markers of the global and Indian twenty-first century: neoliberalism. While India has gone through several stages of opening up the economy (Desai 2016), the Structural Adjustment Programme of 1991 stands out as it 'intensified India's encounter with global capital', thus ushering in the new experience of neoliberalism (Oza 2012: 2). This 'intensified' growth of foreign multinational corporations operating and investing in India, the expansion of the middle class and its mass consumerism, as well as India's growing emphasis on shaping its image abroad, both to connect with its Non-Resident Indian (NRI) population as well as the large foreign markets now open, influenced some of the great changes the country experienced post-1991.[5]

Exploring neoliberalism's effects on masculinity, Andrea Cornwall notes how the accelerated and amplified access to local and global ideas and commodities has brought the 'promise of new freedoms [which] has produced new desires, new identities and new ways of relating and being' (2016: 1). However, while possibilities abound, access to them for different genders, classes and religions has remained stratified as neoliberalism has not brought the means of realising these desires for all. Further, the responsibility of obtaining these desires is passed from systems to individuals, leading to some of neoliberalism's anxieties as 'its emphasis on self-making and self-management' result in 'the pressures of entrepreneurial masculinity [and] individualization of success and failure' (2016: 10). The increased pressure on the individual to control and craft one's own identity through one's work, family, love and body leads to an identity journey that has the potential to be fatiguing or consuming as it is never settled.

Neoliberalism's increased pressure on the individual, compounded by the erosion of systemic support, has over the years resulted in growing insecurity and power gaps that new groups have risen to fill, notably Hindutva and its biggest party, the Bharatiya Janata Party (BJP).[6] Though neoliberalism's political implications in India will not be discussed here, the rise of Hindutva is worth noting as it has created its own particular national masculinity impacting the social and cultural sphere. Rupal Oza argues that as a result of this intensified neoliberalism, India has begun to lose '. . . control onto national culture and identity', to which it has responded by the 'fortifying [of] rigid gender and sexual identities' (2012: 2). Hindutva, whose increasing political power drives this move, has responded by building an image of an undefeatable warrior masculinity, that manifests in the 'hypermasculinity' seen in films. From Salman Khan to Hrithik Roshan, the hero has become a muscular demigod able to save himself, loved ones and the nation from corruption and injustice or the threats of 'outsider' others (increasingly named as Pakistani or Muslim terrorists). This image is not only used locally to garner pride, but has also become an important exportable commodity, as 'the Indian male body, inscribed with the country's nationalistic ambitions and symbolic of a heterosexualized hypermasculinity' (Balaji 2014: 2) carries the image of a strong Indian nation overseas.

As represented in society and onscreen, this image threatens to prolong a situation in which masculine dominance is 'seen as immutable and natural' and free from examination (Banerjee 2005: 7), leading to patriarchal power and the gender violence it can enact.[7] Yet this also comes at a time when the neoliberal impetus for self-reflection and self-making, as well as the growing space for previously subordinated or silenced discourses, has made masculinity a point of examination that needs to justify the forms it takes. While questioning notions of gender identity may lead to, as Judith Butler noted in her seminal work about feminism, a 'certain sense of trouble' (1990: vii), she reminds that a sense of trouble should be embraced rather than feared. This point of reflection and inflection of masculinity can thus at once hold a sense of conflict and unease while also the promise of new possibilities, as currently seen onscreen in the diverse portrayals of masculinity. While *Kabir Singh* and its protagonist take for granted masculinity as the dominant discourse and seem to fear the trouble of questioning it, *Gully Boy* finds some necessary trouble with presumed dominance and faces the questions that this trouble brings. Though both films bring to the fore the challenged notion of masculinity in the midst of a painful transition, Akhtar's film presents a dynamic portrayal of these struggles and the grace with which they can be navigated and represented. As the male hero continues to hold this influential and dominant place onscreen, this chapter will examine what is happening in cinematic representations of different aspects of masculinity, from values to politics, being negotiated in this moment. Further, it will ask what exactly do the films of Zoya Akhtar, written, directed and now even produced by women,[8] contribute to this discussion of twenty-first-century Indian male identity?

THE NEOLIBERAL STORY OF SELF-DISCOVERY

Arjun: 'Dude, it's your life.'

Akhtar's films are journeys of self-discovery. Her first film, *Luck by Chance* (*LBC*), follows the intertwining stories of Sona (Konkona Sen Sharma) and Vikram (Farhan Akhtar) as both struggle to become Bollywood actors. When Vikram falls into a leading role by luck, and a few well-placed lines with the right people, he is propelled into a consuming stardom where he becomes so focused on his goal that he leaves behind those who supported him. In the end, Vikram realises what he has lost through his self-absorption and tries to repair the relationship with Sona that he squandered on his rise to fame. However, his realisation comes too late, for in the meantime she too has come to her own realisation not only about Vikram's true narcissistic character but about what makes her happy.

While *LBC* culminates in the self-realisation that will lead the protagonists on separate journeys, Akhtar's second film, *ZNMD*, is filled with moments of introspection and self-discovery for three friends who set off on a literal journey through Spain. It is here, on the road and away from family, partners and jobs, that they learn to put aside societal concerns and embrace the new freedoms of a neoliberal society in which they are responsible for their lives. The film supports this value shift as it becomes a journey of discovery for each protagonist, who, supported by his friends, works to find his own values. Arjun (Hrithik Roshan) must learn to choose between money/career and happiness, Imraan (Farhan Akhtar) confronts the question of what loyalty and family mean and Kabir (Abhay Deol) must ask himself if he really wants to get married or is doing it because of pressure from his fiancée Natasha (Kalki Koechlin) and family. The film is set up to promote and aid them in this journey of self-discovery in several ways. First, they are removed from their home and placed in a foreign land. Second, their road trip consists of them undertaking adventure sports, where each must confront a fear. Finally, the forced proximity to each other as well as the time pauses allowed by a road trip create a perfect space for reflection.

The thrill of the adventure sports they undergo together is juxtaposed with meditative moments where the characters are shown grappling with these questions on inner journeys. This is a marked shift from past journeys of the male protagonist in films where there is little time for self-reflection. In the films of the 1970s and 1980s, Amitabh Bachchan's 'Angry Young Man' characters 'are always doers, achievers, always on the move. They never sit or meditate . . . There is no hesitation either, no moments of self-doubt; they are quite clear about what they want and how to achieve it' (Kazmi 1998: 140–1). The romantic heroes of 1990s superhit family dramas like *Hum Aapke Hain Koun. . .!* (Sooraj Barjatya 1994) or *Dilwale Dulhania Le Jayenge* (Aditya Chopra 1995) know who they love and must convince the family, whose desires are still placed above those of the individual, to support them. *ZNMD*, on the other hand, gives space for and emphasises the importance of contemplation. In that sense it mirrors *Dil Chahta Hai* (2001), a watershed film by Akhtar's brother Farhan Akhtar on which Zoya Akhtar worked as first assistant and casting director. Highlighting the importance of male friendship in providing support in shifting times, *DCH* too encouraged self-reflection and growth of the male protagonists whether through their friendships or other relationships.

Akhtar emphasises these spaces of self-reflection in *ZNMD* more; there are moments of underwater majesty when Arjun dives with Laila (Katrina Kaif) and then is unable to speak afterwards because of the impact of the dive, or silent moments of long car rides when the friends have nothing to do but stare at the passing scenery. Some of these moments are accompanied by instrumental background music, others with Imraan's poetry (written by Javed Akhtar) which speaks of the life questions the protagonists are experiencing. It is exactly these moments when they are silent, not doing or achieving, that they are able to retreat from their reality to confront self-doubts and grow with new understandings.

This is a journey about individual growth and development in which the 'hero' is no longer asked to use his masculinity to right a greater societal wrong but rather himself. Though encounters with others help shape him, he is in charge of creating change, with the neoliberal focus being on 'self-making and self-management' (Cornwall 2016: 10). Thus, when Arjun reminds Kabir that he doesn't have to marry Natasha and it's 'his life', he does not volunteer to tell Kabir's fiancée and family that the engagement is off, nor does he even say Kabir must break off the engagement, he leaves Kabir's fate in his hands only. Similarly, while Laila makes an intervention in Arjun's life, reminding him to embrace the things that make him happy, she is not the one who tells Arjun he must quit his consuming job, he must come to this decision himself. On their last adventure of the trip, the Pamplona Bull Run, each friend makes a vow of how he will improve his life. The film affirms the neoliberal dream of self-creation and, given the protagonists' class, caste, education, affluence and gender, depicts a situation in which this self-creation can be fully realised.

CONFLICTED AND CONFUSED   153

Figure 8.1 Each of the protagonists in *ZNMD* runs towards his own fate.

Though they have many advantages that allow them to undertake this journey and realise neoliberalism's growth potential to the fullest, the film still highlights friends as key supports. While social structures decay, adding to the anxiety of this period, *ZNMD* is a refreshing story that upholds the human bonds that alleviate an individual's pressure for self-realisation. This is why Kabir can finally admit that he is not ready to marry Natasha and can count on his friends, not his family or fiancée, to support him in making the decision that is best for him. The emphasis on friendship also highlights that on this path to self-discovery one has to rely on people of the same generation who are exercising similar values to help fully realise one's own values.[9] The journey to self-discovery is thus at once individual but also tied up with various influences, from the global to the societal group with which one most closely identifies. Undertaking a journey of self-discovery that confronts generational differences presents distinct conflicts that are also part of identity construction, as examined by Akhtar in her next film.

MEDIATING MASCULINITY ACROSS GENERATIONS

Pluto Mehra: '. . . man has the power to change.'

Setting and following one's values in pursuit of realising one's identity is hard enough to negotiate when among friends and becomes even more difficult when mediated across generations. Akhtar's third film, *DDD*, follows the Mehra family as they embark on a Mediterranean cruise. While the family members struggle to come to terms with their own identities and values, they must also take into consideration their family's wants and desires which heavily impact the course of their lives.

Though the film follows all four family members, each one's journey is tied to Kamal (Anil Kapoor), the patriarch. Kamal is the first character introduced. While the narration employs a bit of sarcasm in noting Kamal's obsession with reminding everyone that he is a 'self-made man', the visuals and positioning of Kamal in the narrative scheme convey his power. Shown executing an admirable golf shot surrounded by well-dressed businessmen, Kamal is presented as the neoliberal ideal, a successful businessman who, through hard work, increased his wealth and elevated his social status and who now enjoys practising Western/global habits of business and leisure. At the same time, he invokes traditional codes of male chivalry, excusing himself from the game for a supposed lunch date with his wife for he 'never keeps a lady waiting'. Kamal is a man of power who controls his shots and gets what he wants professionally and personally.

His male heir Kabir (Ranveer Singh), who is introduced as 'god's gift', also carries implicit power imbued in his position as the one who will carry on the family's name and legacy. Kabir, however, is in conflict as he does not want to uphold the family legacy. Though he goes through the motions of the business role his father wants him to pursue, he is neither content nor successful doing so. Only when he is shown happily flying the plane that his father is threatening to sell is it clear where his true passion lies.

The film emphasises the conflict between parents' wants and their children's desires through several interwoven family stories. Pluto Mehra, the canine narrator whose poetic insights (like in *ZNMD*, Javed Akhtar writes the poetry) bring voice to that which the characters cannot see or say, comments on the relationship between parents and their offspring by observing, 'It is hard for a parent to accept that their child is now able to live life on their own terms. They remain involved in their children's lives even if it is not required.' This commentary accompanies a montage of younger characters begrudgingly being told by their parents what to wear, who to talk to and, more seriously, how to conduct oneself in marriage. Lessons are passed between generations, yet these lectures are ignored as they do not fit the new generation's reality. While their parents tell them one thing, once away, the younger generation are seen figuring out and discovering their own life rules that make them happy.

Both of the younger Mehras embody this neoliberal focus on self-creation and self-fulfilment seen in Akhtar's films. Kabir does not want to become the CEO of his father's company, nor does he want to marry the person his parents have chosen for him as part of a calculated business deal. His sister, Ayesha (Priyanka Chopra), does not want to be a housewife (which she remedies by starting her own business without support) nor does she want to continue in her unhappy marriage. The younger generation are only able to express these thoughts with each other, and, as such, the film is continually divided in juxtaposing scenes in which they act out their dreams among themselves but struggle to find this same voice in front of their parents. For example, though she tells her brother she is unhappy in her marriage, when Ayesha tries to tell her parents her desire to divorce, they are hostile and dismissive. When she is brought in front of the whole family to explain, the confidence with which she expressed her wishes to a supportive Kabir is lost and she looks down at the ground with fear, barely able to reply to her parents' and mother-in-law's interrogation. Achieving her self-realisation is hampered by the different generational beliefs which, in the end, she must confront in order to truly achieve her dreams.

Though Kabir, like the wealthy, transnational young men of *ZNMD*, is still discovering and establishing his own values, his inherited position of male power gives him enough authority to mediate across generations. He is the one who has the most potential to confront his father's patriarchal practices and their resulting conflicts and begin to redefine masculinity for the next generation. This confrontation is essential for, as Cornwall reminds, 'what is hegemonic about certain idealized forms of masculinity . . . is that they have such a grip on men's – and women's – sense of what men should be and do that they are virtually unquestioned' (2016: 1).[10] It is the continued unquestioning adherence to male authority that leads the Mehra family to the breaking point and it is finally the open questioning of this, led by the younger male generation, that offers the possibility of resolution not just for the men of the family, but the women as well.

This generational confrontation is enacted at the film's turning point when societal roles and pressures become too much and the patriarch falls, literally and figuratively. He is rushed to the hospital where the feuding family gathers around him with concern. Though it is revealed to be but a severe case of gas, what appeared to be a near-death experience brings the family together in a space where they are finally able to talk and question. Kabir, exercising his position of gendered familial power, confronts his father while Ayesha silently supports her brother's efforts. Their parents are shocked when Kabir reveals that he never intended to follow through on their marriage proposal/business deal for him as he instead wants to fly planes and be with a Muslim dancer. They chastise him and Ayesha for not having their values. However, while the older generation scoffs at these 'new' values, Kabir criticises them in return as his father's unquestioned sense of entitlement allows him to preach values but ignore them in practice. It is only when Kabir can underline his parents', especially his father's, hypocrisy that Kamal's power begins to crumble, making way for a new world order.

Once Kamal's status as the patriarch is questioned, once he too is shown to have human faults and the system that he upholds to have cracks, he is able to let go of his power and release others from it as well. Opening himself up to change, Kamal is able to reconcile with his wife Neelam (Shefali Shetty) who, because of societal norms, has never left him despite his cheating. Kamal stands up for Ayesha, giving his blessing for her divorce. Finally, he supports his son in following his dreams, even going so far as to rescue him as he jumps into the ocean to swim ashore to repair his relationship with his true love.

The Mehra family come to show the importance of confronting the changing roles of masculinity and questioning structures of power within family and society. It is when these sometimes opposing forces meet and are mediated that resolution is allowed and growth occurs. While this confrontation happens within a family with the financial luxury and power that eases change, the meeting of generations and new lifestyles is sometimes met with other obstacles as well. Ranveer Singh's next role in *Gully Boy* is also that of a dreamer. However, as somebody from the Mumbai slums, his path of identity creation is not only dictated by the challenges of finding one's own values or presenting them to a domineering father, but the roles and expectations of class as well.

ESCAPING CLASS CONFINES

Gemma: 'He's just a boy from the Gully.'

Gully Boy is Akhtar's transition from the cinema of high society to a cinema of the streets, embodied most literally in the name that Murad and the film take: *Gully Boy*, or *'Street' Boy*. Murad is from the streets of Dharavi 17, one of the world's largest slums, yet global neoliberal possibilities lead him to have aspirations that are not that different from those of the male characters in *ZNMD* and *DDD*. Though he may have similar dreams, in Murad's case the difficulties presented by trying to find a new value system and bridging generational divides are compounded by his class and lack of economic, social and religious capital. By returning to the streets, *Gully Boy* presents a key question of India's phenomenal economic growth and entrance into a globalised life and market: what happens to those who are left behind?

The film starts out highlighting the streets of the economically disenfranchised, the ones that many 1990s Bollywood megahits had largely 'anesthetized and supplanted' as Bollywood carried out 'the projection of India into the global commodity fantasy' (Govil 2008: 209). Here lights are dim, shops are closed and only a few people shuffle about as one man walks down the pavement as if he commands these streets. While this confident young man might appear to be the protagonist, proud and in charge of the *gully*, it is soon revealed that this character, Moeen (Vijay Varma), is a friend on his way to meet Murad hiding in the shadows. Murad, in contrast, stumbles in this first scene as he is unwittingly and unwillingly dragged into his friend's plans to steal a car. While Moeen commands space, Murad must learn to negotiate this space as he forms his identity.

Murad is from the streets, but he is also his parents' hope to escape the slums and move up to a lower middle-class stature once he graduates college and gets an office job with his uncle. This thrusts him into an uncomfortable position between spaces. Though his parents want something different for him, Murad is still tied to the space and identity dictated by his class and upbringing; he is expected to follow his father's rules and must even temporarily take on his father's job as a driver when he is injured. His attempts to escape his position in society are continually thwarted by his father; in the beginning he tries to aurally block out his father's second marriage by listening to American hip-hop, only to have his father yank out his earphones and force him to listen to his soundtrack of a shehnai announcing the arrival of his new wife. He opposes his father's decision to take a second wife and, by defending his mother, eventually loses his place in the previous generation's house and must set out to establish his own household with his mother and brother in tow. Even after he has been kicked out, however, his father continues to reappear to try to keep Murad on track to achieve the lower middle-class dream his parents have made for him.

Outside of his house, Murad finds himself negotiating spaces as he defines his identity. This intensified wave of neoliberalism brings the 'increasing consumption of media, fashion, music, and mobility' (Desai 2004: 194) and Murad at once is able to dream of and embrace aspects of this consumption while also being shut out of it. He consumes music and media and even though he can't afford it, is aware of the fashion trends, fully appreciating his friend MC Sher's (Siddhant Chaturvedi) American sneaker collection. In terms of mobility, Murad is at once able to traverse the city – several shots show him moving through it by bus or car – yet at the same time he is continually shut out of spaces, from nightclubs to apartment buildings, due to his class. The spaces he inhabits are different from those of the rich: Murad lives in a house that foreign tourists visit to stare in awe at how many people fit in such a small space, while his friend Sky (Kalki Koechlin) has her own flat whose bathroom, as Murad measures, is comparable in size to his family's whole house. Murad continually finds himself confronting these barriers to mobility as he tries to gain a sense of self and control, and access to new neoliberal identity-making spaces. It is no coincidence that Murad's first recorded song, '*Doori*' ('Distance'), showing images of Mumbai's extreme poverty, speaks of the divide that both he and the people in the video struggle to cross.

In his case, being male does not imbue Murad with inherited and unquestioned patriarchal power. Instead he has been forced to learn to shape his identity in spite of being stripped of power because of his class and religion. It is those of his generation, most notably his girlfriend, Safeena (Alia Bhatt), and MC Sher, that teach him to form an identity in which he incorporates not only where he has come from but where his dreams are taking him. It is Safeena who teaches Murad to follow his dreams because, as she simply puts it, the only reason she is able to achieve all she wants to do (which contradicts what her society's gender, class and religious values ascribe to her) is by being brave. It is MC Sher who teaches Murad to embrace where he is from and use the fire sparked by his social condition to help him get ahead.

These lessons, embedded in a hip-hop biopic which consists of the rags-to-riches storyline, allow Murad to find his new self. He is able to stand up to previous generations who tell him to keep his head down and appreciate his office job, even confronting his father to say that his advice to blindly follow the path life has seemingly dictated for him is wrong. In his final rap battle, reminiscent of B-Rabbit's (Eminem) battle in *8 Mile* (Curtis Hanson 2002), Murad is able to listen to the class-based abuse dealt to him and triumph by embracing those class realities and showing that he has accepted and worked his way around them, a message he embraces in his winning song '*Apna Time Aayega*' ('My Time Will Come'). In the end, Murad regains some of the control that his gender no longer unquestioningly affords him and, despite his class, realises his dream of becoming a hip-hop star.

Though Murad, like the real-life rappers Divine and Naezy who inspired his character, is able to escape his poverty and realise his dream, at the end of the film it is he, and not the exclusionary spaces, that has changed. The story is at once the neoliberal dream of an individual's determination bringing him up from poverty, but it is also a reminder that this dream is for the individual and not for society. The neoliberal reality is that despite vast economic growth and the swelling of the middle classes, there are still large parts of the population who continue to face traditional divides of space, class, religion, generational values and gender that do not allow for easy mobility. Thus, *Gully Boy*, as will also be seen in *Made in Heaven*, reinforces that it is the individual who must negotiate change and, hopefully within these increasingly public negotiations, influence societal change as well.

THE PERSONAL IS POLITICAL

Karan: 'My life is going without any confrontation, so why bother?'

Karan (Arjun Mathur), one of the protagonists of Akhtar's and Reema Kagti's 2019 series *Made in Heaven*, lives his personal life as a gay man in twenty-first-century India in the shadows. Though his sexual activities were still criminalised under Section 377 of the Indian Penal Code during the time the series takes place, he manages to carve out for himself a patchwork existence where he is able to pursue his love interests and at the same time operate within a society and family that do not accept all parts of his identity. Karan's lifestyle reflects some of the far-reaching effects this British Colonial law has had on the LGBTQ+ community in India legally and socially. Trying to escape the emasculating treatment by the British, India's post-independence identity construction centred on a certain type of masculinity as 'a foundation stone equating it to rationality, chivalry and moral superiority', continuing to marginalise 'sexuality and effeminacy (a form of non-masculinity) [which] had no place in this new rhetoric' (Dasgupta and Gokulsing 2013: 11). This exclusion from the national narrative, and the legal ramifications it holds, is driven home for Karan when he finds himself in jail for his identity. As much as he has tried to separate the two, he realises that the personal is political and he has to decide whether to fight to be accepted as who he is or continue living a part of his life in the shadows.

Though the marginalisation and punishment that Karan faces are the result of systemic problems and not necessarily those perpetrated by one individual, the only way he has to combat the system is through his individual decisions that must be used as political statements. Karan's political identity is built alongside his personal identity, as the show follows him finding his place in business and life. Karan, like his wedding-planning business, is quickly revealed to be struggling behind the glossy veneer of a successful, middle-class entrepreneur that he presents to the world. Personal and societal pressures to be financially successful push him to keep trying in business, though he is repeatedly faced with financial failure and relies on family and friends to bail him out.

Like in business, Karan's personal life as a gay man in a country where homosexual relations are illegal leads him time and again to familial and societal trouble. When his landlord, who is attracted to Karan, is caught by his wife secretly filming Karan's sexual relations, he must turn Karan in to the police to save himself. Karan thus finds himself in jail, where he is not only held in squalid conditions, but is tortured and sexually abused by his jailers. For Karan, this is the point where the private and public sphere collide and the personal becomes political.

Karan is released, but he now must make the decision as to whether he continues with his life or he politicises this experience. Influencing his decision are his memories of his previous experience with violence as a result of his sexual orientation. Flashbacks of his young love affair culminate in his mother finding the two boys together in the shower. She beats Karan with a cricket bat, instilling in him a fear of taking his private life out in public. Karan decides to press charges against his landlord who, in filming him in his home and turning the tapes over to the police, has destroyed the barrier between these two spheres that Karan had constructed to protect himself. At the same time, Karan realises the oppression he must confront is not just represented by this one man, or even just his mother. When he drops the charges against the landlord, his lawyer inadvertently confirms this by sighing and saying, 'Sending one landlord to jail won't change anything in this country.' In order to enact the change that will not just create a space for him but others in society, Karan must become political. While he has friends and some of his family behind him, this decision to self-create his identity as political carries the greatest weight out of all Akhtar's works, for though others in their self-realisation risk losing something, Karan must literally put his life on the line for his actualisation.

Rather than pursuing his case against one landlord, Karan files a Public Interest Litigation against Section 377. He is both embraced and threatened by the public; he makes presentations about homosexuality to captive (younger) audiences while at the same time being threatened by political and religious groups that see his work as an abomination. He receives wedding contracts from people who want to support him to make their own political statements and yet is told by others that they do not want him working for them. He must also reconcile on the personal level and finally confront his family. Here Karan finds his father, from whom he has always hidden this part of his identity, to support him, while still experiencing dismissal from his mother. Karan must become vulnerable, and try to survive the consequences, so that this part of masculine identity can find a place in a world that still violently threatens to deny it.

In the series, Karan is shown to finally take a stand, and though he suffers because of it, he is also celebrated for using his personal life to change social viewpoints. The first season ends with a text saying that Section 377 was finally repealed in 2018, making it no longer a crime for consensual sexual relations between adults of the same sex.[11] The personal stance is thus tied to the political outcome, emphasising the strong links between the spheres. Further, it is finally by taking this stance that Karan can truly realise his own identity. After he makes his case political, he finds the willpower to confront his parents as well as his true love, who he betrayed and lost. By taking this action, Karan both returns to the self-centred neoliberal values, yet at the same time connects them to society, showing how not only the individual but society needs to work through and negotiate gender and sexual orientation roles. Karan's actions, as well as the show itself, contribute to this by creating an open space for this negotiation of the rapid changes and identities brought on by neoliberalism. Karan may find his identity and masculinity in a state of change, but though he is conflicted about what to do and who to be, he also has the liberty to explore those conflicts and prepare both himself and society for the identity he chooses in the next phase of his journey.

THE JOURNEY CONTINUES

Zoya Akhtar's films do not always end on a high note. In fact, the happy ending only happens in the closing credits which show, for example, Arjun and Laila's marriage and Kabir and Natasha's break-up in *ZNMD* or Murad's celebration of success and rediscovery of himself in his community in *Gully Boy*. That these endings occur as a backdrop to the credits underscores that these journeys of finding new identities are not ones to be neatly concluded and then cast aside as the dramatic effects of the increased speed of change under neoliberalism lead to a continual process of negotiating identity in terms of values and generational, class and political differences. A key factor in these negotiations is the question of gendered identity in which, as the characters in Akhtar's works find, masculinity as part of identity is no longer a given dominant discourse but is itself at a point of inflection and creation. It is a continued negotiation that is hard and will lead to clashes and confusion as it doesn't give clear answers of what a man, or anybody, should be, nor does it give the guarantee that those answers exist. However, one concrete lesson that the characters learn is that even if those answers do not exist, one still must undertake the journey of discovery. What distinguishes Akhtar's work is her celebration of this identity journey for all characters in which it is all right to have an identity that is unsure, it is all right to question and be confused and that accepting this allows for growth.

Embracing uncertainty leads to another distinguishing mark of Akhtar's work: her ability to highlight male vulnerability. In his exploration of the 'crisis in masculinity' exposed in Anand Patwardhan's documentary *Father Son and Holy War* (1994), Rustom Bharucha specifically highlights the 'silencing' of male vulnerability as the missing piece that keeps the film, and society, from being able to address fully the political and social consequences of a changing male role and identity (1995: 1614). As heroes in mainstream cinema become inflated caricatures of men whose ever-growing muscles keep them safe in films like *War* (Siddharth Anand 2019), or, as in *Kabir Singh*, never face any consequences for their actions, they never experience real vulnerability and thus this important point of reflection is continually missed. However, in Akhtar's works, it is this vulnerability that is the turning point that leads to growth. It allows Arjun to realise that his material drive is not leading to happiness, it inspires Murad's music and his coming into his own identity, and it gives space to Karan to confront his family, his ex-lover and his society that have hurt him and begin to find peace. Opening up to this vulnerability allows for an examination of the constructed nature of masculinity as well as the possibilities to reconstruct this identity. Embracing the gender trouble this brings, Akhtar offers a space to examine and work through the evolution of gender roles not just for men, but for a local and global society that finds itself in the midst of a greater discourse on the construction and changes of gender and identities.

NOTES

1. Though *Section 375* portrayed a male film director tried for the rape of a female crew member, it hardly captured the issue's gravity. Told through a male point of view, it follows lawyer Tarjun Saluja's (Akshaye Khanna) fight to free the accused rapist who, the

film concludes, is the unjust victim of his ex-girlfriend's revenge. The film thus reinforces the dangerous 'men as victims' claims that arose in the #MeToo Movement.
2. The highest-grossing 2019 Indian films, in order, were: *War* (Siddharth Anand), *Kabir Singh* (Sandeep Reddy Vanga), *Uri-The Surgical Strike* (Aditya Dhar), *Housefull 4* (Sajid Khan/Farhad Samji), *Bharat* (Ali Abbas Zafar), *Good Newwz* (Raj Mehta), *Mission Mangal* (Jagan Shakti), *Kesari* (Anurag Singh), *Total Dhamaal* (Indra Kumar), *Saaho* (Sujeeth), *Chhichhore* (Nitish Tiwari), *Super 30* (Vikas Bahl), *Dream Girl* (Raaj Shaandilyaa), *Dabangg 3* (Prabhu Deva), *Gully Boy* (Zoya Akhtar). Numbers from boxofficeindia.com.
3. See Thomas 1995, Gopal 2011, Dwyer 2014, Joshi 2015 and Elison et al. 2016.
4. Beyond cinema, works like Sikata Banerjee's *Make Me a Man! Masculinity, Hinduism, and Nationalism in India* (2005) or Michiel Baas' work on gym culture in India (2016) combine anthropological fieldwork, cultural studies and history to highlight the connection between the male body and nation.
5. The NRI population has been so important in India's neoliberal economic development that it is its own 'legal category . . . designed for Indian diasporics who contribute to the national economy' (Rajan 2006: 1107). In this era, NRIs also represented a large new market for film consumption, leading to several 'NRI cinema' blockbusters like *Dilwale Dulhania Le Jayange* (Aditya Chopra 1995) and *Kabhi Kushi Kabhi Gham* (Karan Johar 2001), as well as the increased use of stars, such as Shah Rukh Khan, as India's global marketing.
6. For an introduction to neoliberalism's impact on the BJP's rise, see Desai 2016. For its implications on masculinity, see Banerjee 2005 and Mubarki 2018.
7. This violence has been examined onscreen through the series *Delhi Crime* (Richie Mehta 2019), based on the 2012 gang rape and murder of Jyoti Singh, and films like *No One Killed Jessica* (Raj Kumar Gupta 2011) and *Chhapaak* (Meghna Gulzar 2020), based on the murder of Jessica Lal and the life of acid attack survivor Laxmi Agarwal, respectively.
8. Akhtar started producing her work with her own production company, Tiger Baby Productions, in 2018.
9. *DCH* is a key turning point in Bollywood history in elevating this mindset.
10. In reference to Tim Carrigan, Bob Connell and John Lee's concept of 'hegemonic masculinity', in which masculinity is seen and practised as the given dominant gender in which power is imbued as a biological, 'nonsocial essence' (1985).
11. The final decision to repeal parts of Section 377 was decided in the case *Navtej Singh Johar and others v. Union of India* in 2018.

WORKS CITED

Akhtar, Zoya (2015), 'Interview', in Nirmal Kumar and Preeti Chaturvedi (eds), *Brave New Bollywood: In Conversation with Contemporary Hindi Filmmakers*, New Delhi: Sage Publications India, pp. 115–38.

Baas, Michiel (2016), 'The new Indian male: Muscles, masculinity and middle classness', in Knut A. Jacobsen (ed.), *The Routledge Handbook of Contemporary India*, New York: Routledge, pp. 444–56.

Balaji, Murali (2014), 'Indian masculinity', *Technoculture*, 4. Available at <https://tcjournal.org/vol4/balaji>

Banerjee, Sikata (2005), *Make Me a Man! Masculinity, Hinduism, and Nationalism in India*, Albany, NY: State University Press.

Bharucha, Rustom (1995), 'Dismantling man: Crisis of male identity in *Father Son and Holy War*', *Economic and Political Weekly*, 30: 26, pp. 1610–16.
Box Office India (2019), 'Top hits 2019'. Accessed 29 July 2020. Available at <https://boxofficeindia.com/years.php?year=2019&pageId=4>
Butler, Judith (1990), *Gender Trouble: Feminism and the Subversion of Identity*, New York: Routledge.
Carrigan, Tim, Bob Connell and John Lee (1985), 'Toward a new sociology of masculinity', *Theory and Society*, 14: 5, pp. 551–604. Available at <https://doi.org/10.1007/BF00160017>
Chakravarty, Sumita (2008), 'The national-heroic image: Masculinity and masquerade', in Rajinder Dudrah and Jigna Desai (eds), *The Bollywood Reader*, Maidenhead: Open University Press, pp. 84–94
Cornwall, Andrea (2016), 'Introduction: Masculinities under neoliberalism', in Andrea Cornwall, Frank G. Karioris and Nancy Lindisfarne (eds), *Masculinities Under Neoliberalism*, London: Zed Books, pp. 1–28.
Dasgupta, R. K. and K. M. Gokulsing (2013), 'Introduction: Perceptions of masculinity and challenges to the Indian male', in R. K Dasgupta and K. M. Gokulsing (eds), *Masculinity and Its Challenges in India: Essays on Changing Perceptions*, Jefferson: Jefferson Publishers, pp. 5–26.
Desai, Jigna (2004), *Beyond Bollywood: The Cultural Politics of South Asian Diasporic Film*, New York: Routledge.
Desai, Radhika (2016), 'The slow-motion counterrevolution: Developmental contradictions and the emergence of neoliberalism', in Kenneth Bo Nielsen and Alf Gunvald Nilsen (eds), *Social Movements and the State in India*, London: Palgrave, pp. 25–51.
Elison, William, Christian Lee Novetzke and Andy Rotman (2016), *Amar Akbar Anthony: Bollywood, Brotherhood, and the Nation*, Cambridge, MA: Harvard University Press.
Gopal, Sangita (2011), *Conjugations: Marriage and Form in New Bollywood Cinema*, Chicago: University of Chicago Press.
Govil, Nitin (2008), 'Bollywood and the frictions of global mobility', in Rajinder Dudrah and Jigna Desai (eds), *The Bollywood Reader*, Maidenhead: Open University Press, pp. 201–15.
Joshi, Priya (2015), *Bollywood's India: A Public Fantasy*, New York: Columbia University Press.
Kazmi, Fareeduddin (1998), 'How angry is the Angry Young man? Rebellion in conventional Hindi cinema', in Ashis Nandy (ed.), *The Secret Politics of our Desires: Innocence, Culpability and the Indian Popular Cinema*, New Delhi: Oxford University Press, pp. 134–57.
Mubarki, Meraj Ahmed (2020), 'Body, masculinity and the male hero in Hindi cinema', *Social Semiotics*, 30: 2, pp. 225–53. Available at <https://doi.org/10.1080/10350330.2018.1547497>
Oza, Rupal (2012), *The Making of Neoliberal India: Nationalism, Gender, and the Paradoxes of Globalization*, London: Routledge.
Rajan, Gita (2006), 'Constructing-contesting masculinities: Trends in South Asian cinema', *Signs*, 31: 4, pp. 1099–124. Available at <https://www.jstor.org/stable/10.1086/500959>
Roy, Abhery (2019), '2018: The year when #MeToo shook India', *The Economic Times*, 1 June 2019. Available at <https://economictimes.indiatimes.com/magazines/panache/2018-the-year-when-metoo-shook-india/2018-the-year-of-metoo-in-india/slideshow/66346583.cms>
Thomas, Rosie (1995), 'Melodrama and the negotiation of morality in mainstream Hindi film', in Carol Breckenridge (ed.), *Consuming Modernity: Public Culture in a South Asian World*, Minneapolis: University of Minnesota, pp. 157–82.

CHAPTER 9

Señoritas at Work: Gendered Work, Aspiration and Leisure in the Films of Zoya Akhtar

Sharanya

This chapter will examine the gendered politics of leisure and work in the films of Zoya Akhtar, analysing the representation of working women, their leisure practices, the role of glamour as labour, care work as leisure and 'workplaces' of leisure. Kathi Weeks likens the 'workplace' to the household, 'typically figured as a private space, the product of a series of individual contracts rather than a social structure, the province of human need and sphere of individual choice rather than a site for the exercise of political power' (2011: 4). Considering in detail Akhtar's first three films, *Luck by Chance* (2009), *Zindagi Na Milegi Dobara* (2011) and *Dil Dhadakne Do* (2015), where there are direct encounters with women at work, this chapter will build on Weeks's formulation of the workplace to interrogate three crucial aspects of Akhtar's representation of gendered work in her films. Firstly, this chapter will examine how the performance of glamour by women subsumes waged work and unwaged work because it is framed as leisure. Secondly, it will analyse the gendered divisions of work and leisure in consuming and occupying luxurious and opulent (cinematic) spaces and how they are thus disguised as sites of aspiration and liberation for women. Lastly, the chapter seeks to highlight how women's work is made invisible as pleasure/leisure, or what I call p/leisure, in how they undertake care, or care work, of familial social structures in Akhtar's films.

In his *Critique of Everyday Life*, Henri Lefebvre interrogates the concept of 'everyday life', asking where it is to be found: work, leisure, family life or life unfolding 'outside of culture' (1991: 31). He goes on to address the dialectic of work and leisure, inferring that while all of the aforementioned elements do make up 'a global system' of everyday life, leisure consists of discrete activities that produce and reflect both passive, 'alienated' attitudes, such as cinemawatching, and active, cultivated leisure activities such as photography, sports and filmmaking (32). In his text *Everyday Life in the Modern World* (originally published in French in three volumes in 1947, 1961 and 1981), Lefebvre's preoccupation with theorising leisure accounts for the fact that leisure can only be acquired as a break from the rhythms of everyday life: while 'pledged time (professional work)' and 'compulsive time (the various demands other than work such as transport, official formalities, etc.)' are dominant in modern life, the nature of everyday work means that 'compulsive time increases at a greater rate than leisure time', the latter defined simply, movingly, as 'free time' (53).

In all of this, the role of 'family life' does not allude specifically to its maintenance, nor to the locus of gendered work, which may include domestic work and other traditionally gendered labour-divisions. The women portrayed across Akhtar's directorial feature films lead complex work lives that cut across class (if not caste), religion and nationality. By interrogating the gendered framing of the work/leisure dialectic with an emphasis on analysing the spaces of aspiration and leisure in Akhtar's first three feature films, this chapter asks: How do Akhtar's films construct a genealogy of women's leisure? In what ways are the gendered underpinnings of work and leisure represented through the women characters? How do the domestic and corporate 'workplaces' in the films create women's ambitions and p/leisure? Is care represented as women's work or as leisure that leads to their betterment? Lastly, how does Akhtar's gaze reinscribe or resist a patriarchal co-option of women's labour in work and leisure?

'BORN TO DANCE': GLAMOUR-WORK AS LEISURE

Stephen Gundle defines glamour as 'an alluring image that is closely related to consumption. It is an enticing and seductive vision that is designed to draw the eye of an audience' (2009: 5). He adds that it could refer to 'people, things, places, events, or environments, any of which can capture the imagination by association with a range of qualities, including several or all of the following: beauty, sexuality, theatricality, wealth, dynamism, notoriety, movement, and leisure' (2009: 6). I wish to dwell particularly on his consideration of wealth, movement and leisure as being 'associated' with glamour. In Akhtar's films, these elements are cultural processes simultaneously imbued with and producing glamour. This is achieved through an aesthetic of global place-politics, elaborated on in the next section, but also through certain women characters in the films *practising* glamour as both waged and unwaged work.

In *ZNMD*, Akhtar's second feature, three friends, Imraan (Farhan Akhtar), Kabir (Abhay Deol) and Arjun (Hrithik Roshan), undertake a road trip to Spain ahead of Kabir's impending marriage to a wealthy interior designer, Natasha (Kalki Koechlin). The trip involves undertaking three communal adventure sports, individually chosen by each of the three men. Even as the sports chosen are depicted by Akhtar with tender sophistication and humour, reflecting fear and pathos rather than traditional machismo, all three men 'overcome' the obstacle of the sports to achieve a more 'actualised' version of themselves by the end. Imraan resolves his issues with his biological father and reinforces his commitment to his writing, Kabir breaks off his wedding to Natasha and Arjun leaves his high-stress banking job to travel the world with Laila (Katrina Kaif),[1] a deep-sea diving instructor whom the men meet when experiencing their first sport.

The first time we encounter Laila, she stands sprite-like on the waterline of the beach, waving a spinning poi in a colourful maxi dress, lost in thought. Imraan attempts to flirt with her, annoying Arjun who is also attracted to her, but Laila turns Imraan down in good humour. Her introduction to the men, and to us as viewers, is through this image of a solitary, lithe, beautiful woman who is revealed, the following morning in slick black gear, as their diving instructor. She is alluring enough to coax Arjun out of his hydrophobia, resulting in the first of a long sequence of erotic instances that culminates in their relationship. In play and work, she satiates the masculine imagination by glamming its possibilities at redemption: the men are worth redeeming because while they are variously immature and money-minded, they are worthwhile as friends and lovers in her spare time, and also double up as excellent students and sources of income in her workplace. But through this process, she continues to be elusive and inaccessible, too glamorous to be 'attained' fully either as a friend or a girlfriend (as opposed to an acquaintance and lover respectively) until the men's redemptive arcs meet their logical conclusions at the end of the film. As Megha Anwer astutely notes of Laila, 'her femininity is so safely seductive that she is able to become one of the guys – without having to shed or forgo her erotic appeal. Her greatest virtue is that she lets the boys be boys, even as she teaches them how to be men' (2019: 309).

Laila's glamour derives in part from her sexual and cultural capital as a global traveller, but also from the blurring of boundaries of work and leisure particular to her job. She is an Indian-American who studies fashion in London for part of the year and spends the rest diving and teaching diving in Spain. Her ability to make a living is never in doubt; in fact, she derives never-ending fun from it, making fun a productive type of glamour, or what I call 'glamour-work': teaching students as she wishes, having seemingly endless reserves of temporal and economic capital and travelling to festivals and Morocco when she isn't teaching or studying. Life is a giant glamorous leisure-circuit, and that takes (unwaged) work. In a scene hued with romance and possibilities, established by an overhead tracking shot that captures the full extent of their intimate attraction, Arjun and Laila lie under the stars, on the grass next to each other, talking. He tells her he has never laid on the grass before, a ridiculous act, because he has a house in London, and she calls him ridiculous for holding such a seemingly mercantile world view. When he replies that living a full life should be learned from someone like her, someone so free, because he spends his life as though he is in a closed box (which is not completely untrue since he works at a desk in a stock market), she takes his hand and quips that a person should only be in a box when they are dead. The scene closes with a shot of the night sky, stars brighter than ever, indicating perhaps that dreams of open-borders tourist travel can be liberation, even for a man who does not fully understand why he should want them. Later in the film, we see free-spirited Laila in yet another glamorous avatar outside work: on her friend Nuria's borrowed Royal Enfield motorbike, corseted up, silky black hair streaming behind her as she chases Arjun, her object of desire, to kiss him and then walk away (only to return towards the end and marry him).

The glamour of Laila's lifestyle is enhanced by the effortlessness of its various components. The representation of the work it takes, from deep-sea diving pedagogy to earning an income, is muted. Other than stray shots of her on the motorbike, we do not see her alone, living this ostensibly free life away from men and the promise of heterosexual domesticity. Laila's glamour-work is what she does for leisure: following on from Anwer, quoted earlier, when Laila isn't teaching the men or being one of them, she is productively turning them into better men.

Much like we first see Laila through the eyes of Arjun and Imraan in *ZNMD*, in *DDD* we are similarly introduced to Farah (Anushka Sharma). We spot her through the eyes of Kabir Mehra (Ranveer Singh), the spoilt brat of the elite Mehra family, holidaying on a cruise ship around Turkey. The cruise journey is supposed to mark the thirtieth wedding anniversary of Kamal (Anil Kapoor) and Neelam Mehra (Shefali Shah), who look the cookie-cutter version of a happy nuclear family in public, but suffer deeply in private. Kamal is a pill-popping businessman on the brink of bankruptcy, Neelam is unloved and unemployed but works just as hard to run the household smoothly and maintain social ties with other wealthy families, trying to keep her binge-eating under wraps. Their son Kabir is bored and unhappy at his corporate job in his family's firm, and dreams of leaving it for a career as a pilot. He pilots a family plane in his spare time, or what is worth calling 'leisure' time in this context, hoping that his father won't sell off the plane. Equally troubled is his older sister Ayesha (Priyanka Chopra), who is in a loveless marriage with the dour Manav Sangha (Rahul Bose), but is also the founder of a successful online travel portal, pining after her childhood friend, who went on to be the acclaimed journalist Sunny Gill (Farhan Akhtar).

Just as with Laila, the glamour of the women marks the beginning of the men's change in romantic fate. Farah, a twenty-five-year-old artist from London, is engrossed in swimming late one night on the cruise ship aboard which the Mehra family is holidaying, but she notices Kabir and the two perform a sensual swim-off, saying nothing. Farah's mystery is revealed soon after when, like Laila, the former transitions from an anonymous seductive swimmer who could have been one of the guests in the same class bracket as Kabir to a vivacious and glamorous cruise-ship dancer and entertainer, pulling off a flapper aesthetic in art-deco architecture with the same ease as a swimming costume. Kabir in *DDD* and the three men in *ZNMD* are struck by the same fact on learning who Farah and Laila are: the women are available, beautiful and able to work and play at the same time, dazzling in both capacities without compromise.

Farah's aesthetic resembles Laila's in spirit: never visibly overworked or underpaid on the precarious gig economy citizenship of life as an entertainer, Farah is glowing, feeding on life's thrills without its commodified excesses. Outside of work, she is chicly turned out, especially on the streets of Turkey. However, in her private moments with Kabir Mehra she is in athletic gym gear, or swimming gear, being, much like Laila, one of the boys but still enough of a woman to be glamorous in her erotic potential.

On one of their 'dates' on the ship, Farah narrates to Kabir how, as a baby, she was so drawn to music she taught herself to dance. When he remarks 'Born to dance', she replies, 'Yes, born to dance' and asks him if he was born to be a businessman. He is unable to own up to his dream of flying, and so he responds that becoming a businessman is what his family has told him to do. Farah responds by saying that she was told by her family that she ought to be a homemaker. She goes on to detail how she ran away from home, and worked her way through odd jobs like bartending and waitressing to put herself through dance school. Kabir is astounded at her independence and strong will, and christens her 'Fearless Farah', calling to mind the glamorous twentieth-century Indian actress and stuntwoman Mary Ann Evans, who was known more colloquially as 'Fearless Nadia'. Farah's allure derives from her commitment to 'the arts', specifically dance, but equally, through the gaze of Kabir and his class, from her ability to live a penniless freelance dance lifestyle without losing the glamour. Unlike Ayesha, who looks and is already moneyed and has to earn her glamour by tunnelling through a heterosexual marriage, substituting a loveless arranged marriage for a passionate one built from mutual love, Farah's solitude and (un)availability is exoticised as devotion to her work. The issue at the end of the film is less about Farah's unemployment, caused by Kabir exposing their relationship, and more that she becomes a glamorous phantom, an outline whose pursuit leads Kabir to make a decision for himself, at last.

Responding to John Berger and Richard Dyer's conceptions of glamour, Lloyd Whitesell notes, 'In one sense, glamour can appear as the content of an image, by its reference to a luxurious, exclusive lifestyle. But in another sense, glamour can be the result of pure form, a vision of perfection created by abandoning oneself to aesthetic principles' (2018: 28). If Laila's is characterised by the former, Natasha Arora's embodiment of glamour-work in *ZNMD* could be read through the lens of the latter: Natasha, as Kabir's rich, high-maintenance interior designer fiancée, is glamorous as a result of her work with, and as a consumer of, affluence. She is essayed as prim, decisive and deeply in love – to the point of wanting to quit her designing job after marriage so as to settle in a domestic routine; a desire that terrifies Kabir, who thought he was marrying the ideal woman: someone who worked *and* played.

Unlike Laila and Farah, Natasha's glamour-work takes work. 'Her stiff upper-class attire marks her as an outsider to the world of globetrotting new age consumers who make travel look easy and recreational – rather than grim business,' writes Anwer (2019: 310). Her sophistication tips over into unpleasantness; Natasha's aspirations to be a housewife are portrayed as unglamorous, and therefore not aspirational: not only is she 'clingy' and keen on dropping work after marriage, she is uncool in her express displeasure (at Imraan's dinner-table antics, at Kabir's socialising with a woman she does not know, at lifestyle-as-commodity) and unwillingness to perform the right kind of leisure (by wanting and appreciating expensive consumer goods such as luxury bags, unlike Laila's laissez-faire attitude to object-as-commodity).

In *DDD*, we are witness to a similar binary between the sacrificial corporate working woman (Ayesha) and the bohemian self-made woman (Farah). Both women are, in effect, independent self-made workers, because Farah has always fended for herself, and Ayesha started her own company from scratch, without access to familial capital or her father's wealth. However, the lack of family income contributes significantly to the production of (or alternatively, lack of) glamour-work on the parts of both women. Ayesha, as a true corporate manager, strikes a perfect work–life balance even while on the cruise. She parties during the social events, and works on her laptop in athleisure or pyjamas late at night. Her glamour-work is similarly proportioned; she is committed to her job but does not work too hard, devoting time to the family escapades and her husband; she always looks like a professional without looking intimidating, dressed in casual chic.

For Laila and Farah, much of this glamour-work in *ZNMD* and *DDD* is waged, because of the public-facing roles these women occupy. In *The Managed Heart*, sociologist Arlie Hochschild examines the 'feeling rules' that entail certain jobs, such as American flight attendants: 'For these workers, emotion work, feeling rules, and social exchange have been removed from the private domain and placed in a public one, where they are processed, standardized, and subjected to hierarchical control' (2012: 153). Their hours outside of the workplace (the beach, the film set, the cruise ship) provide the only leisure-time for the women in Akhtar's films to pursue their non-work-related interests such as travelling, but primarily falling in love, and consequently, investing in romantic and familial care duties (addressed later in this chapter).

SPACES OF GENDERED P/LEISURE

This section examines the spatial construction of gendered pleasure and leisure in the workplace across Akhtar's first three films. According to M. K. Raghavendra, a shift can be witnessed in Indian cinema: where previously the nation state or family unit could be said to be the locus of 'stable relationships', today it is not work but lifestyle patterns that appear to bring characters together, resulting in the absence of 'transactions' of loyalty or love as in films like *Delhi Belly* (Abhinay Deo and Akshat Verma 2011), *Dil Chahta Hai* (Farhan Akhtar 2001) or *ZNMD* (2014: 201–2). Raghavendra defines a transaction as when 'the effort that a person makes towards another in a relationship, creates a debt to be repaid in some way [. . .] Revenge, for instance, is transactional' (198–9). His contention is that a film like *ZNMD* does not involve these affective transactions geared towards family or nation-building because it is a shared lifestyle that brings the characters together; for Raghavendra, lifestyle and livelihood are disparate issues. 'With Hindi cinema increasingly addressing a more affluent public from the metropolitan cities in the new millennium, the nation is becoming more asymmetrically constituted', he writes elsewhere (2011: 28).

Akhtar's films could well be viewed as examples representing this asymmetry in nation-building. The films mainly take place in the metropolises of Mumbai and Delhi and on a more international scale, in Spain, Turkey and London. The first three films represent tenuous and unstable relationships with a unified notion of 'India'. However, the 'transactions' (to use Raghavendra's term) are classed and gendered in both national and transnational contexts. The women in *ZNMD*, and indeed, in all of Akhtar's films, enact these transactions in the performance of glamour, heterosexual romance and care work.

This occurs partly through the role of women being at work/play in glamorous environments such as dancing halls on cruise ships (*DDD*), Spanish beaches, road trips (*ZNMD*), luxury apartments (*LBC*, *ZNMD* and *DDD*) and opulent film sets and outdoor shoots (*LBC*). While these spaces are dominated by men pursuing entertainment and leisure practices in search of self-improvement, the women who are either romantically partnered with these men or in familial kinship with them enable the entertainment and self-improvement because these spaces double as work and leisure spaces for them.

For instance, after seeing Farah dance as part of an evening's entertainment on the cruise ship (a dance where Ayesha spontaneously joins in, rendering the song a double-act between Farah and Ayesha, but also Anushka Sharma and

Priyanka Chopra, the film's two lead heroines; a uniquely gendered demand of mainstream Bollywood acting work), Kabir visits the crew quarters in search of Farah. He encounters her in the middle of a rehearsal and, bypassing the two security crew members, swaggers in. He shouts across the empty auditorium and asks her to lunch, demanding a yes or a no. She agrees, tells him to meet her in Istanbul's Taksim Square later, and when questioned by her colleague, who reminds her of the code of conduct or what Hochschild calls 'feeling rules' – in this case, the strictly professional but cordial relationship that is to be maintained between a guest and a crew member – Farah replies, 'Who says I'm going?'

The auditorium, the same space that was once a site of luxury, excess and pleasure for Kabir, becomes a site to trespass by extension of that consumer logic even when the nature of the room has morphed from being a dancehall to a workspace. However, that transformation to a workplace happens for everyone but Kabir: for him, wanting to talk to the beautiful, anonymous dancer is an exercise in pleasure. When she meets him in Taksim Square later, Farah greets a smiling Kabir with a warning about workplace behaviour: the rules are that we can't get personally involved with guests, she says, so if you can't stop yourself from visiting my rehearsal, keep your volume down. While not expressly telling him off for visiting, she makes clear her professional stakes, boundaries and the p/leisure possibilities available to her as a single woman, and a single woman at work.

This is the beginning of their flirtation and the rest of their relationship is constrained not merely by her workplace rules, but also by Kabir's disregard for them. This is representative of the power dynamics in their relationship: he is a guest on the ship while she is there for work. It is also indicative of the spatial imbalance of global capital and consumption practices. The cruise ship exists as a site of elite pleasure fulfilment, offering a utopian palate of seamless border crossings and doses of culture. The well-travelled middle-class voyager consumes enough of everywhere, but not too much of anywhere, and certainly not enough to be changed by the cultural politics specific to a place. At the beginning of the film, we are witness to a montage of Kabir flying his plane, finally relaxing. He transitions from work to leisure to family and back, but unlike with the women in the film, regardless of the country, we see what he does for fun, and how much it matters to him.

Akhtar's eye dwells with interest in the various locations where she chooses to film; Spain is distinct from Turkey – one encounters the Tomatina festival in the former and Hammam baths in the latter – but Spain is also Turkey inasmuch as both places become feasting and display grounds of cultural capital for the global traveller. 'The spectacles of consumption that litter the landscape in absolute space and time can generate senses of relative deprivation', writes David Harvey. 'We are surrounded at every turn with manifestations of the fetish desire for money power as the representation of value on the world market' (2019: 113). British passport-holder Farah may experience border-free travel much more easily than visa-holder Kabir, but their access to inherited wealth, or the lack of it, clogs those borders in unexpected ways. Farah holds value as a cruise-ship entertainer precisely because she cannot access the familial luxury to which the Mehras are entitled. The scene in which Kabir and Farah's relationship is seen to end, mirrors the aforementioned scene in the auditorium: Kabir is back at a rehearsal, trying to talk to Farah, demonstrating his aggression with a male crew member, who is her colleague. This time, instead of humouring him as she did when he first asked her out, she cuts short his snivelling about the elaborate ruse of which he was a part. Reminding him yet again of her relationship to the place, she asks him to save his games for his father, to get out, as this is her 'place of work'.

Jayashree Kamble discerns that 'the leisure practice of touring Europe in *ZNMD* is specifically tied to the notion of escaping work and daily life, and to early capitalist ideology that travel is a way to self-realization' (2015: 4). The men partake in cultural activities unique to Spain, moving from one posh apartment to another in expensive cars, each more elegant than the last. They all appear to have strained relationships to money, and they come from different income backgrounds: Arjun is self-made and rich but has no familial wealth, Kabir is wealthy but is marrying partly in order to keep that wealth intact, and Imraan is neither rich nor has a family who can support him in Mumbai, and is self-conscious about it, making copious fun of an expensive bag that Arjun gifts Natasha and Kabir for their wedding. In spite of their rocky relationships to economic capital, none of the men appear to think twice when spending that money in social and cultural leisure activities requiring economic participation. They drink, they dance, they go to prison without the slightest fear of deportation. Their leisure is budget-less, border-less and they are all trying to do less work. Kamble elaborates, '[*ZNMD*] superficially critiques the Western economic and cultural practices spread by globalization, particularly as initially exemplified by Arjun, but glamorizes a version of leisure that is but another manifestation of that system and dependent on it for its continuation' (2015: 5).

In contrast, Laila's workplace is the ocean and the beach, where she is constructed as liberated and having it all. While she is 'at home' in the opulence of those environments, hers too is a workplace romance. In a now-famous underwater romance sequence, she and Arjun have an erotic moment that emerges out of pedagogy: she is trying to lessen his fear of the water, he is moved to be shown a beautiful woman's favourite coral-reef hideout. Even here, the consumption of the 'experience' of swimming with and watching a water-spirit who is also a diving professional is an act of class citizenship. Arjun could always have everything he wanted with the money he made, but he now can have it all because he has been convinced of the value of the spectacle that is Laila opening his eyes to the wonders of the world.

Weeks argues that 'the work site is where we often experience the most immediate, unambiguous, and tangible relations of power that most of us will encounter on a daily basis' (2011: 2). This rings true for the representation of working women across the first three of Akhtar's films, but especially for her debut *LBC*. A film that is focused on work, ambition and fortune within the Hindi film industry, *LBC* contrasts the fates of Sona (Konkona Sen Sharma), an 'outsider' from North India, and Nikki Walia (Isha Sharvani), the daughter of the once-leading actress Neena Walia (Dimple Kapadia), against Vikram Jaisingh (Farhan Akhtar), a fame-hungry young man who has left his home and his father's family business in Delhi to train at the modest Nand Kishore acting school so that he may become a leading hero. As Anne Ciecko writes on the title sequence of the film:

> [It] unfolds to display an array of direct-camera gazes by 'invisible' personalities behind the scenes, and above- and below-line talent including prop makers and masters, costume manufacturers and fitters, makeup artists, stunt performers and extras, security guards, projectionists, billboard erectors, hair stylists, sound technicians, catering staff, playback singers, and camera crew members and grips on the job. (2018: 30)

LBC is in love with the production and *work* of cinema as much as it is enamoured with the promise of glitter and opulence that accompany the world, specifically stardom.

Of the three films explored in detail in this chapter, this is perhaps the only film that is about the trials and successes of a work life that is distinct from a life of leisure. Like *ZNMD* and *DDD*, *LBC* too entails workplace romances at the heart of the conflict: Nikki and Sona both want Vikram and aspire to strong careers, and Vikram enjoys the attention and intimacy with both women, but he only wants to be a star. Unlike Nikki and Vikram, Sona and Vikram don't meet at work but they share the same dreams and contacts. On the single occasion that Sona, on her time off from work, travels to meet him at a shooting location with the hopes of surprising him, Vikram is cold and embarrassed. She asks to stay with him in his hotel room, and he declines, citing work ethics and the need to be professional to cover up for the affair he's having with his co-star Nikki. In this way, Sona is never allowed proximity to that opulence, only to the expectation of it. As the film unfolds, Sona is confined to her small, drab flat, as Vikram continues to ride the waves of luxury following his rise to fame. Nikki, in contrast, having been 'born into' the privilege of being Neena Walia's daughter, does not embrace a change in lifestyle. It appears from the start as though for her, p/leisure and work – when it is revealed in a tongue-in-cheek admission that she wanted to be a vet and then decided to go into films instead – have always overlapped. When Nikki is not entertaining her mother, a photo-shoot crew, Vikram or her friend Tanya, all for work and pleasure, we are not witness to how her life passes. Interiority, it appears, takes leisure time.

The 'emotion work' that the women do at the workplace across the films also codes as leisure, because it involves partaking of leisure-like activities at spaces of opulence and global capital: enjoying ice cream by the pool at a five-star hotel, swimming in luxurious apartments and hotels, dancing on a cruise ship, deep-sea diving and being liberated at a festival in Spain, cycling in Istanbul. The unwaged nature of it is represented as the residue of the working relationship: when Laila dines with the men after their deep-sea diving lessons, it is because, as a frustrated Kabir explains to his fiancée, she is their diving instructor. Farah is an entertainer on a cruise ship, who likewise has to socialise with the guests to keep them happy. Nikki has a photo shoot for her debut film in her pink-as-confectionery room, which her co-star Vikram visits later as a part of a work-related dinner. These are gendered expectations too, and they manifest as such primarily because the jobs Farah, Laila and Nikki do are in proximity to luxury. Their glamour-work is premised on delivering leisure as affect for the consumption of the male gaze, which is not restricted to the men in their films, but also extends as an invitation to us as potential consumers of luxury and glamour. Come to Spain, come to Turkey, come to Film City, they indicate, where leisure is in abundance.

THE PLEASURABLE POLITICS OF CARE WORK

Megha Anwer observes of *ZNMD* that 'all the women who do the physical labor of servicing the hyper-mobile men-on-vacation are also available for the emotional labor of entertaining men and facilitating the expansion of their horizons' (2019: 309). Laila oils the trio's friendship, while Natasha organises the wedding with almost no input from Kabir. Due to the attention devoted in scholarly literature to this line of argument with respect to *ZNMD*, the final section of this chapter will focus on how the women in Akhtar's first and third films, *LBC* and *DDD*, perform care work as a form of leisure.

Jean Duncombe and Dennis Marsden note that 'women in paid employment are still largely compelled either to perform the "double-shift" of work and housework, or to do emotion work on themselves to lower their standards of cleanliness and tending' (1995: 164). In *LBC*, the representation of Sona's indifference to domestic life is framed as ineptitude, contrasted with Vikram's lifestyle, which evolves slowly from living with his aunt in a small flat – where he lives after moving from his parents' home in Delhi – to finding a flat for himself at the top of a tower block of flats in Versova, a cosmopolitan Mumbai

Figure 9.1 Sona stares at the domestic apparatus Vikram won.

suburb that is in proximity to film studios. On his first visit, when Vikram asks Sona why she doesn't have a fridge, she replies that her old fridge is broken and she does not have time to order a new one, so she pays to use her neighbour's fridge. Sona complains openly about her lack of desire for cooking when Vikram chides her for not eating healthily. In the same scene, at a grocery store, Vikram fills in a caption contest that eventually wins Sona a fridge. Framed towards the end of the film as the only light in a darkened flat, the fridge represents, if not a traditional fridging of Sona's character arc,[2] a cruel reminder that while she enabled his career by passing on his headshots in a gesture of romantic goodwill, all he left her was a piece of domestic apparatus.

Here, Sona's aspirations in 'making it' are directly at odds with her ability to tend to housework; her 'double-shift' is a single one, geared towards becoming a parallel lead in a blockbuster production. This changes when she and Vikram become romantically involved; in addition to offering him emotional support during his momentary lapse in confidence, Sona also makes decisions about films, keeping his status as a leading hero in mind. She turns down a small role in the same film as him (and fires her manager when he questions her decision to make career decisions around men), and eventually when Vikram snubs her on her surprise visit to the set, she descends into the throes of domestic hell, not leaving her flat and refusing to see friends. Her 'single shift' becomes a 'triple-shift', juggling her career, his career and his feelings, until she loses all three and her care work, or its potential, fails to rebound on herself.

Even in representing the sexism of the industry, Sona's role in *LBC* is of a woman who is foolish enough to perform care work for a man who only cares for his career. In her final conversation with him on the set for a TV show in which she has won a lead role – another instance, as in *DDD*, of a man who intrudes on his romantic interest's workplace – Sona confronts his need to frame her as an anchor in his life. Flitting between states of distress, anger and vulnerability, Sona finally refuses to work the one-way system of emotional care that bloomed as a fungus in their relationship, calling him selfish, before losing resolve to commit to her refusal. To soften the blow, she takes his hand and says it's not really his fault, some people just are like that. Sona is caring towards Vikram, even in her most powerful act of self-care, which is to stop caring for him and cease ensuring his comfort over hers. As Ciecko observes, 'In *Luck by Chance*'s ultimately bleak view of the foibles of the film industry and gender imbalances, Vikram succeeds in becoming a star not primarily because of talent, but because he is a man who learns to manipulate effectively' (2018: 33).

Sona emerges, however, as the protagonist of the film. Where Vikram moves from being an ambitious actor to a famous one, Sona's character arc is uneven but captivating, as she transitions from being an earnest, ambitious actor to a more sober, chastised one. Her refusal of Vikram marks a break with the traditional expectations of heterosexual romance, but also with the prescribed neoliberal dreams of an industry aspirant. Weeks argues:

> From the perspective of the refusal of work, the problem with work cannot be reduced to the extraction of surplus value or the degradation of skill, but extends to the ways that work dominates our lives. The struggle against work is a matter of securing not only better work, but also the time and money necessary to have a life outside work. (2011: 13)

LBC aspires less to the politics of anti-work and functions more as an ode to the myth of meritocracy and hard work, and the odd thrill of the fate–work duet. It is notable that it is the only film out of all of Akhtar's films to reckon with the failed and false premise of the work ethic, and indeed the melancholia of self-enquiry that follows a fallen dream. In *ZNMD* and *DDD*, while the men ostensibly attain self-awareness in the neoliberal pursuit of their 'dream' jobs over the ones they have at the beginning of the films (corporate inheritor, stock market banker, copywriter), the women's stories close with the unification of their family or social units (for Laila, her wedding to Arjun, for Farah, a return to her gig-economy life and possibly a reunion with Kabir that we are not witness to, and in the case of Ayesha, her union with her old flame and nuclear family).

LBC, however, claims Sona as the protagonist whose relationships to her work and to herself mature. The film opens with a close-up of Sona's face, freshly arrived in Mumbai and enquiring about screen tests to the producer of Pinky Productions, and being told derisively that screen tests are futile; the director's eye, she is told, is the camera ('Maker *ki aankh* camera *hoti hai*'), and in this moment we see both the truth of the statement, as Sona will go on to have an unmemorable career partly because she has no enviable social connections, but also the meta-theatrical nod towards the position and role of the director herself; Zoya Akhtar, who has cast most of her immediate family and industry A-listers like Aamir Khan and Shah Rukh Khan, among others, in bit roles in the film, is the eye of the industry camera.

The film's closing scene alludes to the same comment, with another close-up of Sona's face as she sits in the back of a taxi after walking through the city. Her melancholic voiceover narrates the story of her arrival, and of the supposed casteless ideal that is Mumbai, which is a contrast to her hometown where she would have had to marry someone from her own caste. In the voiceover, she says that she does not lament her failure to make it as a big actress; she is still able to do good work, and earn her own living in the city. It is an acknowledgement of the capitalist con of urban class ambition, rather than a chastening over the 'degradation of skill'. In their ethnographic study of women's leisure within heterosexual romances, Kristi Herridge, Susan Shaw and Roger Mannell note that 'in romantic relationships, women who have internalized a lack of sense of entitlement to leisure and an ethic of care may place more importance on their partners' leisure over their own leisure choices and preferences' (2003: 275). In the end, Sona's ethics of care extend to the fulfilment of her dreams over someone else's, even as her dreams are a consolation prize: while she is not a famous film star, as her dreams at the start of the film indicate, she is a central character on a television soap.

In contrast to Sona's arc of self-discovery, Nikki Walia's arc is cared for almost entirely by her former star mother, Neena Walia. Neena is fussy. She wants the best for Nikki's debut film: the best clothes, the best hero, the best diet, the best interview narratives. Nikki's condescension towards her climaxes in an outburst from Neena at the end of the film, where she lists all the sacrifices she had to make and the abuses she faced in order to become a superstar in her time. Neena's anger is deeply gendered, but is ultimately care work: she is upset because she wants her daughter to have a better life. Even her vulnerability has a purpose, and it is the same purpose that we have been privy to from the beginning: Neena's motherhood, which has replaced her (waged) work.

In *DDD*, the mother–daughter relationship has more friction. Even as they turn away from each other, Neelam and her daughter Ayesha perform care work as leisure for other family members. Ayesha is the perfect, sacrificial daughter, ignoring her mother-in-law's jibes about her work, swallowing her sadness at being overlooked continuously by her parents, until she isn't; she leaves her marriage and refuses to become pregnant. But her last act in the film, when she jumps into the lifeboat with her parents so as to save her brother, is in line with the emotional work she has done throughout on a family holiday. She commits to another relationship, and then does all she can to save the nuclear family ideal.

CONCLUSION

While the films do not always pit the women against each other as much as contrast different gendered inhabitations of work and leisure, the gendered 'workplaces' of leisure/work constructed in the films represent both a glamorised and seamless view of work-*as*-leisure, as well as work as a pleasurable site of neoliberal aspiration and heterosexual romance. Through glamour-work – involving the performance of wealth, femininity and movement through leisure – care work and inhabiting spaces of work that blur as leisure, Akhtar's gaze actively frames her women characters working in patriarchal spaces of leisure. Laila, Farah and Nikki are all hard at work in so far as the sexual capital derived from their work is channelled as pleasure – and indeed, leisure – for the respective male romantic leads in question. The same is true for Neena, Ayesha, Sona and Natasha in relation to care work more broadly. Women's work is framed in Akhtar's filmic spaces as a gendered form of glamorous leisure, accessible in and through patriarchal networks of kinship and heterosexual romance.

NOTES

1. The characters of Laila and Natasha are played by actresses who are white or part-white; the implications of the casting are beyond the scope of this chapter, but may be explored in future iterations of this research.
2. 'Fridging' was coined as a term by comics writer Gail Simone in 1999, after a *Green Lantern* comic (1994) in which the hero discovers his dead girlfriend Alexandra DeWitt stuffed in a fridge, murdered by his nemesis Major Force. The term now refers to a narrative mechanism through which women characters are erased, often by death and through violent means but not always, thus accelerating the character development of male protagonists who react actively to the disappearances of women. The removal of women from the story becomes the very impetus for privileging and enhancing the complexity of male character arcs.

WORKS CITED

Anwer, Megha (2019), 'Consumer pleasures and Hindi cinema's en-gendered distribution of moral capital in *Hum Aapke Hain Koun* (1994) and *Zindagi Na Milegi Dobara* (2011)', in Saswati Sengupta, Shampa Roy and Sharmila Purkayastha (eds), *'Bad' Women of Bombay Films: Studies in Desire and Anxiety*, Palgrave Macmillan, e-book, pp. 297–312.

Ciecko, Anne (2018), 'Reflexive global Bollywood and metacinematic gender politics in *Om Shanti Om* (2007), *Luck by Chance* (2008), and *Dhobi Ghat* (2010)', *Diogenes*, 62: 1, pp. 24–37.

Duncombe, Jean and Dennis Marsden (1995), '"Workaholics" and "whingeing women": Theorising intimacy and emotion work – The last frontier of gender inequality?', *The Sociological Review*, 43: 1 (February), pp. 150–69. DOI: 10.1111/j.1467-954X.1995.tb02482.x

Gundle, Stephen (2009), *Glamour: A History*, Oxford: Oxford University Press USA - OSO. ProQuest Ebook Central.

Harvey, David (2019), *Spaces of Neoliberalization: Towards a Theory of Uneven Geographical Development*, Stuttgart: Franz Steiner Verlag. ProQuest Ebook Central.

Herridge, Kristi L., Susan M. Shaw and Roger C. Mannell (2003), 'An exploration of women's leisure within heterosexual romantic relationships', *Journal of Leisure Research*, 35: 3, pp. 274–91. DOI: 10.1080/00222216.2003.11949994

Hochschild, Arlie Russell (2012), 'Between the toe and the heel: Jobs and emotional labor', in *The Managed Heart: Commercialization of Human Feeling*, Berkeley: University of California Press, pp. 137–61.

Kamble, Jayashree (2015), 'All work or all play? Consumption, leisure, and ethics under globalization in *Zindagi Na Milegi Dobara*', *South Asian Popular Culture*, 13: 1, pp. 1–14.

Lefebvre, Henri (1991), *Critique of Everyday Life*. Vol. 1. Translated by John Moore. London: Verso.

— (1984), *Everyday Life in the Modern World*, New York: Routledge, e-book.

Raghavendra, M. K. (2011), '*Zindagi Na Milegi Dobara*, *Delhi Belly* and the imagined nation', *Economic and Political Weekly*, 46: 36 (3–9 September): pp. 27–9.

— (2014), *The Politics of Hindi Cinema in the New Millennium: Bollywood and the Anglophone Indian Nation*, Oxford University Press, Oxford Scholarship Online. DOI: 10.1093/acprof:oso/9780199450565.001.0001

Weeks, Kathi (2011), *The Problem with Work: Feminism, Marxism, Antiwork Politics, and Postwork Imaginaries*, Durham, NC: Duke University Press.

Whitesell, Lloyd (2018), 'Concepts and parameters', in *Wonderful Design: Glamour in the Hollywood Musical*, New York: Oxford University Press, Oxford Scholarship Online. DOI: 10.1093/oso/9780190843816.003.0002

CHAPTER 10

Self-made vs Self-respect: The Politics of Belonging in Zoya Akhtar's Films

Vijeta Kumar

Bollywood has had a steady preoccupation with the hero's journey towards his self-realisation. Over the years, the idea of the male *Bildungsroman* as seen in *Maine Pyar Kiya* (Sooraj R. Barjatya 1989) up to *Lakshya* (Farhan Akhtar 2004) has not evolved and it is rare that the hero arrives at his 'self' on his own. There is usually a female lead, as in *Wake up Sid* (Ayan Mukherjee 2009), or a parent, as seen in *Waqt* (Yash Chopra 1965), to guide him through this journey. In these films, the hero is already rich because his father is, so to become successful is not the objective. The goal, rather, is to achieve some sense of self-sufficiency and an emotional emancipation from paternal authority.

In these cases, even the self-realising act of obtaining a job and the identity and dignity that comes with it is not the main focus, as what is highlighted is rather the new, freer way of seeing themselves after they get a job. Unlike the strong identity or self-realisation place that the job holds for women characters in films, the heroes' job doesn't draw much attention to itself because there are very few jobs in the 'outside' world that are considered 'not for men' and therefore their obtainment represents less self-actualisation and struggle. The heroes have a clear sense that 'rich' does not mean self-made and they take time to arrive at the realisation that, unlike their fathers, they are not self-made. In contrast, rarely do we see a woman in Bollywood on the quest of finding herself. Beyond biopics, the woman heroine either knows what she is good at and must deal with traditional obstacles to continue doing it, as occurs in films like *Dil Bole Hadippa* (Anurag Singh 2009) or *Tumhari Sulu* (Suresh Triveni 2017), where 'the self' is tied to the women's jobs as professional, or she finds that she has nothing left to do but discover her 'self' after a partner has left her, seen in *Queen* (Vikas Bahl 2013) or *Dear Zindagi* (Gauri Shinde 2016). The question remains: Where does that leave women who cannot or do not lose themselves in work or sport? How often do we come close to watching a woman's discovery of herself in Bollywood without the notion of her 'self' attached to the job?

Women as active participants in their own *Bildungsroman* is something we are yet to see more of. The word *Bildung* is the German for 'self-cultivation': Bollywood takes the self-cultivation of its heroes seriously and their 'self-made-ness' even more so. What we are left to imagine then is where and how women fit into Bollywood's idea of the *Bildungsroman*. Zoya Akhtar is perhaps one of the few filmmakers who invests in this curiosity. Interestingly, in her films it is the women who play mother/aunt and do not appear to have a job who are the ones who carry the burden of finding themselves in more ways than one. And this is especially important if we are to ask ourselves what the idea of a self-made woman includes, and whether it is also inclusive of women who cannot work or do not want to. Akhtar offers us a place from which to view these women who cannot hide behind the glamour of independence, women who find that they have to constantly keep doing things to belong in their marriages or in their own lives.

With the men, Akhtar does something even more interesting. She questions the idea of being self-made by confronting it with social realities, something that the films mentioned above do not do, and something that Bollywood is accused of being blind to. In *Gully Boy* (2019), *Dil Dhadakne Do* (2015), *Zindagi Na Milegi Dobara* (2011), *Luck by Chance* (2009) and the Amazon web series *Made in Heaven* (2019), Akhtar gives us a range of men and women who jump through various social obstacles, sometimes invisibly, to become self-made and search for belonging.

In this chapter I will examine how Akhtar puts men and women through both similar and dissimilar challenges to 'make' themselves. In her portrayal of men, Akhtar shows that even though men in society are granted a certain gendered power, other social factors impact that power and lead to different journeys of self-realisation. Following this line of argument, the first section explores the father–son relationships in *Gully Boy*, *ZNMD* and *DDD*, and observes how they are bound by caste and class realities to the ideas that the fathers in these films pass on to their sons about success and being self-made. The second section focuses on the women in *DDD*, *Made in Heaven* and *LBC* who stand at the periphery because of gender but are motivated by a desire to belong. The average Bollywood woman-centric film needs its women to be 'strong' leads. An absolute investment in their selves, their work becomes the defining aspect of what makes the film 'women-centric'. In the popular 'women-centric' films produced across the 2000s (*Chandni Bar* [Madhur Bhandarkar 2001], *Chameli* [Sudhir Mishra 2004], *Chak De! India* [Shimit Amin 2007], *Kahaani* [Sujoy Ghosh 2012]), we do not get to know the women beyond their work, as the filmmaker appears to be checking a list without really paying attention to what and who the women are outside of and without their work. Akhtar departs from this tradition in more ways than one. This chapter will explore how her approach to women in her films separates her work from the range of 'women-centric' films that Bollywood produces. Though these struggles may be dissimilar at the surface level, Akhtar shows how both men and women, even if they seem to belong, must actually go through their own journeys in their fight to belong.

SONS AND FATHERS: LOOKING FOR POWER IN FAMILY

In *Gully Boy*, Aftab Ahmed (Vijay Raaz), a Muslim man, lives with his family in Mumbai's Dharavi slum. We do not know much about him, such as where he works or why he is having the TV set moved into the only bedroom of his house, and we only begin to form a judgement of him when we see him bringing home a second wife. This early glimpse of him already sets him out as an inconsiderate man. In relation to this, we see Murad (Ranveer Singh), Aftab's son, standing mutely by the entrance of this house, wearing earphones, listening to A$AP Rocky's 'Everyday', and glaring as his father and the new wife walk into the house. Before he goes in, Aftab tears out one of Murad's earphones, causing an abrupt shift in the music, which is replaced by the sounds of shehnai announcing the wedding. Murad glares at his father and replaces the earphone and we shift back to 'Everyday'.

The rest of the scene unfolds wordlessly as 'Everyday' continues to play. We look at this scene through Murad's eyes who, still standing, looks around at the gathering of people celebrating his father's second marriage, and then looks at his mother, Razia (Amruta Subhash), and his brother who are serving beverages to the guests. What is pronounced in the scene is twofold: Aftab's violence and the helplessness of Murad and his mother.

We aren't given a backstory to Aftab's decision to remarry (not that this knowledge would make him any less inconsiderate) and we do not know at this time that he works as a driver in a wealthy house. These are things we only begin to find out as Murad's backstory is further developed. There is not enough to gather about Aftab but what is palpable is the mounting tension between the father and son, which is felt at various points, often ending in Aftab beating up Razia and his sons mercilessly. To understand this as patriarchal violence is one thing; to understand it as the result of class violence in which a working-class man must keep his head down through the day, only to vent his frustration by beating his wife and children, is another. But both views are reductive in their perspectives of understanding the powerlessness of a Muslim man living in a country that is becoming more and more Islamophobic.

SELF-MADE VS SELF-RESPECT   183

Figure 10.1 Aftab's demonstrations of patriarchal violence are present throughout *Gully Boy*.

Something that Aftab repeats through *Gully Boy* that often loses ground to more ideal arguments is how he perceives the world as a Muslim man. He warns Murad on the first day of his job replacing Aftab as a personal driver to his wealthy employers, 'Do as you're told, no need to do heroism.' Right before that scene, Razia, who has had big dreams for Murad, is heard arguing with Aftab. She does not want Murad to be sent to do a '*phaltu*' (menial) job. 'You said he'd do an office job', to which Aftab replies: 'Next time you dream, make sure you look around first and match those dreams with our realities', and then adds, 'Who asks after us Muslims anyway these days?'

Aftab is primarily framed in terms of his failures and violence as a husband and father, and we rarely see his powerlessness as a Muslim man. There is no doubt that his violence towards Murad and Razia is brutal. But it is brutal also because it is visible. The scenes that depict him as a powerless man, however, are just as brutal, although not as visible. Here again, Aftab is not just painted as a one-dimensional character that is a victim of the system. The viewer must work at imagining his powerlessness outside of the home. We never get to see Aftab at work or dealing with the world, like we see Murad do. We catch a fleeting glimpse of Aftab's every day when we watch Murad in his father's employer's kitchen, looking at a tray of breakfast being prepared by Aftab's second wife: juice in a glass flask, cereal with exotic berries and a bowl of grapefruit.

Even when we see Murad in the spaces that his father occupies on a daily basis, we cannot get the full sense of Aftab's disenfranchisement in this world that he is so far removed from. Murad has received a college education, is familiar with English and is more immersed in the global culture that gives him at least some exposure to this distant world he is entering. When he drives the daughter of a family to the nightclub, he is drawn towards the entrance because he knows the music that she and her friends are listening to and also likes it. Though he is brusquely told to move away and back to his place, he is much more familiar with at least the culture of this world, as opposed to the circle of the other drivers who exchange recipes and talk about aspects of their daily life from which Murad seems removed but which we know Aftab might fit into more easily even if we never see him at work.

At one point when Murad is driving the family to a New Year's Eve party, the father comments to his daughter who has just received her BA and is avoiding graduate school, that even the driver has a BA and she must do better than that. While it is clearly understood that Murad is in no way viewed as an equal, there is some sense that the knowledge and power Murad holds is different from his father's. Murad looks up and sees and understands aspects of the world around him, while Aftab has walked through life with his head down outside of the house and now struggles to look around him.

Towards the end of the film, when Murad's newly launched song goes viral on the internet, we get to see an Aftab we have not seen before, underscoring his disenfranchisement from society and its changes. He stares emptily into Murad's phone when Murad shows him how many people have watched and liked his video. 'See what people have written about me? Read, read!' Murad says. Murad tries to demonstrate to his father that, walking with his head up, he has obtained a voice in a society that is structured to disregard him. Aftab – quickly, angrily, shifting his gaze away from the phone demands – 'What of it?' Persistent in his belief that likes and comments on songs mean nothing, he reminds Murad who they are and who they will continue to be – servants who shouldn't dare to dream big.

From somewhere and nowhere, a stunning scene from Nagraj Manjule's Marathi film *Fandry* (2013) comes to mind where Jabya (Somnath Awghade), a Dalit boy in love with Shalu (Rajeshwari Kharat), an upper-caste girl, writes a love letter to her in Marathi. But before he is able to give it to her, his father, Kachru Mane (Kishor Kadam), finds the letter.

The viewer comes to this moment well prepared from having watched and perhaps known from experience that love letters getting caught by parents is bad. But to watch a Dalit man who toils day and night, barely surviving, managing somehow to send his son to school only to find the son's love letter in his school bag is worse. We worry for Jabya and expect something terrible.

Instead, his father looks puzzled, then annoyed, and complains about Jabya's schoolbooks being scattered everywhere. The fact that Jabya's father does not know how to read is not broached again nor shown to us in any hard-hitting final way. In *Fandry*, Kachru Mane's illiteracy is not an event, nor a non-event. It is curious that Manjule has chosen a very precarious scene in the film to add that moment, making it easy to miss if you are not looking carefully.

Jabya can read, write, love and dream of a future, whereas Kachru Mane is continually shut out of society and now even his son's life. This dichotomy between a father who has learnt to keep his head down and a son who is learning not to, can result in the growing anger the son holds against the father. Dalit parenthood often deals with this 'special' anger that is understood popularly as teenage angst in mainstream *savarna*[1] discourse. This is why when the son of a Dalit or a Muslim man dreams of becoming self-made, we cannot afford to overlook the context that produces this dichotomy in the first place. In *Gully Boy* this question is raised time and again whenever Murad and Aftab's differing world views are played against each other.

Vetrimaaran's *Asuran* (2019), a Tamil film based on a novel written by Poomani called *Vekkai*, is perhaps one among very few Indian films that depict the struggles of a Dalit father and offer an interesting point of entrance into the question of how societal hierarchies affect fatherhood. It is the story of a man moving between the shifting dilemmas that these identities bring. Following Sivasaami (Dhanush), a Dalit farmer trying to protect his land and family, the film shows him resiliently accepting public humiliation inflicted by upper-caste landlords, much to the agitation of his sons. However, while showing this now powerless side of Sivasaami, the film also gives us a glimpse into his past, where we see in his youth an abundance of the resilience that his sons would like to see in the present. As a young man, Sivasaami certainly wouldn't have agreed to fall at the feet of men. His past reveals a quicker, angrier and vengeful man, an attitude for which he was made to pay a heavy price. His resistance to caste violence was considered 'too big for his boots' by the upper-caste landlords who set fire to the Dalit colony in the village, wiping out Sivasaami's entire family. Oscillating between the extremes of resilience and anger, *Asuran* is one of the rare films that shed light on the complexities of Dalit fatherhood.

As fathers, we are given a little more of Kachru in *Fandry* and Sivasaami in *Asuran* than of Aftab in *Gully Boy*. The violence against Kachru and Sivasaami is far more brutal and explicitly directed by caste. But within the interiority of fatherhood, Aftab too struggles with the complexities of raising a child in a world where he himself has been deemed powerless. The powerlessness of Aftab, although not entirely similar to that of Kachru's or Sivasaami's, is muted in relation to the powerlessness of Murad who, like Jabya, is in love and has aspirations that are continually encouraged from those who can help him become 'self-made.'

Which is why we might have to pause, rewind and ask ourselves if we know for sure whether Aftab can read. It may not be something that the film itself cares about, but nevertheless it is still relevant to our understanding of the man whose son dares to write and perform, which brings us to the question: Is Aftab wrong when he says, 'Life is not easy for people like us. We cannot take big steps. We must learn to keep our heads down and walk'? Is he holding

Murad back and imposing his own powerlessness on the next generation, or simply keeping his son safe, as he fears, like Sivasaami, the negative repercussions his son might face if he gets 'too big for his boots'?

Aftab's character thus holds for us another entrance into the power dynamics the film examines. Here we can see how Aftab's own disenfranchisement is passed down to his son, who must not only fight the world but also his father to realise his dreams. Neither Murad nor the film can be held accountable for not knowing whether Aftab can read and what is his own complex story of power struggles in a society where he has been forced to keep his head down. In Akhtar's films there appears to be room enough for the viewer to ask these questions.

At the other end of society is Kamal Mehra (Anil Kapoor) from *DDD*, Akhtar's third film. Kamal also struggles with power, though in a completely different context. While he lives in a world that is miles away from Aftab's, he still believes, in theory at least, that he has had to struggle as hard as Aftab. Though he has built a business empire and has the money to exert his power in various ways in a capital-based society, his struggle with power is retaining that 'hard-won' power as its loss is always just around the corner, either through the impending bankruptcy of his company or his fall from the position of unquestioned patriarchal power in his family.

When we are first introduced to Kamal Mehra, the narrator (Aamir Khan) tells us that Kamal built his business up from scratch and is what they call a 'self-made man'. For the viewers, this is an introduction as well as a warning. The narrator points out that Kamal insists on constantly reminding everyone that he is 'self-made'. Neelam (Shefali Shah), Kamal's wife and biggest critic, is the quickest to roll her eyes at this. Their daughter, Ayesha (Priyanka Chopra), and son, Kabir (Ranveer Singh), are just as aware of this but roll their eyes less publicly. Kamal's claim to being self-made is broached and ridiculed at the very beginning when the narrator says, 'If he is self-made, he could've made himself a little better.'

We are often reminded by the narrator and others in the film that we are not to take Kamal or his references to his own hard work seriously. The first time Kamal mentions it is at the start of his lecture to his son. 'I have worked very hard, Kabir. I took the bus to work and when there was no money, I went walking. The soles of my shoes would be worn out.' Neelam interrupts him at this point to sarcastically ask, 'Really? What happened after that? We have not heard this story before at all.' In fact, we never do find out the rest of that story. It lies there, ridiculed at the Mehras' dining table, and we never return to it.

Even if Kamal's tales of hardship do hold some truth, he is still pointedly removed from Aftab. While Aftab has also worked very hard, taking the bus every day to his job of driving people like Kamal Mehra around town, he has never had anything to show for it. Thus, while both fathers try to use their life experience as a lesson to their sons, the lesson itself is very different as they come from dissimilar places and offer disparate outcomes. Aftab tries to advise Murad out of fear and anger at the world, and Kamal does it out of a bittersweet nostalgia for his own struggling years, and the belief that without him, Kabir will suffer in the 'real world'. What middle-class and upper-middle-class, upper-caste Hindu parents mean when they use the phrase 'real world' is perhaps being born as Dalits or Muslims in a country that makes their survival very difficult. This is the world that Kamal wants to keep Kabir out of, while at the same time it is this 'real world' that Aftab is, to his mind, trying to help his son survive in.

Ranveer Singh's role, as a son listening to the *gyaan* (wisdom) of his fathers in both *Gully Boy* and *DDD*, is particularly interesting here. Kabir, though he does not want to follow in his father's footsteps exactly, does enjoy the life of wealth that his father has provided and can see, even if he doesn't admit it, a positive outcome of this path of hard work. When he meets Farah (Anushka Sharma), a woman he falls in love with, who tells him the story of how she ran away from home to be able to do what she really wants to do, he does offer some recognition that he would not be able to follow that hard path of truly fighting for his dreams. Murad, on the other hand, has no incentive whatsoever to follow in Aftab's footsteps and must fight for his dreams. Yes, Aftab might have survived life by not dreaming big, but this beaten-down survival is not the dream that Murad has, and he chooses to aim for something better, without the security net that Kabir has.

Akhtar's father-characters Aftab and Kamal arrive at being self-made in vastly different ways. Owing to caste and social capital, Kamal is able to hold his head high and climb the ladder, while Aftab has to keep his head down to retain what remains of his self as a Muslim man in an Islamophobic country. Either way, the notion of being self-made when it comes to fatherhood serves to confront social realities, which is more than what one can expect from a mainstream Bollywood film. Unlike the quintessential Bollywood sons mentioned at the beginning of the chapter who take up the journey to become self-made out of a romantic passion, here Akhtar manages to give us a range of characters who think and act like people not entirely devoid of social contexts. The criticism often levelled against Akhtar is that she only makes films 'about the rich for the rich', which, after *Gully Boy*, changed to 'she should stick to making films about the rich'. Both of these claims become reductive when one begins to pay attention to the subtexts in her films, which are lined with characters who are as real as the caste, religion and class realties that produce them.

WHO BELONGS HERE? CONFRONTING GENDER, CLASS AND CASTE BARRIERS

The father figures in Akhtar's films struggle with using the different degrees of power they have to become some version of a self-made man that society will allow them to become. How they shape themselves is based, to some extent, on patriarchal power that allows them to take on this mantle. The women, however, do not start with that stepping stone of power, and while struggling for the power to be self-made, they must also contend with creating a sense of self-respect as something equally, if not more, valuable.

The contrast between the male and female approach to being self-made, and especially the societal hurdles and conceptions around this, can be clearly seen in the trajectories of Vikram Jaisingh (Farhan Akhtar) and Sona Mishra (Konkona Sen Sharma) in Akhtar's directorial debut *LBC*. Both are aspiring actors who come to Mumbai like thousands do, aspiring to become Bollywood film stars. They arrive with no connections and no back-up plan. Though seemingly starting out from the same place, there are actually large power gaps at play that give Vikram advantages from the start. Arriving as a young, educated, comfortably middle-class male with a family member to stay with, Vikram is able to use his charm, small-time connections and cunning to land a leading role in a big film project.

Sona enters the film world at a different level, her story at once exposing the gendered power dynamics of the industry and offering a more nuanced look at the balancing act between being self-made and carrying self-respect. We are given a hint about the affair she has with a married producer, Satish Chaudhry (Alyy Khan), who lures her with the promise of a big role in a film. We aren't shown this affair as explicitly as we are shown Vikram's, who, when he begins shooting for his film, has an affair with the female lead Nikki Walia (Isha Sharvani). The Vikram–Nikki affair conducted privately but easily with a romantic song thrown in is carried in equal parts by Vikram and Nikki, whereas the Sona–Satish affair, although conducted equally privately, is carried mostly by her. Women are plagued to a larger degree than men by the belief that self-respect is more important than success. There are consequences, we are cautioned again and again.

That success always ends up interfering with sincerity in the film and modelling profession is something that is deeply explored in films like Madhur Bhandarkar's *Fashion* (2008) and *Heroine* (2012). These films convey a moral lesson for the female leads who allow success to 'change' them at the cost of their self-respect. Akhtar pushes Vikram and Sona into a similar position but is far more in control of the narrative and less willing to submit her film to an easy fate than Bhandarkar was.

Akhtar's focus is on Sona's survival, not as a moral lesson but for the sheer pleasure of watching a woman become someone she had long aspired to become, with or without love. The obstacles faced by Sona are professional and personal in nature, and she must constantly reinvent different, newer forms of self-respect to deal with changing situations. One instance is when she arrives at Vikram's shooting location to surprise him and is hurt when he behaves coldly and distantly towards her. Her friend, Laxmi (Megha Narkar), tells Sona about his affair with Nikki. Betrayed, she decides to confront him, and right when it looks like Sona is losing herself in the relationship, Laxmi reminds her, 'Our self-respect is in our hands.'

After that, it is liberating to watch Sona collect herself and break all contact with Vikram. He comes back twice: first, to confront her, assuming she leaked news of his affair with Nikki Walia to a gossip magazine and accusing her of trying to grab a share of his fame; second, to apologise to her after he finds out that Sona had nothing to do with the magazine article. Between the first and second time, Sona seems to have found the 'self-respect' that Laxmi reminded her of. She does not go after him, even to explain her innocence to him.

The film picks up a somewhat different register after this and shifts focus from Vikram to Sona. That Vikram's film is doing well is something we see through other sources. It is curious that, after having closely followed his journey to success, we do not celebrate it. The film itself has moved on at this point. Towards the end of the film we see Sona at her apartment, giving an interview, talking about her independence and how happy she is acting in TV serials, which aren't as glamorous as acting in films but still allow her the independence she seems to value more than glamour. As we approach the last scene in the film, we see a huge billboard of Vikram as Sona gets into a taxi and rides away.

In some sense, self-respect is pitched against being self-made, as something equally, if not more, valuable. At one point in the film, when Sona is refused a role in a big project after it was promised to her, she is on the verge of giving up. 'It's not in my destiny,' she says, and Vikram tells her that 'destiny' is a word for people who do not have the courage to make their own life. In principle, Kabir (*DDD*) lacks this drive and Murad (*Gully Boy*) becomes the poster boy for it.

Though Sona herself does not share the same social capital as Vikram, in an industry where female leads or co-leads are still under-represented and under-paid, Sona as a character is given equal time and development as her male counterpart. Akhtar does not have rigid ideas about what a 'main' role or a character in a film is or should be like. There is a certain democratic charm we see in the shift of focus between Vikram and Sona. We see a similar sentiment in *ZNMD*, where the idea of a 'lead' actor seems somewhat ruptured since there is no 'lead character' or 'lead story' as such.

Akhtar does not make these distinctions,[2] which allows for a certain kind of freedom in which all characters can become noticeable and memorable for something they say or do. There is a certain non-uniformity in the range of characters we get to see, who often struggle to belong to the world of those more uniformly of a certain class and caste. Because of this we see several perspectives and positions of people finding their way through the world and can see through these power dynamics that play out as they make attempts at belonging.

In addition, it is often the women who seem to have trouble belonging. Whether it is through clothes, mannerisms or 'good English', they are often reminded that they will always be outsiders. One example is Jaspreet 'Jazz' Kaur (Shivani Raghuvanshi) from *Made in Heaven*, Akhtar's web series co-created with Reema Kagti. Jaspreet works at Made in Heaven, a high-profile wedding-planning company run by Tara Khanna (Sobhita Dhulipala) and Karan Mehra (Arjun Mathur). She comes from a lower-middle-class Delhi family and, in the first few episodes, finds it hard to make friends with her colleagues who are mostly from upper-middle-class families.

In the second episode, Jazz causes a social blunder by sharing private wedding party pictures on social media. The picture is of the bride, a Dubai princess, who is kissing a celebrity guest at her wedding party the night before she is to be married. The picture goes viral and Jazz is yelled at by one of the seniors and warned, 'The next time this happens, you can catch a bus and go back to Dwarka or Rohini or wherever the fuck it is you're from.' Dwarka and Rohini are in West Delhi, an area that is neither posh nor affluent, as opposed to the clientele of Made in Heaven. Its reference here is significant in reminding Jazz of her social location in the hierarchy.

Later in the series, she uses the company credit card to buy an expensive outfit for herself, and although she intends to return it after wearing it once, the incident is discovered, and she is immediately fired. In the beginning, Jazz might have us believe that she is a stereotypical small-town girl who dreams of an elite social life. The outfit incident, and earlier in the series, when we are given generous scenes of Jazz enjoying her limited time at an expensive hotel room, are all ways in which she is reaching for something that appears to be just within reach for a brief moment.

She may not always reach these dreams, but Akhtar has different plans for Jazz. Like with Aftab, who is not pushed towards easy victimhood, and with Sona, whose narrative is not submitted to moral lessons, Jazz is given a raunchy sex life with a man who works at a garage in her area. Jazz hides this from everyone and doesn't seem to want anything except sex from him. This is in equal parts surprising and liberating to watch. One way of humanising people, who we are accustomed to seeing as victims by Bollywood standards, is to show them as people with the ability to think for themselves. Jazz is by all means a thinking character. She doesn't just survive – she fights, lives and fashions her own way of becoming self-made and finding self-respect, enough to say 'no' to Kabir Basrai's (Shashank Arora) flirtations until she is ready to start a physical relationship with him. She seems to like him too, and a little further into the story is heartbroken when she finds that he has a relationship with another girl. But Jazz is not willing to compromise on what she is looking for in a man and doesn't mince her words when she tells him this without hesitation. By not letting go of what is important to her – the ability to make a choice even at the cost of love – she doesn't give the viewer more reasons to pity her. There is something admirable in the way she balances her fight to be a certain way while still carrying the challenge of remaining an outsider.

Incidentally, Tara Khanna, who co-owns Made in Heaven, is also an 'outsider' by that logic, as she is originally from Laxmi Nagar, an area like Dwarka and Rohini in East Delhi. Though Tara has carefully constructed her life to give off a glowing veneer after marrying her former boss, top industrialist Adil Khanna (Jim Sarbh), her hold on this facade is tenuous. She must constantly prove her worth and her belonging because she can never undo the fact that she is from a place that her husband calls 'filthy'. Before joining as a secretary at Adil's firm, Tara takes an etiquette grooming course at 'Princess Grooming Academy'[3] ('Hands off the table, walk straight, do not make noise when you chew, smile even if the wine is bitter, do not step out before blow-drying your hair'), learning the ways of the elite world she wants to enter. While Tara is able to overcome class anxieties and develop tolerance for what she is unable to overcome – a suspicious mother-in-law, for instance, who exclaims 'business is not everybody's cup of tea', referring to the money Adil invests in her wedding-planning company – she is still not fully able to belong. And here, the viewer must ask whether this is covertly also about caste. She is desperate for a baby, in the hope that becoming a mother to the future heir of Adil's family wealth would solidify her position in the family. Marriage, contrary to what Tara hoped, has not seemed to have done that. This more permanent place in her marriage and Adil's family that she so desires is also a deeply rooted caste anxiety, something that women who marry into upper-caste families are often challenged with.

Tara's life comes apart after she discovers her husband's affair with her best friend and also his family friend, Faiza (Kalki Koechlin), who had previously made Tara feel welcomed in Adil's world of *khandani* (inherited) richness. But that was before Tara became, in Faiza's words to her therapist, 'All styled out, branded from head to toe.' Unable to hold her rage over the Faiza–Adil affair any longer, and after one of the many sorry messages Faiza sends her, Tara arrives at Faiza's house and trashes the place, breaking glasses, windows and mirrors. Later, when Adil picks a fight with Tara about this, he says, 'At the end of the day, class just fucking shows up, doesn't it? You can't buy it, it can't be taught, and it can't be married into, clearly. They could have you arrested. Then we would all be involved, publicly. Maybe think about it next time before letting your *jaat* (caste) show.'

It is not uncommon for people to use caste and class synonymously, often interchangeably. Curiously enough, Adil uses both class and caste in the same sentence but not interchangeably. He could have just as easily said 'class' instead of 'caste', the way so many upper-caste Indians do, but *jaat* is the word he is looking for. Class doesn't quite cut it, if what he really wants is to insult her and mean it. Oddly, he doesn't use the anglicised 'caste', which assumes a political flavour, and instead uses its more social, more local, Hindi counterpart. We do not know what Tara's caste is, but we can now take a guess. What we do know for sure is that Adil is aware of it enough to know that it is definitely not upper-caste.

Akhtar uses the insider–outsider equation to draw our attention to things that aren't overtly spelled out for the viewer. In *DDD*, she accords a certain newness to the rich lifestyle of the Mehras, and particularly Neelam Mehra. Though Neelam doesn't face the same class and caste anxiety as Tara, she does struggle with the fight to belong. When we are introduced to them, Kamal is playing golf with other businessmen. He has established himself enough to be here, giving us the impression that he owns whatever is around him. Neelam, on the other hand, has to rely on the materiality of things to be able to belong – clothes, mannerisms and, most importantly, silence. In many ways, her reputation is more at stake than Kamal's. Not long after she is introduced, the friends she is dining with speak behind her back about Kamal's affairs in a way that we do not see Kamal's friends do. Neelam, although well aware of this, must continue to behave as if everything is alright.

Kamal and Neelam eloped when they were young and have been together ever since. She stood by him when he was building his business, and even after he'd established himself enough to forget her and have extra-marital affairs, which cause Neelam great emotional trauma. We are given generous shots of Neelam privately dealing with her depression and its resulting eating disorders. In a particularly jarring scene, after she encounters Kamal openly flirting with a woman, we are shown a distraught Neelam stuffing cakes in her mouth. We see a similar, albeit differently motivated, shot of Kamal taking anti-anxiety medication to cope with the anxiety about his company's bankruptcy.

There is no doubt that Kamal and Neelam have both been rich for a while, but they've had to learn to adapt and develop an acquired taste and tolerance for the things that rich people are expected to do: expensive cruise vacations for family and friends, private planes, overt generosity and the inability to accept bankruptcy. When Kamal's manager's son, Sunny (Farhan Akhtar), returns with a cheque for Kamal, repaying in full (plus interest) the money Kamal spent on his Yale education, Neelam disapproves and feels he shouldn't have accepted it. Kamal says that he wasn't going to take it but had to because Sunny insisted. Generosity is an acquired taste, sometimes not acquired wholeheartedly. In the same scene, Sunny gives them an Egyptian artefact and Kamal and Neelam exchange praises about how beautiful it is, revealing a small performative joy at knowing what to recognise as good art.

Herein lies Akhtar's finesse. None of the four families that we get to know in *DDD* are alike. They might be the same kind of 'Dilli' (Delhi)-rich, but there are pointed differences in the way they dress and speak English. Perhaps less anxious to belong, compared to Akhtar's other characters, is Prem Mehra (Pawan Chopra), who occupies an interesting position in the Mehra family. Prem is Kamal's brother and works under him in an almost secretarial capacity. Kamal often gives orders to Prem publicly, something of which his daughter, Ayesha, disapproves. On the other hand, Prem's wife, Indu (Ayesha Raza), carries more social anxiety. While Prem is accepted to a certain degree because of his brotherhood and job, Indu can only look for acceptance in the gossiping circles of women who are as ruthless with their friends as with their foes. While we do not know them outside of their vacation behaviour and can only see how they act on the cruise with others, this high-pressure parade gives us a glimpse into Indu's fight for belonging.

At breakfast one morning, Indu is annoyed with her daughter, Divya (Sarah Hashmi), for not making an effort to look presentable. 'This is not your bedroom,' she says as she remarks on her daughter's outfit choice. She makes this observation after she notices Rana Khanna (Vikrant Massey), an eligible bachelor and another guest at the Mehras' anniversary, eyeing the affluent and posh Noorie Sood (Ridhima Sud). 'Look at Noorie,' she tells Divya in the hope that Divya will learn something about attire and etiquette from Noorie who is wearing a white minidress.

In a hilarious misunderstanding, Prem, Indu and their daughters, Divya and Putlu (Khushi Dubey), arrive for a family lunch dressed up in costumes because they thought it was a theme party. Divya, the first to realise that it is not, leaves immediately. Manav (Rahul Bose), Ayesha's husband, approaches them with a camera in hand, and takes their picture even as Indu looks visibly embarrassed, but Prem is seen smiling sweetly, posing for the camera. Indu, however, is mortified, again reminded that they are not quite part of this group.

There is nuance in the way the film is able to demonstrate the difference between inherited wealth or what is called '*khandani*' rich and the newly rich. We see a certain degree of performance in the way Neelam makes an effort with clothes, much like Tara. Although similarly lost in their respective marriages, Neelam and Tara both invest solidly in how they appear to friends and relatives as a way of keeping themselves 'belonged' to the world they have married into. And by that extension, they both have had to work hard to belong and are seen working harder to remain that way. But in their refusal to be victims, Neelam, Tara and Jazz exhibit a toughness that reflects Akhtar's reluctance to push people towards complete villainy or victimhood.

This is something that many reviews of *Made in Heaven*[4] and *DDD*[5] seem to have missed. Most argue that Akhtar's interest in showing the problems within elite families is an absurd height of privilege and that very often she ends up glamorising the very thing she sets out to ridicule. This, however, can be a premature assessment to make if, like the letter scene in Manjule's *Fandry*, the viewer has missed Adil's casteist way of taking Tara to task in *Made in Heaven* and the many ways in which Indu and Neelam have trouble belonging in *DDD*. Even at these levels, there is still a fight to be self-made and have self-respect that each woman must realise in her own way.

CONCLUSION

Caste and social capital allow one the opportunity to become self-made. Neither *Avarnas* (those outside the Varna/caste system) nor Muslims can afford to be self-made easily when the focus is on survival. The various versions of fatherhood in the films discussed are made to encounter these social realities. With Aftab–Murad, Kamal–Kabir and Prem, Akhtar stretches out possibilities of various kinds of fatherhood that are each governed by social structures just as they are by masculinity, patriarchy and control. This shift from a mainstream, loving father–son duo in Bollywood to one that is governed by religion, caste and class inequalities is visible as a necessary shift in Akhtar's films.

Another familiar aspect of her films is how they demonstrate a deliberate inattention to female characters who break the ceiling. The focus instead is on female characters who aren't able to do so, which makes them refreshingly familiar to what we may have grown up seeing in our families. In creating ordinary characters who could very well be a nosy, gossip-loving next-door neighbour, a friend trying hard to belong at a workplace, a wife from a wealthy family struggling to remain wealthy and a 'wife', Akhtar removes the burden on women to necessarily shine at their jobs to be successful, in order to recognise women who are usually forgotten. She makes us acknowledge them as people who have similar, if not more, complicated struggles with their identities, again as a result of social inequalities.

Akhtar's films do not seem to buy into the distraction of creating work and independence as easily for female characters and instead give us complicated characters who are on the other side of the curtain: mothers and aunts dependent on their husbands who seem to have made it but who find themselves stuck with a self that no longer fits their world. They deal with caste and class realities without entirely drawing attention to either, even if the very basis for their struggles is rooted in class and caste. And this stands out because their struggle to be noticed is not the subject of the film itself, thus abandoning entirely the checklist to make 'women-centric' films. The core argument of these films is that women do not have to do extraordinary things for a film to be 'women-centric'. The attention given to the nuances of a woman's ordinary struggle and interiority in her life is enough.

NOTES

1. *Savarna* – those with *Varna*, a caste Hindu, used for those within the *Varna* system. The phrase '*savarna* discourse' is used here to refer to the mainstream discourse surrounding father–son relationship portrayals in popular cinema, which shows a glaring lack of acknowledgement of how caste determines relationships between family members.

2. The desire for a strong, almost always male, lead is still present in the Bollywood film industry, leading to a lack of fully developed and intriguing supporting characters, especially when it comes to women's roles. In an Instagram post, actor Abhay Deol notes how with *ZNMD*, in which he played one of the three leads, 'Almost all the award functions demoted me and Farhan from main leads, and nominated us as "supporting actors". Hrithik and Katrina were nominated as "actors in a leading role". So by the industry's own logic, this was a film about a man and a woman falling in love, with the man supported by his friends for whatever decisions he takes.'
3. The sign appears written as such, with 'Acadmy' misspelled, signifying to the viewer that this is not an elite grooming school of the upper class, but a more modest version for working-class women.
4. 'Weddings, especially Punjabi weddings would make eminent viewership sense – has not Bollywood proved its efficacy in the box-office long enough? But while turning the lens to the hideousness behind these multi-crore affairs, *Made in Heaven* ends up glorifying them' (Sharma 2019).
5. 'Akhtar has tremendous fondness for the widely reviled one per cent. Akhtar luxuriates in beautiful clothes, accessories and experiences that only a few can afford, and her refusal to judge her well-shod characters beyond mild knocks at their self-absorption and naiveté allows us to forgive them their preciousness and vicariously take a vacation at their expense' (Ramnath 2015).

WORKS CITED

Ramnath, Nandini (2015), 'Film review: *Dil Dhadakne Do* is an empty vessel that makes a pretty noise', *Scroll*, 5 June 2015. Available at <https://scroll.in/article/732250/film-review-dil-dhadakne-do-is-an-empty-vessel-that-makes-a-pretty-noise>

Sharma, Sanjukta (2019), '*Made in Heaven* review: Strong performances and sharp writing, but the weddings get in the way', *Scroll*, 9 March 2019. Available at <https://scroll.in/reel/915796/made-in-heaven-review-strong-performances-and-sharp-writing-but-the-weddings-get-in-the-way>

PART IV

The Word and the Screen

CHAPTER II

Deconstructing the Perception of 'The Elite Class Filmmaker': A Critical Analysis of Mainstream Film Reviews of Zoya Akhtar's Cinema

Ruchi Kher Jaggi and Mudita Mishra

Zoya Akhtar's journey as a director in the Hindi film industry has had four key milestones, each represented by her feature films: *Luck by Chance* (2009), *Zindagi Na Milegi Dobara* (2011), *Dil Dhadakne Do* (2015) and *Gully Boy* (2019). Until the release of *Gully Boy*, most mainstream reviews of Akhtar's films criticised her focus on telling stories of affluent people and their 'first-world' problems. The popular narrative of the critics' opinion was premised on the constant interactions between the story of the films and their nouveau riche characters. She has also been criticised for using her industry network to get big film stars on her projects and that even as a woman filmmaker, her focus is on men's stories.

The broad themes of the popular reviews in English of Akhtar's films, in our opinion, are oversimplified assertions, if not exactly reductionist. What adds to this reductionism is that as one of the few female filmmakers in the industry working on big budget, mainstream productions, Akhtar is forced to face certain expectations that her male counterparts are not. Any filmmaker who has attempted to tell complex stories of the film industry, male bonding and the hypocrisy of the urban elite, with a deep understanding of the audience and the marketplace, certainly deserves an engagement at a more nuanced level.

This chapter, therefore, conducts a critical discourse analysis of the popular criticism of Akhtar's directorial ventures by combining an analysis of Akhtar's films' reviews with our interviews with select film reviewers and critics in India. These film reviews and reviewers have been limited to English-language newspapers, magazines, websites and the reviewers thereof, respectively. Consequently, film reviews written in and reviewers writing in other languages have not been the focus of this study. This chapter discusses the perceptions of a successful woman filmmaker in the Indian context, especially in comparison to her male counterparts, where the pressure to tell a story in a certain manner may possibly be a function of her gender and lineage. This chapter is particularly significant as professional film reviewers have not been studied in this way and an engagement of this nature in the professional film review landscape in India is inherently missing. This contextualisation also provides an anchoring point for a much-needed academic reflection.

THE RELATIONSHIP BETWEEN FILMS AND THEIR REVIEWS

The impact of film reviews forms the central premise of this study. In this chapter, we begin to deconstruct certain perceptions around Akhtar as a filmmaker, while operating within the framework of the reviews of her films and related discussions with film reviewers. It follows from this contextualisation of the current study that the role of film reviews (and by extension, the respective reviewers) be examined theoretically, by enlisting a few key studies that underline the importance of reviews in creating public perceptions, and therefore in creating larger discourses for films and their makers.

Several studies have explored the relationship between films and their reviews, in that the latter affected the reception of the former. These studies are situated across a spectrum of social and economic contexts, primarily driving ideological and economic-gratification-related conversations on the impact of film reviews on their readers.

Gerda Gemser, Martine Van Oostrum and Mark A. A. M. Leenders address the relationship between the discourse generated by film reviews as an extension of the overall discourse around a film. The authors state that film reviews have two kinds of effect – influence effect (which impacts the decision to watch a film) and prediction effect (which impacts people's perception of whether a film will be successful or not) (2006: 44). In writing about the expertise and professional capacity of reviewers to affect discourses, Ilona K. E. de Jong and Christian Burgers studied the differences between the film reviews written by professional film critics and the reviews posted by the audience. They argue that though audience reviews are overwhelmingly present in the online space, the discourse around films in particular is driven much more by what professional reviewers say (2013: 79).

Another widely cited study in this context by Morris B. Holbrook constructs, argues and comments upon the conflict between the popular appeal of films and expert judgements. The study is contextualised in a discussion that emerges from the negative criticism of how the media has debased high forms of culture through commercialisation and commodification, and that there exist different criteria for film critics and audiences in evaluating films and 'formation of their tastes' (1999: 145).

In an experimental study, Christer Thrane found that the better the expert review of a movie, the more likely it is that people will see it (2017: 9). However, the study also pointed out that the extent of the effects of expert reviews is somewhat genre-specific and gender-specific, with a tentative connection identified that states that the effects of favourable reviews on motion picture decisions were stronger for women than men for certain genres. Gabriel Weiman also refers to the film critic as an influencer or opinion leader, once again asserting the idea that film reviews and their respective reviewers have an advantage in affecting opinions, thus holding the power to affect perceptions and discourses around films, filmmakers, actors or any other elements of films that they review (1991: 267–79).

So far, all the studies that have been reviewed in this section have a broad social sciences context and largely find themselves at the intersection of business studies, economics, marketing and consumer studies. Hence there is a significant presence of the political economy context and an investigation of the impact of film reviews largely from the commercial point of view. There are references to the concept of cultural capital in some of the studies but the engagement with film reviews as cultural capital, and consequently ideological discursive constructions around a film have not been addressed directly. This research gap problematises the need for our research to look at the discourse generated by film reviews and reviewers from a cultural and ideological frame, where political economy, institutional frameworks, production practices and audience response intersect. Since our study is situated specifically in the Indian context, it also fulfils another significant research gap at the level of cultural geography. Following from the discussions on cultural and ideological gaps, this study uses the theory of encoding/decoding by Stuart Hall (1973) to make sense of these intersections in the context of Akhtar's work.

Film reviews remain one critical source in crafting these narratives of perception around the filmmaker and her cinema, as not only do they reach the masses by way of print and online channels but as established earlier in this section through multiple studies, they also impact the audiences in how they perceive a filmmaker and her cinema. In this context, Hall's encoding/decoding model helps situate the role of a film review, which can be personified as an 'encoder' of meaning structures, as derived from the knowledge frameworks of the reviewer writing the reviews. John Fiske supplements Hall's theory by emphasising the agency of the audiences in not only being active audiences and deriving meanings of text, but also in engaging with the content by way of participating in communities created by them to celebrate the content (1989). The reviewer, by way of this interpretation, becomes a part of the extended community that a film may create, thus allowing the audiences to engage with the reviewer as a key player in meaning-making and deriving their perceptions of the film (or of the filmmaker) from the reviewer.

Bill Yousman, whose research paper revisits Hall's encoding/decoding model, quotes Hall thus: 'I don't think audiences are in the same positions of power with those who signify the world to them' (Hall et al., cited in Yousman 2013: 202). Yousman posits that in light of this articulation, it would be fair to assert that while one may look at audiences as agentic in the process of meaning- making (decoding), 'in the act of encoding there is always an attempt to fix meaning in a particular way' (202). This powerful summation brings us back to the significance of film reviews which must be studied for the purposes of understanding the perception created around Akhtar's cinema.

A SUMMARY OF MAINSTREAM REVIEWS OF AKHTAR'S FILMS

To analyse the discourse around Akhtar's films, it is essential to first engage with the interpretations of various film reviewers in India with respect to her cinema, before exploring their thoughts via interviews. This section attempts to understand, through their reviews, the ways in which film critics have evaluated and commented upon Akhtar's growth as a filmmaker over a decade, thus laying significant groundwork for creating the aforementioned social perception with respect to her identity as a director.

For this purpose, the film reviews have been chosen from some of the leading English-language national dailies and magazines in India, along with a few prominent websites. While the scope of selection of these reviews was as wide as the available sources themselves, we have tried to restrict their selection to those written by key reviewers, including (but not limited to) the ones who have been interviewed in later sections, to achieve parity of argumentation between this section and the interview section.

Beginning with *Luck by Chance*, Akhtar's debut film and perhaps one of her best works as per the reviews, Akhtar was able to accomplish a difficult task, that of staying away from the label of a star-kid coming from a family background of rich artistic legacy in the industry. The media reviews, which could have been premised in a comparison with her father (Javed Akhtar, scriptwriter/screenwriter and lyricist), her mother (Honey Irani, actress, screenwriter and director) and brother (Farhan Akhtar, director, actor, screenwriter and producer), surprisingly stayed away from that narrative and focused instead on her directorial talents as a newcomer.

This film lay the foundations for Akhtar's capabilities in handling multiple, complex characters, which would continue to be seen in her subsequent work.

The reviews appreciated her telling an insider's story of the film industry, fraught with the protagonists' struggles and their negotiation with the grim realities therein. Shubhra Gupta in her review in *The Indian Express* is perhaps the kindest to this particular work of Akhtar's, appreciating the then-debutant for 'great cinematic moments and roundedness of characters' (2009). Mayank Shekhar in his review in the *Bangalore Mirror* observed that it was to Akhtar's credit as a director that the 'unreal' world of the film industry was depicted as close to reality as possible, born out of Akhtar's extensive research of and exposure to this world as an insider. He concluded that *LBC* was a 'personal breezy neighbourhood film about free spirited people of the industry' (2009). In a recent interview with Ushnota Paul, reviewer for *The Telegraph*, Akhtar mentioned that *LBC* was by far her most 'personal film' (2019). Perhaps this element that stemmed from her personal struggles, experiences and motivations as a debutant allowed for the raw honesty in *LBC* that was observed by film reviewers across the fraternity and earned the film appreciation in the years to come.

Zindagi Na Milegi Dobara bore the burden of very high expectations from Akhtar as her second directorial venture after a critically acclaimed debut. The film was labelled a 'bromance' in most of the mainstream reviews. Kaveree Bamzai, in her review in *India Today*, wrote that she was 'convinced that no one can make bromance as beautifully as a woman' (2011). While most reviews did appreciate her aesthetic sense in showcasing the most beautiful locations and capturing breathtaking adventures undertaken by the three male protagonists, they were not so kind in evaluating her choice of narration and the story itself. These criticisms were fraught with inadvertent comparisons to her brother Farhan Akhtar's debut venture, *Dil Chahta Hai* (2001), on which she worked as an assistant director, which had a similar storyline and a much too similar trio of male protagonists (Shekhar: 2011). *DCH* was a coming-of-age film, not just for the characters in the film who, very much like in *ZNMD*, were urban men exploring their freedom and identities, but also for the industry that saw a celebration of male bonding like never before. Having said that, Mayank Shekhar in her review pointed out that keeping aside the parallels with *DCH*, Akhtar maintained 'a firm voice of her own' and kept things 'artistic, without any pretensions', despite the focus on philosophy through poetry. Ajit Duara in his review in *Open* magazine observed that the issues addressed in the film may not have been profound, but 'Zoya's felicity in weaving together picture, prose, music and poetry' and tying them to Spanish culture was unique (2011). He very astutely observed that 'writing or making a movie about the rich doesn't necessarily make the content superficial', even though he began his review by quoting F. Scott Fitzgerald on how the rich were different and difficult to understand. Overall, there was a definite appreciation for this film riding on emotions and having a female gaze to a story of male bonding, which perhaps lent it its sensitivity towards exploration of life.

Akhtar's third feature film, *Dil Dhadakne Do*, came after a filmmaking gap of four years. *DDD* was criticised for undermining the 'perceptive power of audiences' by oversimplifying what could have been the critical issues by way of using a family pet as the voice of the film, as reviewed by Anuj Kumar in *The Hindu* (2015). Shubhra Gupta in her review in *The Indian Express* lamented 'crucial sharpness (going) missing' from the film in Akhtar's pursuit of keeping things 'bubbly and bright' (2015). Deepanjana Pal, in her review in *Firstpost*, brushes away the criticism around portraying stories of the rich and instead applauds Akhtar's talent to showcase the pains and thoughts of the privileged class, as she had done in *LBC* and *ZNMD*. However, Pal reviewed *DDD* as 'pretty but artificial, with a tissue-thin story told through flat characters played by gorgeous actors' (2015). Ajit Duara in his review in *Open* magazine has a similar viewpoint when he reviews the film as 'flat and tiresome, with little beyond the banal fixations of the idle rich' (2015). Overall, the only redeeming factors of the film that the mainstream media acknowledged were in its (isolated) handling of good character portrayals, along with eliciting a few good acting performances from its key actors.

Gully Boy, the latest of Akhtar's films, was clearly an example of an underdog winning. Not only was the film appreciated for being an empathetic tale of the country's lower-class struggles, it was also recognised for placing rap as its central theme, around which not only the protagonist, but the entire story and narration revolved. Two noteworthy aspects that seemed to hit a chord with the reviewers were that one, Akhtar let go of her 'elite' comfort zone to tell a story of the marginalised, and two, that she facilitated the leading actor (Ranveer Singh) to internalise the strife and urgency of the character being played to perfection and with conviction. When Swetha Ramakrishnan, in her music review for *Gully Boy* in *Firstpost*, mentioned that 'the *Gully Boy* album is a game changer', there was an inherent credit given to Akhtar's acknowledgement of rap culture and the social class it represents. In addition to depicting Mumbai's social milieu in a simple and straightforward manner, as observed by Namrata Joshi in her review in *The Hindu* (2019), Akhtar also managed to capture, according to Rachit Gupta in *The Times of India*, 'emotional intelligence' (2019) in not only the characters, but throughout the unravelling of the film. Ajit Duara reviewed the film in *Open* magazine as 'a refreshingly different film on a subject not normally trodden by mainstream cinema' (2019). Mayank Shekhar in *Midday* labelled the film as a 'new kind of "Angry Young Man" movie, in effect – seamlessly merging sub-culture with pop mainstream' (2019). He also observed, very significantly, that it was Akhtar's intellectual ability to lend the female gaze to her work that made it possible for the female character in the film (portrayed by Alia Bhatt) to stand out and display the depths of her character even in a film focused on an overpowering male character on a rap journey to break class and identity barriers.

In an attempt to articulate the underlying meanings in the reviews for Akhtar's work and to study the ensuing perceptions thus created by these reviews of her identity as a director for a certain high society, we arrived at a few observations. The reviews by mainstream media, over a decade, project Akhtar as having come of age, and certainly hint at her progressing towards an artistic maturity; they have observed her finding synergy between who she started out as and who she has become. This proposition could be interpreted in light of the reviews received by her first film, *LBC*, and by her most recent film, *Gully Boy*. As charted by various film reviewers, Akhtar's development as a director saw hues of raw talent and honesty in storytelling in her first film. This was indicated via the oft-referred-to 'personal' touch to the film in multiple reviews. Clearly, the reviews for *LBC* positioned Akhtar as the amateur, an untouched, uninfluenced but talented auteur who had a penchant for connecting real-life struggles with the reel ones.

In contrast, while the reviews for her films *ZNMD* and *DDD* were in parts appreciative of her aesthetic sense and ability to create great characters, they were more critical of her tackling the 'issues' of the privileged. Despite that, Akhtar earned favour with a few critics, who asserted that there was nothing wrong with her showcasing stories of the upper urban class, as long as she was able to do justice to the treatment of human emotions and who the people beneath these emotions were. It is interesting to observe here that Akhtar's stories of relationships and emotions have been appreciated by the reviewers more in the context of a social background of struggle, as against that of comfort and privilege.

This argument also found resonance in the reviews of *Gully Boy*, where she was applauded not only for portraying the struggles of the non-privileged, but also for interplaying those struggles with the same passionate emotions of heart and ambition as were showcased in her films before this, and for staying true to her strong and layered characterisation of people in her story. Akhtar played to her strengths, and those were highlighted against the backdrop of honest storytelling, very similar to her first film. Utpal Borpujari, national award-winning filmmaker and film critic, and one of the interviewees of this study, told us, 'The realism of her debut film is missed in her subsequent films. *Gully Boy* in some ways marked her return to realism within the realm of mainstream storytelling, but the freshness of *Luck by Chance* was remarkable.' This seems symbolic, in a way, of her coming full circle in touching base with the same fresh talent that she began with, albeit seasoned with experienced maturity earned through her journey of a decade of filmmaking.

All of this is indicated as an achievement of the reviews proclaiming Akhtar's growth, underlining once again the criticality of the message transferred from the reviewers to their readers in an act of affecting the latter's perceptions, even if not as an explicit intention to do so.

INTERVIEWS WITH FILM CRITICS: THEMATIC ANALYSIS

Following from earlier discussions about the criticality of film reviews in creating discourses around a film and its filmmaker, this section captures the opinions and interpretations of film reviewers themselves on those ideations, which help to meaningfully encapsulate, under various themes, the different threads of this study's discussion. The interviews created an insightful framework for engaging with different components of Akhtar's filmography and they helped to develop a cogent structure to understand the components (or the lack of them) in professional film reviewing, with significant self-reflexivity being demonstrated by a few interviewees.

The interview questionnaire we created addressed two broad categories of questions. First, it focused on understanding the reviewers' ideological positions as commentators on films and seeking their critical responses on Akhtar's body of work as well as on the popular criticism of her films. Using purposive sampling, we reached out to thirteen professional film critics. The reviewers for the interviews in this section include Ajit Duara (affiliated with *Open* magazine, an English-language Indian magazine), Mayank Shekhar (affiliated with the Indian English-language newspaper *Mid-Day*), Pradeep Menon (affiliated with the Indian news website *Firstpost*), Swetha Ramakrishnan (affiliated with *Firstpost*), Ushnota Paul (affiliated with *The Telegraph*, an Indian English-language newspaper) and Utpal Borpujari (national award-winning filmmaker and former national award-winning film critic affiliated with multiple national publications). Five of the six interviews were conducted through emails and one was conducted on a messenger app. The reviewers will be identified by their initials in the chapter: AD, MS, PM, SR, UP and UB.

The questions that addressed the reviewers' own positions asked them to define their approach towards film criticism. This was crucial because it helped us to contextualise their responses to questions posed later in an ideological framework. With respect to their opinion and insights on Akhtar's body of work, our questions addressed some key themes, including diversity (or its absence), character development, focus on men's stories, treatment of women characters, technical and aesthetic competence and narratives of the affluent class of society, among others. Two themes were fleshed out in detail: Akhtar's treatment of male and female characters through concepts like gaze and feminism, and whether her work has repositioned a discussion on class by viewing/representing elites as having fragmented identities, vulnerabilities and struggles, a lens that has not been applied to engage with her work. The following section discusses the themes that emerged from the interviews.

FILM REVIEWERS AS ELITES, ENTERTAINERS AND AUTEURS

Won H. Chang uses three labels to describe film critics – elites, entertainers and auteurs (1975: 721–5). When we asked the film critics interviewed for this study to describe themselves in these categories, AD (Ajit Duara), MS (Mayank Shekhar) and PM (Pradeep Menon) identified themselves exclusively as auteurs. SR (Swetha Ramakrishnan) identified herself as an entertainer, while UP (Ushnota Paul) placed herself at the intersection of elite and entertainer. UB (Utpal Borpujari) did not place himself in any of the categories, identifying himself purely as a film critic, and not a reviewer.[1] This description was insightful to see the trajectories in which their responses evolved in the later parts of the interview. For example, AD, who described himself as an auteur, also has formal qualifications in film scholarship and teaches film courses at university level. His ideological position is very different from the rest, and their subsequent responses establish a more independent voice, with minimal influence of popular opinion. One of the reviewers, PM, who is identified as an auteur, is also a filmmaker, and the artistic insight is evident in his responses. The reviewer who put herself in the category of elite and entertainer, UP, vacillated between justification of the commercial context and strong political and aesthetic perspectives. An auteur by identity, MS says, 'Cultural commentary by and large has been an elitist pursuit. That said, film reviewers, given the mass nature of the medium they comment on, attempt to, as they should, make their works accessible to wider audiences.' This backdrop helped the authors to understand the nuances of their responses and also helped to view film reviews as a deconstructive engagement on the part of the film critic rather than a mere popular comment on a film. For instance, one of the interviewees, PM, says, 'I believe a film critic must be an "artist" in their own right, every film review striving to be a work of art in itself, however minor.'

As creators, reviewers must also ask the question of their social responsibility. Asked about this position, all the reviewers deconstructed the social responsibility of film reviews/reviewers in different ways, except AD, who states, 'I don't feel any social responsibility to viewers.' They focus on being authentic and unbiased as their primary responsibility. This may mean responsibility towards the readers of their reviews or facilitating the decision-making for the movie audience by, for example, 'break[ing] down a subplot, a character's arc, a dialogue or technical choices to simpler understanding' (SR).

The critic's identity and ideology are central to this discussion. UP says, 'If I need to call out the blatant sexism in a film like, say a *Kabir Singh*, and be blatantly honest about how it's problematic, then yes, I will.' This is endorsed in an article in *The Guardian* which states that it is imperative 'to hear critical voices offering a different perspective. The result of a greater increase in female critics being heard could signal a shift in the sort of films we see lauded' (Salmon 2018). UB sums up, 'Critics always have a social responsibility to dispassionately and qualitatively critique a film.' MS adds, 'Social responsibility is a completely subjective thing – a work-in-progress; operating in the subconscious (ideally); and shaped also by feedback from consumers.' The instrument of social responsibility and agency of the film critic in legitimising a film or calling it out for its problems is therefore extremely critical.

ZOYA AKHTAR'S CINEMA: DIVERSITY OF EXTERIORITY OR INTERIORITY

An overarching theme in the critique of Akhtar's cinema has been that of limited diversity. The experts interviewed for this study deconstructed diversity from different positions. Their responses focused on two concepts: diversity of exteriority and diversity of interiority. They all more or less agreed that the entire body of Akhtar's work may not come across as diverse. The accompanying arguments and explanations were, however, very different for each interviewee. One of the arguments was that since her films are based primarily in urban settings, she has not explored truly diverse stories. However, it was also pointed out that her familiarity with the urban spaces that she has been a part of may be a delimiting factor which, as she explores them more over time, may help her diversify her range. *Gully Boy* was a case in point by most respondents, to comment on the diversity of exteriority that has begun to be reflected in her work. In the words of PM, 'She is young and has a long career ahead of her, so you can expect her to truly diversify with time, once she is more prolific, more successful, and hungrier for subjects that challenge her. In fact, if you look at her filmography through primarily this lens, you will see that she has, indeed, constantly moved farther away from her core comfort zone with every subsequent film, from *LBC* to *Gully Boy*.'

There was significant engagement with the concept of diversity of interiority in Akhtar's work. The interviewees discussed the diversity of treatment, characters, writing and voice. Another argument that emerged was about her grip on her stories, especially from the point of view of the writing quality where there were repeated references to her writing partnership with Reema Kagti, which, in the words of PM, 'seems to be a well-oiled machine that has a strong control over their scripts'. SR states, 'She is a viewer's director. Letting her scenes go when we are in the flow, and holding back to create viewing tension. That is a skill very few directors possess in India.' The critics elaborated on diversity of interiority through Akhtar's development and treatment of the characters in her films. The diversity of interiority in her work was also mentioned in the context of her understated tone of storytelling which, according to them, is deep and nuanced. AD calls Akhtar an intelligent filmmaker who understands how to treat her subjects with diversity. However, he is quick to point out that she is extremely conscious of the importance of the star system, and casts and tailors her script according to the comfort level of the actors she selects. UB observes, 'I find Zoya Akhtar to be a very interesting filmmaker from the context of the way she views the world around her. The films she has made have been unpretentious and have had a lot of heart. And she chooses stories, at least she has done so till now, from a world that she is apparently familiar with thematically and/or geographically.'

THE WOMEN AND MEN OF AKHTAR'S WORLD: REFINED GAZE, POWER DYNAMICS AND THE MARKET LOGIC

The discourse surrounding Akhtar's body of work also speaks of her focus on men's stories and using her industry network to cast big film stars in her projects. The narrative that emerged in our interviews with the film critics offers a deeper insight into Akhtar's cinema through the lens of gender and power. AD, for example, says, 'She knows that the male movie stars have the ability to draw the audience to the film.' UP refers to Akhtar's lineage and industry connections: 'Maybe, because she is influenced by the two strong men in her life, her father Javed Akhtar and brother Farhan Akhtar. She has said in multiple interviews that she does read out her scripts to these two people and takes note of their feedback during the pre-production stage.'

While there is a broad agreement on her roping in top male actors in her films, the interviewees engage with it at a more complex level. PM mentions, 'I think a blanket statement like "she focuses on men's stories" does not do full justice to Zoya Akhtar's work. They are much more about relationships, with men and women sharing equal space.' SR argues that it is unfair to say that Akhtar focuses only on men's stories and that it is important to engage with every piece of work she has created individually. UB says, 'An important factor in her films is that she creates strong women characters even if the story is told from a male character's view. *LBC* and *Gully Boy* are two fine examples of that. Even in *DDD*, the female characters had strong heft. Only in *ZNMD* the focus was almost totally on the three male protagonists, but then, it was a buddy film of three friends who happened to be male.'

The gender dynamics of Akhtar's films, both in the context of their position in the film industry ecosystem and as independent works of art, emerge as a critical and complex theme in the interviews. It is important to note that the gendered nature of market logic comes across as justification from the critics themselves. PM, for instance, argues, 'Zoya Akhtar, at the end of the day, is likely to have the same ambitions in terms of audience reach that any of her contemporaries would have. And the market, particularly the "blockbuster" market, still unfortunately favours the male audience far more.' The discussion evolves in two directions: the gaze she focuses on and the power dynamics between the men and women in the film's universe. One of the interviewees argues that many of Akhtar's films usually have women characters who closely follow stereotypes. But for all these women characters, these films also have at least one female character who breaks every stereotype, almost attaining a 'hero's arc'.

The character played by Alia Bhatt (Safeena) in *Gully Boy* deserves special mention here, as most critics took it as an example to argue their perspective. According to SR, 'Alia's character gets to play the angry young woman – a trope that has been reserved for men across generations of Bollywood. She gets to be the possessive lover, the one who fights for attention and has to "win over" Murad. This is a very keen subversion by Zoya.'

PM explained his perspective on how gender and power interact in the context of the same film by using three distinct moments in the film which eventually seem to flow out of the preceding moment:

> There is also some mastery of visual craft with how Murad and Safeena play off each other. There is this one particular action with their hands that the two share, which speaks of the longing they have for each other. The first time they perform this little action in the film is when Murad is yet to start on his rap journey. Safeena is up in her room, looking out her bathroom window, while Murad is down on the ground outside, seated at the foot of a staircase to an undefined place. This staging seemingly hints at the balance of power between them, the fact that Safeena as a medical student is further ahead in her personal journey than Murad. The next time they perform this action, Murad has just qualified for the finals of the rap competition. They show him scaling the walls and climbing into her bathroom to tell her this and also repair their relationship. Once he climbs in, they perform that action before they reunite. The third time they perform the same action is at a railway station right at the end of the movie, after Murad has become a star. This time, he is on a foot over bridge, while Safeena is looking up at him from the platform. Murad has gone ahead of her now, purely in terms of outside success, yet that action binds them together throughout, keeping them as equals in their relationship.

AD, however, argues, 'Akhtar's most independent character is Safeena in *Gully Boy*, but she is still the spunky woman of a male categorisation of the kinds of women who men may encounter. At no point do other women in the film, one being Kalki Koechlin, form any sort of feminine bond. They just compete for the man.'

Her films may seem to be stories of male protagonists performed by commercially successful male actors from the Hindi film industry, but the detailing of all her characters – men or women – and the way her characters are crafted with equal attention, indicates that her treatment is, indeed, feminist. Akhtar's treatment of her female characters is expectedly more sensitive to women than any of her male contemporaries. But what emerges from the interviews with the critics is that there is also a very clear effort on her part to put as much work into every character, big or small, carefully designing both male and female characters in service of the story she wants to tell. As one of the interviewees, PM, summarises:

> Even when she is telling a man's story, the perspective and gaze is distinctly her own, a woman's gaze, that woman being Zoya Akhtar, a sum total of her own experiences as a human and an artist. If one observes how the hero of *Gully Boy* and the hero of *Simmba* (another film by a male director where Ranveer Singh played the lead role) are visually framed, you will learn as much about the directors as you will about the versatility of the actor playing those two distinct roles.

NARRATIVE OF THE ELITE OR MISPLACED CRITICISM?

Mainstream reviews of Akhtar's films appreciate her visual brilliance, production design and cinematographic vision on the one hand, and critique her focus on telling stories of affluent people and their 'first-world' problems on the other. The popular narrative of the critics' opinion is premised in the constant interactions between the story of the films and their nouveau riche characters. When we discussed this dimension of the reviews of Akhtar's films with our expert interviewees, their opinions were far more nuanced and varied. A scholarly gap exists in studying the Indian elite class in the post-liberalisation era in the sociological context and Akhtar's film *DDD* is a novel narrative on the lives of elites and their 'anxieties, vulnerabilities, desires and aspirations' in the contemporary Indian context (Bhandari: 2017). One of the interviewees opines that this is the kind of critique that the work of a filmmaker like Akhtar deserves. Another critic states that such scholarship would throw a very different light on both Akhtar and her work, and should be able to place her films in a different context. SR, in fact, breaks it down and comments, 'Zoya is not the kind of filmmaker who commits to one tone while portraying the elite. In *ZNMD*, the tone is aspirational, while in *DDD*, the tone is cheeky, almost holding a mirror to the elite about issues that are seemingly brushed under the carpet.' UP reasons out the conflict by explaining her cinema's connection with the audience and states,

> The first world problems of the people in Zoya Akhtar's films can only be considered a 'problem' by a certain niche elite class in contemporary India, seen through a lens of rose-tinted glasses. The majority of the movie-going audience in a country like India would not be able to connect with it (like they can with a *Gully Boy*, or maybe even a *LBC*). But would they not enjoy watching it irrespective? Of course they would. And maybe even get a certain voyeuristic pleasure while getting a glimpse into the world of the elite Indians, a lifestyle they probably aspire for someday.

What emerges is a discursive engagement to understand that Akhtar is telling character-driven stories of affluent people which also seem to be aimed at as wide an audience as possible. UB rationalises the liberty of a filmmaker thus: 'As a critic and now a filmmaker, I always believe that a filmmaker will tell a story about a world that she or he feels aware of or is interested in. We cannot grudge a filmmaker for choosing to tell stories from only the affluent world – that is his or her choice. The analysis, I feel, should be more from the aspect of whether the filmmaker is able to portray that chosen backdrop in a believable way.' AD reflects on the harsh criticism of her portrayal of the elite and states, 'Reviewers generally expect condemnation of privilege in India, and this Zoya refuses to do. Hers is a more Hollywood depiction of our capitalist aspirations, which I feel is honest.' PM also reflects on the fundamental lack of depth in the ways in which her films have been perceived and spoken about in mainstream reviews. SR discusses that as Akhtar continued making films over the years, film criticism as an art also evolved, with more mainstream publications having their own in-house critics, some of whom were millennials capable of catching the pulse of young audiences. AD, in fact, states, '*Schadenfreude* is a German word which describes the pleasure that people take in someone's failure. This word is applicable to the Indian context. We are never objective in our assessment of films, and very personal in our judgments of filmmakers, especially a woman director from a film family.'

CHALLENGING CLASS LABELS OR POLITICAL CONFORMITY

When Akhtar's last film *Gully Boy* was released, there was trepidation about how someone who had only told stories of rich people would engage with the subaltern – Indian Muslim rappers who have emerged from the ghettos of Dharavi, one of Asia's largest slums, that exists in the heart of Mumbai. MS observes, '...the lead character is Muslim, but that's not all there is to his identity. By not focusing on his religion too much (Ranveer in *Gully Boy*), or at all (Farhan in *ZNMD*), she normalises it for her audience. This has a stronger effect through entertainment than pamphleting and preaching ever could'. Another respondent, PM, is appreciative of the way Akhtar's treatment of the film was a sharp departure from the 'lowest common denominator' stories that do not belong to any particular cultural time or place. However, two of the respondents invoke the argument of Akhtar's socio-political vision as being conformist. SR takes the example of her debut film *LBC*, where she took a bleak view of the foibles of the film industry and its gender imbalances, and argues that it was one of her best films but commercially unsuccessful, which possibly led her survival instinct to press the 'conform' button. She refers to the dilution of the inherent politics of the *gully* rap genre in *Gully Boy* by romanticising the caste/class conflict, abject poverty, lack of opportunities and issues of discrimination and creating a more sanitised version of poverty for a much wider audience consumption. AD comments on Akhtar's adherence to conformity by saying, 'The graph of all her scripts follows this conformism. So, you have the traditional three-act structure playing out in her movies – first, the situation is described, then a conflict occurs, and finally a resolution of the conflict is arrived at. It will be noticed that the resolution she arrives at is always politically and socially correct.' While working with recognisable and thus arguably conforming forms, Akhtar's work still leaves open to debate how much she is pushing the envelope.

CONCLUSION: POPULAR OPINION AND MULTIDIMENSIONALITY

The central premise of this chapter was based on the unidimensional discourse surrounding Zoya Akhtar's films in the mainstream reviews. The interviews with expert film critics helped expound the several layers that exist in the art, craft and substance of her cinema that creates several points of interaction and engagement that, in the words of two of the interviewees, one can 'chew on, mull over and discuss'. Reaching this juncture to deliberate on the discursive possibilities created by her cinematic contributions from the stage of monolithic perceptions available in mainstream reviews by self-reflexive and introspective engagement of the film critics themselves is a crucial transition. In the framework of Hall's theory of encoding/decoding, this emerges as a moment of meaningful discourse, where the frameworks of knowledge and relations of production interact to encode and decode layers of meaning structures. As PM remarks, 'I do not think that it is the film critics that are entirely responsible for any shift that she has shown in her work, but certainly the overall discourse around her films will play at least a minor role in her own journey as a filmmaker.' And while that remains one crucial takeaway from this research, it is hoped that this endeavour to deconstruct some of the perceptual frameworks around Akhtar as a director is successful, in that it allows academics and audiences alike to emerge from the previously mentioned singular dimensionality of thought and celebrate her for the distinctive filmmaker she is.

NOTE

1. Correspondence with AD (Ajit Duara, email to the authors, 28 March 2020); MS (Mayank Shekhar, personal communication to the authors, 12 June 2020); PM (Pradeep Menon, email to the authors, 8 April 2020); SR (Swetha Ramakrishnan, email to the authors, 1 April 2020); UP (Ushnota Paul, email to the authors, 3 April 2020); UB (Utpal Borpujari, email to the authors, 6 May 2020).

WORKS CITED

Bamzai, Kaveree (2011), '*Zindagi Na Milegi Dobara* review: A grown up bromance', *India Today*, 15 July 2011. Available at <https://www.indiatoday.in/movies/reviews/story/zindagi-milegi-na-dobara-movie-review-137555-2011-07-15>

Bhandari, Parul (2017) 'Towards sociology of Indian elites: Marriage alliances, vulnerabilities and resistance in Bollywood', *Society and Culture in South Asia*, 3: 1, pp. 108–16.

Borpujari, Utpal (2020), email to the authors, 6 May 2020.

Chang, Won H. (1975), 'A typology study of movie critics', *Journalism Quarterly*, 52: 4, pp. 721–5. Available at <https://doi.org/10.1177/107769907505200417>

Ciecko, Anne (2015), 'Reflexive global Bollywood and metacinematic gender politics in *Om Shanti Om* (2007), *Luck by Chance* (2008), and *Dhobi Ghat* (2010)', *Diogenes*, 62: 1, pp. 24–37.

De Jong, Ilona K. E. and Christian Burgers (2013), 'Do consumer critics write differently from professional critics? A genre analysis of online film reviews', *Discourse, Context & Media*, 2: 2, pp. 75–83.

Duara, Ajit (2011), '*Zindagi Na Milegi Dobara*', *Open*, 20 July 2011. Available at <https://openthemagazine.com/cinema/zindagi-na-milegi-dobara/>

— (2015), 'Movie review: *Dil Dhadakne Do*', *Open*, 10 June 2015. Available at <https://openthemagazine.com/cinema/dil-dhadakne-do/>

— (2019), '*Gully Boy* movie review', *Open*, 15 February 2019. Available at <https://openthemagazine.com/cinema/gully-boy-movie-review/>

— (2020), email to the authors, 28 March 2020.

Fiske, John (1989), *Television Culture*, London: Routledge.

Gemser, Gerda, Martine Van Oostrum and Mark A. A. M. Leenders (2007), 'The impact of film reviews on the box office performance of art house versus mainstream motion pictures', *Journal of Cultural Economics*, 31: 1, pp. 43–63.

Gupta, Rachit (2019), '*Gully Boy* movie review', *Times of India*, 14 February 2019. Available at <https://timesofindia.indiatimes.com/entertainment/hindi/movie-reviews/gully-boy/movie-review/67981331.cms>

Gupta, Shubhra (2009), 'Movie review: *Luck by Chance*', *The Indian Express*, 30 January 2009. Available at <http://archive.indianexpress.com/news/movie-review-luck-by-chance/417117/0>
— (2015), '*Dil Dhadakne Do* movie review: Heart develops a big beat for Mr and Mrs Mehra', *The Indian Express*, 7 June 2015. Available at <https://indianexpress.com/article/entertainment/movie-review/dil-dhadakne-do-movie-review/>
Hall, Stuart (1973), *Encoding and Decoding in the Television Discourse*, Birmingham: Centre for Cultural Studies, University of Birmingham.
— (1994), 'Reflections upon the Encoding-Decoding Model: An interview with Stuart Hall', in Justin Lewis and John Cruz (eds), *Viewing, Reading, Listening: Audiences and Cultural Reception*, Boulder: Westview Press, pp. 253–74.
Holbrook, Morris B. (1999), 'Popular appeal versus expert judgments of motion pictures', *Journal of Consumer Research*, 26: 2, pp. 144–55.
Joshi, Namrata (2019), '*Gully Boy* review: A feel-good movie for the underdog in each of us', *The Hindu*, 14 February 2019. Available at <https://www.thehindu.com/entertainment/movies/gully-boy-review-a-restive-soliloquy-to-liberation/article26266429.ece>
Kumar, Anuj (2015), '*Dil Dhadakne Do*: It needs a pacemaker', *The Hindu*, 6 June 2015. Available at <https://www.thehindu.com/features/cinema/cinema-reviews/dil-dhadakne-do-it-needs-a-pacemaker/article7286441.ece>
Kumar, Nirmal and Preeti Chaturvedi (2015), *Brave New Bollywood: In Conversation with Contemporary Hindi Filmmakers*, New Delhi: Sage.
Lauret, Maria (1991), 'Feminism and culture – the movie: A critical overview of writing on women and cinema', *Women: A Cultural Review*, 2: 1, pp. 52–69.
Menon, Pradeep (2020), email to the authors, 8 April 2020.
Pal, Deepanjana (2015), '*Dil Dhadakne Do* review: Priyanka, Anushka, Ranveer star in Zoya Akhtar's celebrity pyjama party', *Firstpost*, 7 June 2015. Available at <https://www.firstpost.com/entertainment/dil-dhadakne-do-review-priyanka-anushka-ranveer-star-in-zoya-akhtars-celebrity-pyjama-party-2280578.html>
Paul, Ushnota (2019), 'Zoya Akhtar's stories: A conversation with the director', *Telegraph India*, 21 October 2019. Available at <https://www.telegraphindia.com/entertainment/zoya-akhtar-s-stories-a-conversation-with-the-director/cid/1713070>
— (2020), email to the authors, 3 April 2020.
Ramakrishnan, Swetha (2019), '*Gully Boy* music review: A rousing, eclectic soundtrack that sets the benchmark for a trailblazing genre', *Firstpost*, 26 January 2019. Available at <https://www.firstpost.com/entertainment/gully-boy-music-review-a-rousing-eclectic-soundtrack-that-sets-the-benchmark-for-a-trailblazing-genre-5963241.html>
— (2020), email to the authors, 1 April 2020.
Salmon, Caspar (2018), 'Who needs film critics? Actually, we all do', *The Guardian*, 20 June 2018. Available at <https://www.theguardian.com/film/2018/jun/20/who-needs-film-critics-diversity-hollywood-oceans-8-wrinkle-in-time>
Shekhar, Mayank (2009), '*Luck By Chance*: Show (you) must go on', *Bangalore Mirror*, 30 January 2009. Available at <https://bangaloremirror.indiatimes.com/entertainment/reviews/luck-by-chance-show-you-must-go-on/articleshow/22226505.cms>
— (2011), 'Mayank Shekhar's review: *Zindagi Na Milegi Dobara*', *Hindustan Times*, 15 July 2011. Available at <https://web.archive.org/web/20110719095357/http://www.hindustantimes.com/entertainment/reviews/Mayank-Shekhar-s-review-Zindagi-Na-Milegi-Dobara/Article1-721577.aspx>
— (2019), '*Gully Boy* movie review: Iska Time Aa Gaya Bhaay!', *Mid-Day*, 22 February 2019. Available at <https://www.mid-day.com/articles/gully-boy-movie-review-iska-time-aa-gaya-bhaay/20404185>

— (2020), personal communication to the author, 12 June 2020.

Thrane, Christer (2018), 'Do expert reviews affect the decision to see motion pictures in movie theatres? An experimental approach', *Applied Economics*, 50: 28, pp. 3066–75.

Weiman, Gabriel (1991), 'The Influentials: Back to the concept of opinion leaders', *Public Opinion Quarterly*, 55, pp. 267–79.

Yousman, Bill (2013), 'Revisiting Hall's Encoding/Decoding Model: Ex-prisoners respond to television representations of incarceration', *Review of Education, Pedagogy, and Cultural Studies*, 35: 3, pp. 197–216. Available at <https://doi.org/10.1080/10714413.2013.803340>

CHAPTER 12

The Final Word: An Interview with Zoya Akhtar

Aakshi Magazine and Amber Shields

Amber Shields: *We wanted to start by learning a bit more about you and your development as a filmmaker. What experiences in your life influenced you to become a filmmaker?*

Zoya Akhtar: It has to be my home. Both of my parents are from the film industry and are writers. When I was a child, my father was a working writer in the industry. My mother had been a child actress. She acted until she was 16 or 17 but stopped when she got pregnant and married. She had me at 19 and my brother at 21. When we turned about 8 or 9, my mother went to FTII [Film and Television Institute of India] to study and we used to go to Pune and spend the weekends with her. She had this huge collection of films and we watched movies with her and my dad. Basically, everything was about movies and the arts. My father is a writer and a poet so there would be a lot of poetry around as well as music, writers and actors. Every film was dissected and discussed. It was just part of our life. We loved the movies, but now I realise I was definitely looking at more than just the surface stuff. That was the biggest influence, as you end up loving movies. You realise that's what you are going to do and that's what everyone in your family does. It's just something that came very naturally.

AS: *So, by the time you went to New York University for a diploma in filmmaking, you were coming in with different experiences and degrees of exposure?*

ZA: Totally. It wasn't just my background; it was also the fact that by the time I went to NYU I was 24/25 years old. I had started working in Bombay when I was 19 years old as a copywriter and then as an assistant in advertising. I got a job with Mira Nair when I was 21. I worked with Mira doing *Kama Sutra* (1996) and then I did a little indie film called *Bombay Boys* (Kaizad Gustad 1998). Only after I had assisted on two films did I go to New York. I had studied literature and sociology, so I had already graduated with a Bachelor of Arts. I had finished my education and I thought I might as well go because I was going to do film, I was already working in the business, I had the resources and I loved New York. By the time I got there I had watched a lot of films and knew a lot about movies. I had worked on a set as an Assistant Director, so I was coming in with considerable experience.

AS: *It would be great to hear about some of your earlier projects, like when you were working with Mira Nair or Dev Benegal or on later projects with your brother [Farhan Akhtar].*

ZA: It was weird for me because I wanted to be a director but was working in a variety of roles mainly on American films shot in India. They had a certain structure which was incredible because at that time Indian films didn't shoot in one schedule or have sync sound. The kind of films we worked on had a very different set-up. The way to handle it, to produce it, to break it down and schedule was very different. Learning all that was invaluable to me because it didn't exist in India at that time.

What I didn't want to do, which is a very Indian industry thing to do, is to take a job with one director, then stick with that director and keep working with that one director until you make a film. I find that most of those filmmakers are an offset of the other, you get a kind of imprint. Me and my friend Reema Kagti, who is also a director, met when both of us were ADs and around 22 years old and we made a conscious choice not to work with only one director. We were just going to work with everyone. At that time, we were the only freelance people that existed. You could call us and we would get on a job and get out and it was great because we did all the foreign commercials and films that came in. We didn't stick with one director and that really taught me a lot. It taught me what to do and what not to do. So, you literally hand-picked things you loved about somebody's work, studied them and learned from them and realised what their strengths are or realised what didn't work or what worked better. I think that really helped me.

What also helped me was that I started doing jobs that weren't necessarily AD jobs. Via Ismail Merchant I got a gig in New York as a PA on an indie film called *Side Streets* (1998) with the director Tony Gerber. I had already been an AD, so I did really well and it was a very good experience for me. Once I finished that, I came back to India and got offered a job to cast by Dev Benegal, who was adapting the book *Split Wide Open* (1999). I hadn't done that before but I took it because my ultimate goal was to direct actors. Casting really helped me in terms of learning how to work with people, listen and believe in people and get something out of them. It taught me how to know when there is no hope and how to have serious empathy with that part of filmmaking.

It was an unbelievable experience working with actors. It really increased my empathy because I was working with people and realised how fragile they are.

AS: *Did anything stand out in particular when you were working on those films in terms of practices you did or did not want to use in your own work?*

ZA: Of course, my experiences with sound really stood out because I grew up in an industry with no sync sound and all the films were dubbed. There were tiny indie films that did use sync sound, but they were like 2 per cent of the industry. The norm was you had big stars who would do eight films at a time, come to the set, shoot and get out. Nobody had the time or the bandwidth to figure out how to shoot sound live so entire movies used to be dubbed. I've never worked on a dubbed film my entire life and I knew I didn't want to work like that. There was the question of how to shoot sync sound on location in a country as noisy as India. That required some serious learning. I worked on this on my brother's film *Dil Chahta Hai* (2001). That year, both *Lagaan* (Ashutosh Gowariker 2001) and *Dil Chahta Hai* used sync sound, and they shared a crew. There was a bunch of technical crews in India that would only work on foreign films and didn't touch mainstream films because nobody worked like that. In terms of production, that was invaluable learning for me from all these players.

Aakshi Magazine: *You knew that you didn't want to work within certain systems like dubbed sound, which is interesting because usually the expectation for people who have a Hindi film industry background is that they would extend that same form or tradition of filmmaking. Instead, it sounds like you were doing different things and trying to figure out what you actually wanted to make. Where did that come from?*

ZA: We were part of the industry, but my parents' life wasn't just the industry. There was a lot more going on with them which really opened up our minds. They didn't really tell us what to do and we were free to explore. Once we were adults, if we wanted to work with this person or get a job on a film my dad just told us to go out and get it. No calls were made for us, so we ended up working in places where nobody actually knew us. It was great. We weren't directed in any particular way; we weren't told where to go or what to do and as a result we had very diverse experiences.

Also, I have always been a mix of very industry and very artsy, that was the kind of culture in my house and that extended to my adult life with my friends. So, on the one hand, I have my industry, hardcore 'Bolly babies' friends with whom I grew up and they are my besties. And then I have this entirely different set of friends, whether it's Nitya Mehra or Reema Kagti or Arjun Bhasin, who came from small towns or from out of town, who are in the film industry but have no history with it, or are documentary filmmakers. My life has always been a mix of cultures and I think that comes out in my work as well. It's a bit of a hybrid. It's industry but it's not industry enough, it's alternative but it's not alternative enough.

When we were growing up, of course we watched all the Indian films. My mom is Parsi so we watched all the musicals, that goes without saying. But we also watched all the American films and then my mom was in film school so we ended up watching films by filmmakers like Carlos Saura and Franco Zeffirelli, things that one wouldn't have seen normally. It was completely eclectic. There would be a Costa-Gavras film and you didn't understand these films but you watched them and if you were bored you fell asleep but they were there so when you got older you watched them again. It was part of my mom's education and we were studying with her, literally.

My mom had a projector. Since my parents were in the industry, we knew all the distributors so they would sometimes send prints before the release and we would watch them. I watched *The Godfather* (Francis Ford Coppola 1972) on our dining room wall when I was maybe 10 and I didn't understand a word but everybody was saying how amazing it was and I was thinking 'this must be really important'. It was that kind of space. At the same time, there were discussions about the box office: what's running, which film worked, which one did not. So, it wasn't all art, but also the feeling that it needs to fly and the commerce aspect was always there.

AM: *Your debut feature film* Luck by Chance *took a long time to make. How did that experience shape the type of filmmaker you are today?*

ZA: How it shaped me is more philosophical than practical. You get a sense that things happen when they're meant to happen. For a while I really pushed for that movie to happen, but it didn't. Six actors said no to it, then my brother said yes. In the meantime, I was supposed to do a dance film with Hrithik [Roshan] and for some reason it wasn't working out between us. He's my friend as well and he asked me, 'What do you actually want to do?' I said, 'I want to do my first film' and he said he would do it. And then I got the funding. So, it was as random as that. You don't know where or when, but things do fall into place. And when they do, and you're in it, you realise that this was meant to happen now. Now I know that it's going to happen and I'm easier with it.

I think what has been really helpful for me the past ten years is that I have grown an incredibly thick skin when it comes to rejection. If one person says no to my film, I come up with another plan and can bounce to the next person in two days, there's no trauma attached. I realised the only person my film really needs is me! You learn to become patient and enjoy it. I love what I do. I'm not saving the world; I'm making films and I enjoy it. I don't want to get stressed about it; I want to love what I do every day, and that's it.

AM: *Looking at the bigger picture, apart from your individual struggles with casting, what was it about the industry at that time that stopped you from making LBC?*

ZA: When I started pitching the film there weren't any multiplexes, there wasn't this kind of narrative. *Luck by Chance* has what India loves to call the 'anti-hero' story. If the male lead is not the great guy who ends up with the woman and saves the day, then he's not the hero. He [the male lead Vikram] wasn't the hero at all. The lead in the film is a manipulative, social-climbing, incredibly ambitious wannabe actor. That's what he wants to do and we know that no integrity comes with that. It was an extremely juicy character. Today, if I had to make that film again and approach the actors in their twenties, I don't think I would have a problem casting it at all. I think the content has changed and the narrative has changed. I keep being asked if it was because I am a woman, but I don't think so, because I would have picked up on that. It was about the part. Actors didn't want to play that part. One actor told me, 'I really love the film, but I don't want to be seen like this so if you can flip it and I become the girl's part and the girl becomes the guy's part then I will do it.' That was what it was like.

AM: *Throughout your film career, you have had an interesting relationship to the representation of class. You faced some criticism for depicting 'first world problems' after* Zindagi Na Milegi Dobara *and* Dil Dhadakne Do. *How do you respond to such criticism?*

ZA: I don't respond to it, it's ridiculous. You can't comment on the characters' economic strata, that is not criticism. You can tell me it didn't resonate with you. You can tell me it's not a film that would connect with the Indian masses, but you're not the producer so what's it to you? I don't understand this criticism. And actually, *Zindagi* is possibly my most popular film, so it's really strange. It's not criticism I can take home and do something useful with; I'm not going to turn around and say that now I am only going to make movies about the middle class. I'm going to do what I want to do, and you have the freedom to buy the ticket or not.

AM: *It's not like there aren't other films made about the same class.*

ZA: Yes, I feel if it is fake, they are okay with it no matter how rich they are. If they have the hardcore Indian morality, then they are okay. If at the end of the day they are all getting married and touching everyone's feet, then they would be fine. If you are going to tell your parents to get lost, then they are not okay with that. It's the morality of it. It's not the only film about rich people, they've been making films about rich people throughout cinema history. When I did *Gully Boy*, they asked me whether I was doing the film in reaction to this criticism and I responded no. Why do you keep asking me about the economic strata of my characters? I also created a show called *Made in Heaven* before *Gully Boy* and it's about very rich people. So, I'm not going to give up, I just laugh it off.

AM: *Many of your films have Muslim characters whose religious identity is neither underlined in the narratives, nor are they represented in stereotypical ways. But then you have that interesting moment in* DDD *where Kabir tells his parents 'the girl I like is Muslim'. Also, in* Gully Boy *the hero and heroine are Muslim, which we haven't seen in Hindi cinema in a while. At the same time, you said in an interview that you didn't want to make it a 'Muslim story' and the emphasis was more on class. Could you talk about your thought process when it comes to writing Muslim characters?*

ZA: I'm an atheist and was brought up as one. My mom's Zoroastrian or Parsi, my father's Muslim. They're both atheists, but technically I'm Muslim. Culturally I'm Muslim, by name I'm Muslim. When we were growing up in the 1970s, there was always Muslim representation. I grew up with *Amar, Akbar, Anthony* (Manmohan Desai 1977).[1] That's the India I grew up in, and suddenly this identity kind of disappeared completely from our screens. But that's not my life. My world is very mixed and that needs to be reflected in the films.

With *Gully Boy* specifically, I decided to make him Muslim because it was a more interesting and a more familiar milieu to me. And because it is a very marginalised society and it helped the story. But it's not about their religion. It's not about Islam. It's about a culture, it's about this person who is there and they're in your life and it's normal. It needs to be treated like that.

AM: *What about in the other films like* ZNMD, DDD *or in your series* Made in Heaven *that have Muslim characters? How conscious is that choice?*

ZA: Yes. It's definitely a thing. You want to see yourself there, you want to represent.

AS: *You often work with large star ensemble casts or have multiple leading characters and yet you always manage to create the space to showcase individual characters' compelling stories. How do you balance this attention in your writing and in your directing?*

ZA: I think the first balancing has to come on paper because I don't like characters that are not rounded or are useless. Even if it is just one scene, there needs to be some kind of understanding, impact, vibe, something. I love ensemble films. I love Robert Altman, Paul Thomas Anderson, and those directors who have done ensembles well. Even Scorsese and Woody Allen have done a bunch of ensembles beautifully. I like those films and I watch them a lot. I like characters and honestly, a lot of the time the supporting characters are way more fun than the lead and you see it when you're writing. Like in *Luck by Chance* I had a lot of fun with Romy Rolly (Rishi Kapoor), though he was not a lead, and his wife (Juhi Chawla). And Nikki Walia (Isha Sharvani). I love Safeena (Alia Bhatt) in *Gully Boy*, I love Natasha (Kalki Koechlin) in *Zindagi*. I have a lot of fun with these characters. I always find them more exciting. You just balance the world out.

With actors you create an environment that is fair. It's gotten easier for me with each film because now people know they're not going to get the short end of the stick in the edit; I take care of the actors and I do actually make sure their parts are balanced. So, there is trust there. You have to make people feel safe. I've realised one thing about actors: when there's more of them, they're all really easy-going. They play off each other, especially the good actors, and they up each other's game. I think no one wants to be the person who created the problem, so everyone behaves well. I enjoy it thoroughly and it's fun to cast and if you get people you like and are good actors it's really thrilling and fun.

My crew is usually the same. There are two options for every department and so everyone knows everyone, and I've repeated most of the actors so it's really comfortable. We're like a well-oiled machine now, everyone just comes in and knows how to do it.

AS: *Your works have complex gender portrayals for both men and women in which they are negotiating their hopes and dreams against societal gender roles and expectations. What is the importance of bringing these gendered aspects of the characters' identity struggles to light? How do you think about that when you're writing these films and how important is that to you?*

ZA: I grew up with a cinema where masculinity was toxic. That's not the kind of men I'm attracted to or interested in. I think I put out male characters I'm hoping to see in the world. One part of it is wishful thinking, but by putting the idea of a better man out there you're making that okay on some level. It's okay to be gentle and to be quieter, to not resort to violence. You're still sexy to me. I find that much more attractive. And that's my experience of men mainly, at least most of my male friends or men I've dated. I think our cinema needs that.

About gender, I don't come from a family or a space where we had gender roles as such. But I am definitely very aware of what is going on in terms of gender politics. Like in *Zindagi*, the character Imraan (Farhan Akhtar) hooks up with a Spanish girl (Ariadna Cabrol). There is this little scene with the two of them in bed where he speaks in Hindi and she speaks in Spanish and there was just this connection there. When we were editing the film, my brother and producer said, 'why don't you just chop that scene, you don't need it' and I said, 'we do need it'. We are in a country where, sorry to say, but a lot of people think white girls should just sleep with you and as a filmmaker you have to be aware of that presumption. The minute we put that scene in, it became a love story, it wasn't just about a hook-up, but about a connection that was deeper. Suddenly everybody didn't just think, 'oh, he just hooked up with the white girl.' You have to be very careful as a filmmaker, you have to be aware of what you put out, especially with our audiences.

AS: *You have so many different roles and you make so many different types of media. What is the most striking difference between working on short films, a streaming show like* Made in Heaven *and directing a feature film? In terms of themes, narrative or style, do you find yourself making different choices?*

ZA: It's . . . amazing, actually. As a writer you have many ideas and some ideas are just half an hour, and are not going to hold longer than that. Like *Lust Stories* is only meant to be 19 minutes. It is succinct and correct. But *Made in Heaven* requires 8 hours of content. So I am actually in a space right now where I can actualise any idea I have, which is a blessing. It's really fun. What goes into it is the same kind of involvement (as a film) – what you want to say, what you want to do, how you want to design it.

Aside from the timeframes, another main difference is box office pressure, especially if you are doing theatrical release in India. Your weekend numbers matter, which is not the case on the OTT [over-the-top] platforms. It really takes the pressure off. It's something that you put out there and the audience can keep growing and keep commenting. I still get messages about *Made in Heaven* because people are still watching it. The second difference is that there is no censorship with the OTT platforms, which there is on theatrical releases, so you can play with different narratives and themes and you can visualise things differently. Even the casting is not as pressurised on an OTT platform as it is with a theatrical release. You need certain things to develop those characters, you need to grow with them, you need that length. I like working in all three. Each one has its own fun sides. Though when you are shooting a show you have to shoot damn fast. *Made in Heaven* was shot in four and a half months. I might shoot three or four pages a day in a movie, but I am shooting eight pages a day on a show. I am shooting like a beast. There's no time to think and it's a bit hectic, but besides that, it's amazing.

AS: *You and Reema [Kagti] are the creators of* MIH *but you don't direct all of the episodes. Are you there for all the shooting as the creators and producers?*

ZA: As creators you can't direct all the episodes. You are there in the beginning. We are there in the writers' room. Nothing on the script can change without our approval. I directed two episodes for *Made in Heaven*. We are doing another show right now for Amazon. Reema is going to direct about three episodes on that and then there will be other directors. When *MIH* comes back, I'll direct an episode or maybe two and then the directors will be there. So as a creator, you are kind of there, you set the tone, you are involved in the casting, you're involved in all the scripts and the design, and all is already decided with *MIH*. It's the same crew, they know what they are doing, and we can just move on from there. But we can't direct everything. Beyond a point it's foolish for me to spend four and a half months just directing something when I can actually set up something completely new.

AS: *That goes into our next question about your collaborations. Can you talk about your collaborations with Reema Kagti, with your father Javed Akhtar and your brother Farhan Akhtar? How do you all work together?*

ZA: I work all the time and I like to work with my friends and family because I don't feel like I am losing out on life. I have no FOMO [Fear of missing out] because everyone is there. My best friend is my costume designer, Arjun Bhasin. A very old friend of mine, Avan [Contractor], does my hair. I've worked with all these people whom I've known since my teens or my early twenties. It's the same crew that keeps working together.

With Reema it is specific because it's very difficult to find a co-writer. She would be very difficult to replace because we just have a system of writing which you can't find with many people. With writers especially, you have to find that person who can write and who can work the way you work and get into the same process. And most importantly, shares your values and politics. You can't write with somebody who is not politically aligned with you. It would be madness. I'd be violent (Laughs). When it comes to writing there's a lot of boxes to tick, which you don't really need with other collaborators. For example, I don't care who my DP votes for, but your gaze has to be in sync with your writer, more than with anyone else.

AM: *This goes back to what we discussed at the beginning about your having eclectic influences. I particularly wanted to ask about your relationship to or understanding of the popular Hindi film form, especially its elements like melodrama, star system and song sequences.*

ZA: I love our Indian actors. We survived the onslaught of Hollywood because of our actors. All the industries that have survived Hollywood did so because of a star system. We want to see our stars. They are great ambassadors and it works really well. I mean, of course, there are problems, but as a system I have no complaints with it because that is how our audience is motivated to come to our cinema.

I love mainstream Hindi films. It is an extension of our form of storytelling. It was an oral tradition accompanied with music that came into our theatre and then to the cinema. So, it is a form that is intrinsic to us and to who we are. Indians love singing and everybody thinks they are great singers! It's just who we are. And I love the fact that though we watch things from everywhere in the world, our cinema is our cinema. Sometimes I will get a pang to see a Hindi movie. And I love that, and I hope that does not change. Of course, we should have room for every kind of narrative and every kind of structure, but I definitely want the musicals to never ever go away because it's really fun and special. And it's ours. And half the globe reacts to it. So, it's good.

AM: *Where does this come from? Is it because you come from a family that has been associated with the popular film form? If we take the example of a film like* Court *(Chaitanya Tamhane 2014), or many of Anurag Kashyap's films, not everyone has this sense of finding continuity with the traditional Hindi film form . . .*

ZA: They don't and that is fine. That's a choice they are making. I mean tomorrow I may have something that does not require music and I won't use it. I can happily make something that is without music. I don't have a problem with that. But if you talk to Anurag Kashyap, he's grown up on Amitabh Bachchan, not Tarkovsky, and that's the truth of it. Their love for film came from that. And they know it and they say it and you can't deny it. In fact, he [Anurag] called me yesterday and said I am watching '*Baawre*' [dance number from *Luck by Chance*] and I want to ask you, 'How do you shoot songs? I don't know how to do it. I love it. And I don't know how to do it.' And I told him there is nothing to 'do'. And we were just having a conversation about it because there are so many things in his films that I am like 'dude, how did you do that?' Does he love it? Of course he loves it! You can't see '*Chaiya Chaiya*' [*Dil Se* (Mani Ratnam 1998)] and not like it. Or '*Dola Re Dola*' [*Devdas* (Sanjay Leela Bhansali 2002)]. I can watch '*Dola Re Dola*' any time if you play that song. It's just beautiful. It's special. And the form will just get better, hopefully.

AM: *In your own films, when you are making choices about whether to have a song, is this ever a concern at the back of your mind? Do you ever think about it in terms of a tradition you would like to continue, or do you see yourself breaking from it?*

ZA: No, I don't. It really depends on the story I am telling and who I am telling it to. Tomorrow, if I am making a film which I know is a tiny film, like if I make a film about the migrant exodus during the Coronavirus, I may have a background score but I am not going to put a song and dance in it. If I am making a film primarily for a South Asian audience, then why would I take away from what they want and what I enjoy also? It depends on what you are saying and who you are saying it to.

AM: *It is said that the multiplex changed Indian cinema because it was no longer necessary to make a film catering to all classes. Does that feel true to you or do you still want to make a 'pan-Indian' film that is for a large audience?*

ZA: Of course you want to make a film for the largest possible audience. You want the whole world to watch your movie. But you also have to know your limitations. You also need to know who relates to you and who doesn't. I know what my bandwidth audience is right now and there will be subjects that will be niche even for them, or there'll be subjects where I could stretch that number. It depends on what I am doing, but I know my budget, what I need to cover and how many people will see it.

AM: *Are there certain choices that you make so that a larger number of people will watch or understand your films?*

ZA: You make certain choices in casting because it helps to get the audience in and it helps you to get the budget you want and make the film the way you want to make. Sometimes you make certain choices just because you are talking to an audience that is so used to being treated in a particular way. When we did *Zindagi*, the film for me ended when the boys were running, with the poem. Then we had focus screenings where we had all kinds of people: students, people that are working in gyms, people that are day labourers, people that only speak Hindi. And for the majority of those people, across the board, the feedback was: did they die?! They did not get it! Now that's not a question you want people to leave with. I had to add that song at the end which I was not planning to do. You have to react to that because that's primarily the audience.

AM: *What about a device like the voiceover. You use that a lot. Is that also a choice you make for the same reason?*

ZA: I like voiceovers. I like poetry. I like it as a device. It lets you internalise things and gives you something more. I know a lot of people say it is lazy filmmaking, but I don't care. It depends on how you use it. *Ferris Bueller's Day Off* (John Hughes 1986) is one of my favourite films ever. It has the most epic voiceover on the planet.

AS: *Could you talk about the launch of your production company Tiger Baby in 2015? Why was it important for you to set up your own production company? How did it come about?*

ZA: Karan Johar is a very close friend of mine and we were out one night, and he asked me why I was not producing. I had been thinking about it. I had also spoken about it with Ritesh [Sidhwani], who was the producer on my other three films. He told me I should have my own space and put out my own content because I have a very strong point of view. He encouraged me to own my own work as an artist. I thought it was time. I decided to stop being lazy and do it, and from *Lust Stories* onwards everything has either been co-produced by Tiger Baby and Excel, or certain things are just Tiger Baby.

It is great to have your own space. I'm really enjoying it, though I work a lot more. When I created Tiger Baby I had to set it up ASAP for *Gully Boy* and *Lust Stories*. My mum became a partner in it. But then when we started to do the show, *MIH*, Reema wanted me to produce it. I told her she needed to own it because she was co-creating it with me. So, then we had a subsidiary company called Tiger Baby Digital and we did *MIH* out of that. But now it's just Tiger Baby and we are working out of one company and that's it. The three of us are partners.

AM: *Now that you've produced some projects under the label of Tiger Baby, has that experience been any different from your earlier work?*

ZA: Yes, because suddenly you are involved in all the deals and you are involved in the marketing at a level that you weren't earlier. It's fun but it's a different ball game. Which is why I don't want to get into that zone of doing everything myself without Excel. That would take away from my and Reema's core strength, which is writing and directing and putting projects together. I should be ideating, saying this would be good, bringing together these actors or directors or writers, and so it makes perfect sense for me to keep working with Excel also and have Farhan and Ritesh [at Excel] be the 'muscle'. Let them do all the other work. It works perfectly.

AM: *What is your reaction to being called a female filmmaker? How do you respond to it?*

ZA: I mean how do you respond to it? Everyone asks how do you feel being a female filmmaker and I say, 'as opposed to when I was male three years ago?' I have nothing to compare it to. What is your point? What is the question? You just have to keep calling it out, you can't get affected. You've grown up in such a sexist society that it can't affect you beyond a point. Yes, I am a woman but why are you talking about my gender, you 'male editor'. It's not perfect being a man and it's not perfect being a woman. Are you a good person? Are you a great artist? Then you are great. I just laugh at people and then they back off. I feel it will change because there are so many now.

AM: *In the context of the #MeToo movement, there has been conversation online about reading more women writers, watching more women filmmakers and so on. In that context, do you think that one can own being called a 'female filmmaker'? Is it necessarily a limiting label? Or is it the context in which it is said?*

ZA: I don't know. Then you have to own being a woman driver. You have to own everything you do as a woman. It's really weird to me. You don't say my 'lady doctor'. You just say my doctor. It's kind of bizarre. There were very few female directors earlier on, so maybe it was a bigger deal back then. But now, there are more of us, and that's the way it is, and people should stop saying it. The Instagram page of my production house, Tiger Baby, pushes a lot of women but we never call them 'female' artists. We just put them out as artists.

Because why should we be doing this constant 'us-ing' and 'them-ing'? If you kept saying the male filmmaker Anurag Kashyap, I'd ask why: are you fascinated, are you shocked? Why are you referring to my gender? In 2020 if you are still commenting on it then we should push back a little bit.

AM: *In what way does your gender impact your work as a filmmaker?*

ZA: I think my gender is my gaze. My experience of life is being female in India. It's very different and has a lot of impact. I don't know any other way so everything I do is operating from this female experience and gaze. It could be anger, or a point to be made, or a lens to be looked through. Everything comes from that zone. It's wild because I grew up with boys. Most of my friends have been boys. I find boys very easy. I find the narrative very easy to come by. But I look at them as a woman. My gaze is just there.

AM: *In terms of dealing with a patriarchal society and film industry, are there instances where you find yourself making certain negotiations that your male counterparts would not — this could be on set while shooting, while promoting a film or how your films are reviewed?*

ZA: Yes, it's in everything. It is so inbuilt. It really bothers me that actors get paid so much more than actresses. It doesn't happen so much with me, I think, because I am a director. I can pull my weight according to how well my last film did at the box office. That kind of standardises it. But those things are hard, and you do have to negotiate certain things. It's changed a lot, but it is still a male space. At the same time, I know how lucky I am and how blessed I am because I grew up in this space, so a lot of the doors were open for me. I grew up in an absolutely gender-neutral home. There was no concept of girl or boy. I figured out sexism as a concept only when I got to college! I was like 'what do you mean you can't go out and your brother can go out?'. It didn't exist for me. So, I feel if somebody was sexist with me a lot of times I didn't catch it. It took me a long time to realise it; now I can look back and see it as it was.

There hasn't been a significant point in my life when I was treated in a particular way because I was a girl that made an impact on me or that hurt me. I don't have scars from it. So, I deal with it very differently. I have friends who get upset with me because if there is a funny sexist joke I will laugh. They will not find it funny, but I will. Yes, it is not right, but nothing funny is right. Even if you laugh at someone falling on a banana peel, it is cruel. You are laughing at someone getting hurt. No humour is politically correct. You just have to balance it. But I am aware of the politics and I will call it out. I get angry because I see it affecting other people. But I don't really let it get to me because I just bulldoze my way through it.

AM: *But as a filmmaker, working on a set, with actors, you must have to manage egos and all of that so you cannot always call it out . . .*

ZA: Actors want to be loved and they want to be guided. If they've agreed to do your film, they've already crossed the hurdle of your gender. They are not going to come in there and be sexist. They just want your approval. It does happen with technical crew sometimes. In my first film, my Steadicam operator would keep going to the film's actor Farhan [Akhtar], my brother, who is also a filmmaker. He would ask him if the shot was okay. Farhan told him he is not the director. Finally, I took him aside and I told him that this is a problem because I am directing the film and you don't seem to believe it. He said, 'no no no, you're like my sister.' And I told him, 'I'm not your sister, I am your director.' And then eventually we became friends. You just have to deal with it in a particular way without letting it get to you. And if everybody knows you know your stuff, they will be okay.

But I know they do give women a hard time. I have friends who have told me they have a very hard time because they are women, and maybe they are more sensitive to it or maybe they are working with more difficult men. There are so many factors that come into play. I mean, the filmmaking business is a sexist space, so you have to handle it in a particular way. But if the film industry thinks you can make them money, you could be man, woman, dog, cat, they will be interested in you.

AS: *You have described your films as not art house enough and not industry enough. Do you see yourself as a part of a kind of movement of a New Bollywood, or do you think such a movement exists right now? Is something happening in Bollywood?*

ZA: I mean definitely things changed with the multiplex space, and a lot of new content is coming in, also with the OTT space. But would I call myself 'New Bollywood'? No. Bollywood has always evolved, always changed, every decade has seen a new influx of people. Every decade has seen a different kind of trend. So, you are new until you are old. Hopefully you are relevant and your work is relevant. I won't call myself new, because if you call yourself new today, you will be calling yourself old tomorrow. Hopefully I am here to stay.

AS: *Alright, we won't put you in that box. But do you view yourself or maybe some other directors as a 'shift' in what Bollywood is doing? How would you describe some of those changes?*

ZA: I think the biggest shift came in 2000, which was the shift in how films were shot, because that was the year they were making *Lagaan, Chandni Bar* (Madhur Bhandarkar 2001), *DCH, Gadar* (Anil Sharma 2001), *Kabhi Khushi Kabhi Gham* (Karan Johar 2001). It was a mix of all kinds of films. And that's when it started being different. Things opened up. Narratives changed. I think it was the 2000s onwards. But is there a shift now, yes with the OTT platform definitely there is a shift. It is in a bit of a flux right now and everyone is finding their audience and I am in that.

AS: *Where do you see the Hindi media industry – film, TV, streaming series, music – twenty years from now? What would you like to see? What do you think you will actually see?*

ZA: It's going to expand because the borders are getting softer. Today I will create a show that is right next to *The Marvellous Mrs Maisel* (Amy Sherman-Palladino 2017–20) and right next to *Fauda* (Avi Issacharoff and Lior Raz 2015–18). You have access to a world audience, but so do others. So, you have to up your game. I see storytellers being able to relate to a larger audience beyond the South Asian audience and that is interesting. I see interesting collaborations coming out of it. I feel there will be all types of Indian representations everywhere, and that is interesting for me to watch. But otherwise I think, for the most part, we are here doing what we do best.

NOTE

1. A hallmark example of the popular *masala* (spice) films of the 1970s, *Amar Akbar Anthony* tells the story of three brothers separated in early childhood who are each raised by families of different religions: Hindi, Muslim and Christian. As adults, the brothers reunite despite their different faiths, thus making the film an example that uplifts harmony between the different religious communities of the country.

General Index

Aabobo Film Club, 65
Akhtar, Farhan, 2, 3, 6, 10, 13, 21, 31, 77, 78, 81, 151–2, 165, 167, 173, 188, 192, 195n, 202–3, 209, 213, 218, 220, 223, 225, 228, 230
Akhtar, Jan Nisar, 115
Akhtar, Javed, 3, 4, 20, 76, 81, 102, 115, 123, 152, 154, 202, 209, 217, 225
Ali, Imtiaz, 65
Allen, Woody, 222
Altman, Robert, 222
Amazon Prime, 61, 63, 64, 126–7, 133–4, 141, 224
Anderson, Paul Thomas, 222
Angry Young Man, 152, 204
Anjali, 63
Arora, Shashank, 190
A$AP Rocky, 111, 182
auteur, 205, 207
Awghade, Somnath, 184
Azmi, Shabana, 126

Bachchan, Amitabh, 117, 128, 152, 226

Badshah, 46–7
Bagri Foundation London Indian Film Festival (LIFF), 62
Bambaiya, 90n, 114–15, 120–2
Banerjee, Dibakar, 6, 10, 59, 63, 67, 71
Bangalore International Short Film Festival, 62
Benegal, Dev, 3, 76, 218
Benegal, Shyam, 77
Berlinale, 62
Bharatiya Janata Party (BJP), 150, 163n
Bhasin, Arjun, 219, 225
Bhatt, Alia, 13, 53, 117, 157, 204, 210, 223
Bhoopalam, Neil, 69
Bildungsroman, 180–1
biopic, 158
Bollylite, 12, 13
Bollywood *see* Hindi Cinema/Film Industry
Bollywoodisation of Indian cinema, 7–8
Bombay *see* Mumbai

GENERAL INDEX 233

Bombay film industry *see* Hindi Cinema/Film Industry
Bombay Talkies, 59
Bose, Rahul, 97, 167, 193
Bose, Shonali, 10
bromance, 203
buddy films, 128
Butler, Judith, 150

Cabrol, Adriadna, 223
Cannes Film Festival, 62
capitalism, 172, 177, 212
Caplan Merwanji, Susan, 110
Carter Pilcher, 66
caste, 152, 177, 181, 185–7, 191, 193–5n, 213
  Avarnas, 194
  Dalit, 56n, 184–5, 187
  savarna, 48, 56n, 184, 195n
censorship, 134, 224
Chatterjee, Basu, 109
Chaturvedi, Siddhant, 78, 157
Chawla, Juhi, 223
chivalry, 154, 159
Chopra, Pawan, 192
Chopra, Priyanka, 11, 13, 43, 94, 154, 167, 171, 186
Chopra, Tisca, 65
class, 67, 70–1, 86, 127, 129, 132, 136, 139, 148–9, 152, 156–9, 161, 182, 287–8, 190–1, 194–5n, 204–5, 211–13, 221–2
colonial rule, 126, 149, 158
consumerism, 131, 133–4, 149, 157, 163n
Contractor, Avan, 225
Copyright Act, 44
corporatisation, 24, 27, 29, 78, 149
Costa-Gavras, 220
couple-form, 32–4

COVID-19/Coronavirus, 63, 64, 226
cultural capital, 166, 201

Das, Nandita, 126
Dayama, Yashaswini, 137
Delhi, 120–1, 137, 170, 173–4, 190–2
Deol, Abhay, 13, 151, 165, 195n
Dhanush, 185
Dharavi, Mumbai/Bombay 17/Dharavi 17, 50–2, 109–12, 114, 122, 156, 182, 213
Dharma Productions, 28
Dhulipala, Sobhita, 190
diaspora/diasporic, 8, 120, 129–32, 134, 140–1, 163n
Disney+, 63
Divine, 39, 47, 54, 55n, 114–15, 123–4n, 158
documentary film, 161, 219
domesticity, 167
Dosti, 128; *see also yaar/yarana*
dowry, 139
Dubai, 190
dubbing, 219
Dubey, Khushi, 193
Dutta, Tanushree, 147

economic liberalisation, 8, 132, 211
Eminem, 158
Emiway, 82
ensemble, 23, 25–6, 37, 75, 78
Eros Now, 63
Excel Entertainment, 6, 10, 227–8

family in crisis film, 93–7, 100
Fearless Nadia (Mary Ann Evans), 168
feminism, 150, 206, 211
Film and Television Institute of India (FTII), 2, 4, 41, 76, 217
Film City, 174

Film Finance Corporation, 41
film festivals, 62, 65
Foucault, Michel, 94–6, 98, 103, 106
Foucauldian, 93, 94, 96, 106

Gautham Menon, 63, 64
gender, 59, 68, 101–3, 131–2, 140–1, 147–9, 150, 152, 155, 158, 160–1, 163n, 199, 209–10, 213, 223, 228–9
generational divides, 147–8, 153–8, 161
Gerber, Tony, 218
Ghazal, 117
globalisation, 109, 127, 131, 133, 156, 161, 172
gully rap, 44, 46–51, 80, 108–9, 112–16, 121, 213
Gulzar, Meghna, 4, 7
Gustad, Kaizad, 76

Hall, Stuart, 201–2, 213
Hashmi, Sarah, 193
'*Hatke*' film, 7, 60, 78
hero, 148–50, 152 161, 180, 210
    anti-hero, 221
heroine, 128, 180
heteronormativity, 129–30, 139
heteropatriarchal, 129–32, 137, 139
heterotopia, 93–9, 102, 103, 105, 106
Hindi Cinema/Film Industry, 11–12, 16n, 21–36, 59, 60, 64, 65, 66, 69, 72, 73n, 119–20, 122–3, 127–35, 147–9, 151, 156, 170, 171, 173, 180–2, 187–8, 190, 194–5n, 199, 203, 210–11, 213, 217–22, 225, 229–30
    also referred to as Bollywood, Bombay Film Industry, the Film Industry

Hindi film romance, 32–4
Hindutva, 150
hip-hop/rap, 46, 55n, 119, 123n, 204–5, 210; *see also* *Gully* rap
Hirani, Raju, 79
Hollywood, 77, 131, 212, 225
homophobia, 126, 131, 133, 135, 140, 144n
homosocialism, 126, 128, 132
HumaraMovie, 64

Indian Censor Board, 126, 141n
Indian Film Festival of Los Angeles (IFFLA), 62
Indian 'middlebrow' cinema, 67, 68, 72, 73n
Indian Penal Code Section 377/Article 377, 126–7, 129, 134, 139–40, 141n, 158, 160, 163n
indie film, 219
indie music, 46
International Documentary and Short Film Festival of Kerala (IDSFFK), 62
International Film Festival of India, 62
International Film Festival Rotterdam (IFFR), 62
Irani, Honey, 2, 4, 5, 17, 76, 202, 217
Islamophobia, 182, 187
Istanbul, 171, 173

Jafrey, Javed, 129
Jaipur International Short Film Festival, 62
Jio TV, Jio Cinema, 63
Jio MAMI Mumbai Film Festival, 62

Johar, Karan, 26, 27, 37, 59, 144n, 227
Joshi, Abhijat, 79

Kaam Bhaari, 82
Kadam, Kishor, 184
Kagti, Reema, 2, 3, 6, 10, 79, 80, 121, 158, 190, 208, 218–19, 224–5, 228
Kaif, Katrina, 68, 73n, 152, 166, 195n
Kapadia, Dimple, 31, 83, 173
Kapoor, Anil, 11, 43, 94, 154, 167, 186
Kapoor, Janhvi, 71
Kapoor, Prithviraj, 31
Kapoor, Raj, 31
Kapoor, Rishi, 27, 78, 223
Kapoor, Sanjay, 31
Kapoor, Shahid, 148
Kapoor, Sonam, 133
Karmarkar, Kiran, 132
Kashyap, Anurag, 10, 59, 61, 65, 226, 229
Khan, Aamir, 102, 177, 186
Khan, Alyy, 188
Khan, Cezanne, 132
Khan, Farah, 1, 4, 6, 17, 23, 36, 37
Khan, Ikhlaque, 104
Khan, Kamran, 4, 23
Khan, Saif Ali, 130
Khan, Sajid, 147
Khan, Salim, 4
Khan, Salman, 150
Khan, Shah Rukh, 78, 130, 163n, 177
Khanna, Akshaye, 161n
Khanna, Rajesh, 117
Kharbanda, Kulbhushan, 129
Kharat, Rajeshwari, 184
Koechlin, Kalki, 13, 53, 63, 111, 138, 151, 157, 165, 191, 211

Kolkata International Film Festival, 62
Kukunoor, Nagesh, 10
Kumar, Akshay, 147

Lefebvre, Henri, 164–5
London, 166–7, 170
Ludhianvi, Sahir, 117

machismo, 166
male body, 149–50, 163n
Malhotra, Pawan, 54
Malhotra-Irani, Smriti, 132
Mamgain, Preeti, 137
masala film, 12, 17n, 231n
masculinity, 113, 121, 129, 147–53, 155–6, 159–61, 163n, 194
    hypermasculinity, 150
    toxic masculinity, 148, 223
Massey, Vikrant, 78, 100, 193
Mathai, Mahesh, 76
Mathur, Arjun, 127, 134, 158, 190
Maurya, Vijay, 3, 81–2 121
MC Altaf, 82
Mehra, Nitya, 3, 219
Mehta, Deepa, 129, 144n
Merchant, Ismail, 218
Merchant, Vaibhavi, 30
#MeToo Movement, 22, 147–8, 163n, 228
Mirza, Saeed, 109
Multiplot film, 78; *see also* ensemble
multiplex, 9, 11–12, 27, 60, 66, 93, 226, 230
multiplex cinema/film, 2, 7, 10, 11–13, 78, 221
Mumbai/Bombay, 108–16, 119–22, 156–7, 170, 172, 174, 176–7, 188, 204, 213, 217

Mumbai International Film Festival, 62
Mumbai film, 109

Naezy, 39, 47, 50, 54, 114, 123n, 158
Nair, Mira, 2, 6, 61, 64, 76, 217–18
National Film Archives, 41
Narkar, Megha, 189
Nas, 110–11, 122
NDTV Prime, 65
neoliberal, 109–10, 112, 114, 116, 119–20, 127, 148–54, 156–8, 160–1, 162n, 176, 178
nepotism, 24, 37
Netflix, 60, 63, 64, 133–4, 141n
New Bollywood, 7, 9, 43, 131, 230
New Economic Policy, 120
New York, 217–18
New York Indian Film Festival (NYIFF), 62
Non-Resident Indian (NRI), 149, 162n
nuclear family, 167, 176–7

Onir, 10
over-the-top (OTT) services, 62, 224, 230–1

Paranjpye, Sai, 14
Patekar, Nana, 147
Pathak, Vinay, 136
patriarchy, 104, 112, 128–9, 131, 139, 150, 154–5, 157, 165, 178, 182, 186, 188, 194, 229
Pednekar, Bhumi, 69
Percept Picture Companies, 27
Pocket Films, 64, 65
polyglossia, 113, 115
Poomani, 185
post-global, 131

Public Interest Litigation, 139, 144n, 160
Pune, 217

Raaz, Vijay, 182
Raftaar, 46–7
Raghuvanshi, Shivani, 138, 190
Rakhee, 4
Rahul Piske, 82
Raza, Ayesha, 136, 193
Rich, Rishi, 115, 123
Rocker, Dule, 48
Roshan, Hrithik, 13, 31, 150–1, 165, 195n, 220
Roshan, Rakesh, 31
Roy, Ronit, 132
Royal Stag Barrel Large Short Films, 64, 65

Sahara One, 27
Salim-Javed, 4, 76, 77, 79; see also Salim Khan and Javed Akhtar
Samos, Sumeet, 48
Sarbh, Jim, 135, 191
Saura, Carlos, 220
Schadenfreude, 212
Scorsese, Martin, 222
Sedgwick, Eve, 127
Sehgal, Baba, 46
self-made/self-creation, 152, 180–1, 186–8, 190, 193–4
self-discovery/self-realisation, 151, 153, 155, 160, 172, 177, 180–1
Sen, Aparna, 31
Sen Sharma, Konkona, 31, 73n, 151, 173, 188
sexism, 131, 175, 208, 228–30
sexual capital, 166, 178
Shah, Shefali, 94, 167, 186

Sharma, Anushka, 43, 100, 167, 170, 187
Sharvani, Isha, 173, 188, 223
shayar, 108–9, 113–16, 119–23
Shetty, Shefali, 155
short film, 59–74
Shorts TV's 24/7 HD TV, 65
Shorts International, 66
Shrivastava, Alankrita, 3
Shiv Sena, 126, 141n
Sidhwani, Ritesh, 6, 227–8
Sikri, Surekha, 71
Simran, 63
Singh, Anhad, 135
Singh, Ranveer, 11, 13, 15, 43, 54, 108, 147, 154, 156, 167, 182, 186–7, 204, 211, 213
Singh, Yo Yo Honey, 46–7
single screen, 11–12
soap opera, 132
social, 12
song-and-dance sequences, song picturisation, 12, 29–32, 59, 225
Spain, 151, 165–6, 170–4
Shrivastava, Srishti, 78
stardom/star system, 31–2, 149, 162n, 209, 225
streaming services, 11, 126–7, 133–4, 141
Structural Adjustment Programme of 1991, 149
struggling actor, 22, 32
subaltern, 213
Subhash, Amruta, 182

Sud, Ridhima, 78, 96, 193
Sundance Film Festival, 62
sync sound, 218–19

Tamil Film Industry, 63, 64
Tanwar, Sakshi, 132
tapori, 23, 108–9, 115, 119–23
Tarkovsky, Andrei, 226
terrorism, 150
Tiger Baby Films, 88, 162n, 227–8
Tiwari, Shewta, 132, 162n
Toronto International Film Festival (TIFF), 62
T-Series, 45
Turkey, 167–8, 170–1, 174

urbanisation, 131, 133
UTV, 27

Varma, Ram Gopal, 9, 10, 23, 51
Varma, Vijay, 53, 71, 78, 118, 156
voiceover, 71, 73, 102–3, 177, 227
voyeurism, 136, 212

Wahab, Zarina, 97
woman filmmaker, 13, 14, 35–7n
'women-centric' films, 181–2, 194

yaar/yarana, 128; *see also dosti*
Yashraj Films, 28
YouTube, 62, 65

Zeffirelli, Franco, 220
Zinta, Preity, 130

Index of Films

3 Idiots (Raj Kumar Hirani 2009), 35
8 Mile (Curtis Hanson 2002), 158
11'09"01 (Youssef Chahine, Amos Gitai, Shohei Imamura, Alejandro G. Inarritu, Claude Lelouch, Ken Loach, Samira Makhmalbaf, Mira Nair, Idrissa Ouedraogo, Sean Penn and Danis Tanovic 2002), 61

Aaina (Deepak Sareen 1993), 5
Aamir (Raj Kumar Gupta 2008), 51
Actress (Balwant Bhatt 1934), 38
Aids Jaago (Mira Nair, Santosh Sivan, Farhan Akhtar and Vishak Bhardwaj 2007), 61
Ajab Prem Ki Gazab Kahani (Rajkumar Santoshi 2009), 35
Ajeeb Daastaans (Neeraj Ghaywan, Kayoze Irani, Shashank Khaitan and Raj Mehta 2021), 63
Amar, Akbar, Anthony (Manmohan Desai 1977), 222, 23In
Anand (Hrishikesh Mukherjee 1971), 128

A Night of Prophecy (Amar Kanwar 2002), 123n
Anuradha (Hrishikesh Mukherjee 1960), 39
Armaan (Honey Irani 2003), 5
Asuran (Vetrimaaran 2019), 185
Awaara (Raj Kapoor 1951), 109, 120

Baiju Bawra (Vijay Bhatt 1952), 39
Bhumika (Shyam Benegal 1977), 42
Billu (Priyadarshan 2009), 23
Bombay Boys (Kaizad Gustad 1998), 6, 217
Bombay: Our City (Anand Patwardhan 1985), 123n
Bombay Talkies (Zoya Akhtar, Dibakar Banerjee, Anurag Kashyap and Karan Johar 2013), 2, 13, 59, 60, 61, 66, 67, 69, 72, 126
Bombay Velvet (Anurag Kashyap 2015), 10
Black Friday (Anurag Kashyap 2004), 10, 51

Chak De! India (Shimit Amin 2007), 28, 181
Chameli (Sudhir Mishra 2004), 181
Chandni Bar (Madhur Bhandarkar 2001), 181, 230
Chaudvin Ka Chand (M. Sadiq 1960), 128
Chhapaak (Meghna Gulzar 2020), 162n
Chutney (Jyoti Kapur Das 2016), 65
Chutney Popcorn (Nisha Ganatra 1999), 144n
Court (Chaitanya Tamhane 2014), 226

Darr (Yash Chopra 1993), 5
Dear Zindagi (Gauri Shinde 2016), 94, 180
De Dana Dhan (Priyadarshan 2009), 35
Dedh Ishqiya (Abhishek Chaubey 2014), 126, 132
Deewar (Yash Chopra 1975), 4, 50, 109
Delhi Belly (Abhinay Deo and Akshat Verma 2011), 170
Delhi Crime (Richie Mehta 2019), 162n
Dev D (Anurag Kashyap 2009), 10, 24
Devdas (Sanjay Leela Bhansali 2002), 42, 226
Devi (Priyanka Banerjee 2020), 67
Dharavi Hustle (Bajaoo 2016), 51
Dhoom (Sanjay Gadhvi 2004), 28
Dil Bole Hadippa (Anurag Singh 2009), 180
Dil Chahta Hai (*DCH*) (Farhan Akhtar 2001), 6, 10, 77, 152, 170, 203, 219, 230

Dil Dhadakne Do (*DDD*) (Zoya Akhtar 2015), 2, 7, 11, 15, 43, 86, 93–107n, 110, 148, 153, 156, 164, 167–70, 173, 181, 186–7, 189, 192–3, 199, 204–5, 209, 211–12, 221–2
Dil Se (Mani Ratnam 1998), 226
Dilwale Dulhania le Jayenge (*DDLJ*) (Aditya Chopra 1995), 8, 42, 95, 152, 162n
Dolly Kitty Aur Woh Chamakte Sitare (Alankrita Shrivastava 2019), 73n
Don (Chandra Barot 1978), 109
Dostana (Raj Khosla 1980), 128–30
Dostana (Tarun Mansukhani 2008), 126, 129–31, 133

Ek Ladki Ko Dekha Toh Aisa Laga (Shelly Chopra Dhar 2019), 126, 132–3

Fandry (Nagraj Manjule 2013), 184, 193
Father Son and Holy War (Anand Patwardhan 1994), 161
Fashion (Madhur Bhandarkar 2008), 22, 188
Fauda (Avi Issacharoff and Lior Raz 2015–18), 231
Ferris Bueller's Day Off (John Hughes 1986), 227
Fire (Deepa Mehta 1996), 126, 129–32, 141n
Four More Shots Please! (Rangita Pritish Nandy 2019–20), 132

Gadar (Anil Sharma 2001), 230
Gangs of Wasseypur (Anurag Kashyap 2012), 10

INDEX OF FILMS

Ghost Stories (Zoya Akhtar, Dibakar Banerjee, Anurag Kashyap and Karan Johar 2020), 2, 13, 60, 61, 63, 71
Ghulam (Vikram Bhatt 1998), 120
Girlfriend (Karan Razdan 2004), 132
Gold (Reema Kagti 2018), 10
Gosford Park (Robert Altman 2001), 103
Guddi (Hrishikesh Mukherjee 1971), 42, 23, 38
Gully Boy (Zoya Akhtar 2019), 2, 3, 7, 12, 13, 14, 15, 16, 38, 39, 73, 80, 81, 85–6, 108–25n, 147–8, 150, 156, 158, 160, 162n, 181–2, 185, 187, 189, 199, 204–5, 208–13, 2213, 227

Heroine (Madhur Bhandarkar 2012), 22, 144n, 188
Hero Hiralal (Ketan Mehta 1988), 38
Highway (Imtiaz Ali 2014), 94–5
Honeymoon Travels Pvt. Ltd (Reema Kagti 2007), 6, 10, 126
Housefull 4 (Farhad Samji 2019), 147
Hum Aapke Hain Kaun (Sooraj Barjatya 1994), 15, 93, 128–9, 152
Hyderabad Blues (Nagesh Kukunoor 1998), 10

I Am (Onir 2010), 126, 130, 144n
I Hate Luv Storys (Punit Malhotra 2010), 23

Kabhi Khushi Kabhi Gham (*K3G*) (Karan Johar 2001), 8, 93, 230
Kabir Singh (Sandeep Reddy Vanga 2019), 147–8, 150, 161, 162n, 208
Kaagaz ke Phool (Guru Dutt 1959), 23, 38
Kaala (Pa Ranjith 2018), 51
Kahaani (Sujoy Ghosh 2012), 181
Kahaani Ghar Ghar Ki (2000–8), 132
Kal Ho Na Ho (Nikhil Advani 2003), 6, 28, 126, 130, 133
Kama Sutra: A Tale of Love (Mira Nair 1996), 6, 217
Kapoor and Sons (Shakun Batra 2016), 94, 140, 144n
Kasauti Zindagi Ki (2001–8), 132
Khamosh (Vidhu Vinod Chopra 1985), 42
Khosla Ka Ghosla (Dibakar Banerjee 2006), 10
Krrish (Rakesh Roshan 2006), 5
Kuch Kuch Hota Hai (*KKHH*) (Karan Johar 1998), 42, 93
Kyunki Saas Bhi Kabhi Bahu Thi (2000–8), 132

Lagaan (Ashutosh Gowariker 2001), 10, 219, 230
Lakshya (Farhan Akhtar 2004), 180
Lamhe (Yash Chopra 1991), 4
Let Them All Talk (Steven Soderbergh 2020), 107n
Like Father (Lauren Miller 2018), 107n
Love Aaj Kal (Imtiaz Ali 2009), 32, 35
LSD: Love, Sex Aur Dhokha (Dibakar Banerjee 2010), 10
Luck By Chance (*LBC*) (Zoya Akhtar 2009), 1–4, 7, 8, 12, 14, 21–37, 77, 82–4, 151, 164, 170, 173–6, 181, 188, 199, 202–5, 208–9, 212–13, 220–1, 223, 226
Lust Stories (Zoya Akhtar, Dibakar Banerjee, Anurag Kashyap and Karan Johar 2018), 2, 3, 13, 60, 61, 63, 69, 71, 224, 227

Main Hoon Na (Farah Khan 2009), 7
Main Madhuri Dixit Banna Chahti Hoon (Chandan Arora 2003), 38
Maine Pyar Kiya (Sooraj R. Barjatya 1989), 180
Made in Heaven (Zoya Akhtar and Reema Kagti 2019), 2, 3, 7, 15, 61, 80, 126–8, 133–136, 138, 140–1, 148, 158, 181, 190, 193, 195n, 222, 224, 228
Maqbool (Vishal Bhardwaj 2003), 10
Masti (Indra Kumar 2004), 126
Mission Mangal (Jagan Shakti 2019), 147
Mother India (Mehboob Khan 1957), 98
Mumbai Cutting (Jahnu Barua, Rahul Dholakia, Rituparno Ghosh, Shashanka Ghosh, Manish Jha, Anurag Kashyap, Sudhir Mishra, Ruchi Narain, Ayush Raina, Revathi and Kundan Shah 2008), 61
Munnabhai M.B.B.S (Rajkumar Hirani 2003), 28
My Brother, Nikhil (Onir 2005), 126

Namak Haraam (Hrishikesh Mukherjee 1973), 108, 113–14, 116–17, 119, 129
Navarasa (Priyadarshan, Vasanth, Gautham Vasudev Menon, Bejoy Nambiar, Karthik Subbaraj, Sarjun KM, Karthick Naren, Arvind Swami and Rathindran R. Prasad 2021), 63
Nayakan (Mani Ratnam 1987), 51
Nina's Heavenly Delights (Partibha Parmar 2006), 144n

No One Killed Jessica (Raj Kumar Gupta 2011), 162n

Omkara (Vishal Bhardwaj 2006), 10
Om Shanti Om (Farah Khan 2007), 1, 23, 24, 31
Oye Lucky! Lucky Oye! (Dibakar Banerjee 2008), 10, 94

Paava Kadhaigal (Sudha Kongara, Gautham Menon, Vetrimaaran and Vignesh Shivan 2020), 63
Palki (Mahesh Kaul and S. U. Sunny 1967), 114
Pardes (Subhash Ghai 1997), 8
Piku (Shoojit Sircar 2015), 94, 95
Pitta Kathalu (Nag Ashwin, B. V. Nandini Reddy, Tharun Bhascker and Sankalp Reddy 2021), 63
Putham Pudhu Kaali (Sudha Kongara Prasad, Rajiv Menon, Karthik Subbaraj, Suhasini Maniratnam and Gautham Vasudev Menon 2020), 64
Pyaasa (Guru Dutt 1957), 49–50, 108, 113–14, 116–17, 119

Queen (Vikas Bahl 2013), 180

Raazi (Meghna Gulzar 2018), 7
Ragini MMS-2 (Bhushan Patel 2014), 132
Raja Harishchandra (Dadasaheb Phalke 1913), 59
Raja Hindustani (Dharmesh Darshan 1996), 128
Rangeela (Ram Gopal Varma 1995), 1, 23, 38

INDEX OF FILMS

Ray (Srijit Mukherji, Abhishek Chaubey and Vasan Bala 2021), 63
Rock On! (Abhishek Kapoor 2008), 39
Rockstar (Imtiaz Ali 2011), 39

Saajan (Lawrence D'Souza 1991), 114
Saaz (Sai Paranjpye 1998), 39
Salaam Bombay! (Mira Nair 1988), 42, 51, 76, 111
Salim Langde Pe Mat Ro (Saeed Mirza 1989), 54, 125n
Satya (Ram Gopal Varma 1998), 10, 109
Secret Superstar (Advait Chandan 2017), 39, 44
Section 375 (Ajay Bahl 2019), 147, 161n
Sholay (Ramesh Sippy 1975), 2, 4, 126, 129
Shor Se Shuruaat (Amira Bhargava, Rahul V. Chittella, Arunima Sharma, Supriya Sharma, Satish Raj Kasireddi, Pratik Kothari and Annie Zaidi 2016), 64
Shorts (Neeraj Ghaywan, Vasan Bala, Anubhuti Kashyap, Shlok Sharma and Gitanjali Rao 2013), 61
Shubh Mangal Zyada Savdhan (Hitesh Kewalya 2020), 126
Shuruaat Ka Interval (Amrit Raj Gupta, Shishir Jha, Ankit Tripathi, Palash Vaswani, Aarti S. Bagdi, Atanu Mukherjee and Rukshana Tabassum 2014), 64
Shuruaat Ka Twist (Sanjiv Kishinchandani, Hanish Kalia, Praveen Fernandes, Heena Dsouza, Avalokita and Gaurav Mehra 2019), 64

Side Streets (Tony Gerber 1998), 218
Simmba (Rohit Shetty 2018), 211
Slumdog Millionaire (Danny Boyle 2008), 51
Split Wide Open (Dev Benegal 1999), 218
Street Singer (Phani Majumdar 1938), 39

Talaash (Reema Kagti, 2012), 79, 80
Talvaar (Meghna Gulzar 2015), 7
Tees Maar Khan (Farah Khan 2010), 73n
Titli (Kanu Behl 2014), 94
The Godfather (Francis Ford Coppola 1972), 220
The Journey (Ligy J. Pullappally 2004), 144n
The Marvellous Mrs Maisel (Amy Sherman-Palladino 2017–20), 231
The Pink Mirror (Sridhar Rangayan 2004), 126, 141n
The SlumGods of Bombay – Hope, Hip-Hop and the Dharavi Way (2014), 51
Tumhari Sulu (Suresh Triveni 2017), 180

Unfreedom (Raj Amit Kumar 2014), 126, 132–3, 141n
Unpaused (Raj and Dk, Nikkhil Advani Tannishtha Chatterjee, Avinash Arun and Nitya Mehra 2020), 64

Veer-Zara (Yash Chopra 2004), 28
Veere Di Wedding (Shashanka Ghosh 2018), 73n

Wake Up Sid (Ayan Mukherjee 2009), 109, 180
Wanted (Prabhu Deva 2009), 35
Waqt (Yash Chopra 1965), 180
War (Siddharth Anand 2019), 161

Zanjeer (Prakash Mehra 1973), 4, 128

Zindagi Na Milegi Dobara (*ZNMD*) (Zoya Akhtar 2011), 2, 7, 12, 15, 35, 43, 75, 84–6, 95, 110, 151–6, 160, 164–5, 167–70, 172–4, 176, 181, 189, 195n, 199, 203–5, 209, 212–13, 221–3, 227

EU representative:
Easy Access System Europe
Mustamäe tee 50, 10621 Tallinn, Estonia
Gpsr.requests@easproject.com

www.ingramcontent.com/pod-product-compliance
Lightning Source LLC
Chambersburg PA
CBHW070340240426
43671CB00013BA/2383